The Encyclopedia of

BRITISH MILITARY AIRCRAFT

Chaz Bowyer

The Encyclopedia of

BRITISH MILITARY AIRCRAFT

Chaz Bowyer

Crescent Books
New York

A Bison Book

Copyright © 1982 by Bison Books Limited
Text Copyright Chaz Bowyer

Produced by Bison Books Limited,
4 Cromwell Place, London SW7

First English edition published by Arms and
Armour Press Limited, 1982

Library of Congress Catalog Card Number : 81
5415
All rights reserved.
This edition is published by Crescent Books,
distributed by Crown Publishers, Inc.

b c d e f g h

Printed in Spain

Library of Congress Cataloging in Publication Data

Bowyer, Chaz
The encyclopedia of British military aircraft.

1. Airplanes, Military.   2. Aeronautics, Military—
Great Britain.   I. Title.
UG1245.G7B67   623.74'6'0941   81-5415
                                          AACR2

Reprinted 1982

D. L. B. 13391-1982

Page 1: a rebuilt Sopwith Pup is preserved by the
Shuttleworth Trust, Old Warden, Bedfordshire.
Pages 2-3: a McDonnell Douglas Phantom FGR2
fires its pod-mounted cannon.
Above: the Supermarine Spitfire PR 19 was a
photographic reconnaissance aircraft.

Contents

Introduction 6
Background 8
Part One: 1912-1918 30
Part Two: 1918-1939 58
Part Three: 1939-1945 90
Part Four: Postwar 146
Part Five: Helicopters 204
Part Six: Airships 212
Index 222
Acknowledgments 224

Introd

Compilation of any form of aircraft encyclopedia immediately involves an author in decisions. Which aircraft should be included? Which omitted? And in what specific format and sequence should the subjects included be presented? An encyclopaedia's *raison d'être* is primarily as a form of quick reference; hence ease of reference must take highest priority. With that in mind, this volume is organised in four main time periods, with separate sections covering airships and helicopters. Within each section subjects are arranged in alphabetical order by manufacturer; all cross-referred in a master index of aircraft at the rear. Final selection of subjects can only remain a matter of personal choice for the compiler. My overall objective has been to offer a single-volume ready-reference to the

more significant *operational* aircraft used over the past 70 years by Britain's fighting air services. Necessarily, in my view, these must include a number of aircraft not of British origin, without which no record of Britain's military and maritime aviation would be 'complete' or balanced.

The interpretation of which aircraft should be considered significant is clearly my own; doubtless many readers may have different views. Equally, I have omitted listing so-called 'manufacturers' in great detail, simply because any comprehensive list would need to include virtually every nut-and-bolt maker who in any way contributed to the ultimate construction, very many of whom were not aircraft manufacturers as such. In the same basic context, to refer to an aircraft as being a Hawker-

uction

Siddeley product is only true of certain designs of relatively recent years; several significant designs originated with private aircraft firms which were subsequently married into the Hawker-Siddeley family.

All technical figures quoted herein have been extracted from such authentic sources as test and trial reports or makers' figures, but a word of caution is offered to those (I hope few) readers who accept the printed word as gospel. Despite the excellence of even the most modern production methods and standards, it remains a simple fact that no two aircraft, even from the same production line, have ever been truly identical in every possible respect. Differences, however slight, become immediately apparent in the air, and in any case are exacerbated by the myriad of additional modifications and refinements – official and unofficial – incorporated locally at unit or squadron level. To give merely a single example, standard production Spitfires of the early marks could, by meticulous attention to detailed refinements, have almost 40 mph added to their makers' stipulated 'maximum' speeds. Thus all figures given in this volume for precise performance and physical parameters are indeed accurate, but for specific examples of the aircraft type and mark indicated. It would be folly to assume that such precise data is automatically concrete for every other aircraft of the same type and mark.

Chaz Bowyer
Norwich, 1981

Backg

Above: a Douglas Dakota of No. 27 Squadron demonstrates a glider pick-up technique at the 1950 Farnborough air show.

Military aviation in Great Britain can be said to have been inaugurated within the British Army in 1878, in which year authority was granted for the experimental production of spherical balloons and their ancillary field equipment at the Woolwich Arsenal, with an initial sum of £150 being allotted for the construction of just one balloon. This official recognition of the possible usefulness of balloons for army purposes was, at least in part, a result of the past endeavours of various individual officers to establish the military worth of balloons. Among many such officers must be mentioned Captains H P Lee of the Royal Engineers (RE), J L B Templer of the Middlesex Militia, G E Grover, RE, and F. Beaumont, RE; this last officer having attached himself to the Federal Army balloonists during the American Civil War for practical, operational experience. By 1880 military balloon instruction and general training had been introduced at Aldershot, and a balloon detachment made its first-ever appearance in that year's Aldershot manoeuvres. In 1885 two small detachments of balloon personnel and equipment were despatched overseas to join army formations in the Bechuanaland Expedition and the eastern Sudan campaign respectively, and on 25 March 1885, Lieutenant R H L Mackenzie, RE, spent seven hours aloft in a balloon basket, accompanying a seven-mile long march of a convoy from Suakin to Tofrik in the Sudan zone – the first operational use of a balloon by the British Army.

In 1890–91 a Balloon Section and Depot were officially constituted at Aldershot and a balloon factory built. Although training and development continued apace, ballooning – as a worthwhile military activity – continued to be regarded with some scepticism by a number of higher authorities in the army. The outbreak of the Boer War, however, provided a great impetus to expansion of the tiny balloon establishment. In September 1899 the first of an eventual three balloon sections was sent to South Africa. A total of 30 balloons was ultimately employed. There the balloon crews provided invaluable services as gun-spotters for the artillery and in general reconnaissance roles. After the Boer War the balloon section at Aldershot continued slowly to expand. In 1906, by then titled the Balloon School, it moved its base, factory and other facilities to South Farnborough. By then the activities of the Balloon School had begun to include experimentation with various other forms of aerial progress, including airborne wireless trials, construction of a full-scale, biplane glider to the design of Lieutenant J W Dunne, and of a full-size aeroplane to the ideas of the extrovert aviation pioneer Samuel Franklin Cody. Further experiments with aeroplanes were, however, soon prohibited by the War Office from April 1909, on the grounds of the 'extravagant' expenditure to date of £2500 on the Dunne and Cody projects!

Before this embargo came into force, the first British Army Airship, Dirigible No. I, popularly titled *Nulli Secundus*, had been completed. Its first appearance was on 10 September 1907 – cylindrical in shape, covered with goldbeater's skin, 122 feet long and 26 feet in diameter, with a capacity of 55,000 cubic feet. It was powered by a 50 hp Antoinette engine purchased in Paris, as no aero engine of British origin was yet available. Carrying a crew of two or three, this non-rigid airship developed a top

THE NEW NAVAL AIRSHIP 'THE BABY'

speed of 16 mph. Though limited in development potential, the *Nulli Secundus* provided valuable practice in the construction, handling and general operation of such a craft, and indeed was used to train selected Royal Navy personnel in airship handling in preparation for the construction of the Admiralty's first venture into airship design. This first RN design, titled somewhat cynically *Mayfly*, was of 700,000 cubic feet capacity and was powered by two 200 hp Wolseley engines. It was a rigid airship, but unfortunately was buffeted by a sudden squall while being extracted from its shed at Barrow on 24 September 1911 and broke its back. It was returned to its shed unflown. This setback resulted in no further interest by the Royal Navy in building airships for the next two years – the First Lord of the Admiralty then being Winston Churchill, who was no protagonist of airships in general. Despite its regrettable misfortune the *Mayfly* – officially titled His Majesty's Airship (HMA) No. 1 – was a remarkable design and had included the extensive use of a German-invented light alloy, duralumin, which not only reduced weight but increased structural strength by virtually 100 per cent over previous wood-frame projects.

In May 1909 the second army airship, Dirigible No. II, often called *Baby*, was launched after reconstruction and enlargement with the designation HMA *Beta*. At the same period a third non-rigid design, the *Gamma*, was in hand, an airship of even larger size which was eventually launched in February 1910. Meanwhile, the development of the 'heavier-than-air' aeroplane for war purposes had been seriously engaging the attention of the government, resulting in a properly constituted system of training in the use of aeroplanes, in addition to balloons and dirigibles, being inaugurated by a special Army Order, dated 28 February 1911. This effectively created the Air Battalion of the Royal Engineers, with effect from 1 April 1911. On that date the Balloon School was absorbed into this new RE Battalion, which then comprised a headquarters at South Farnborough, and two companies; No. 1 (Airship) Company at South Farnborough, and No. 2 (Aeroplane) Company at Larkhill. Thus this latter company became the first British military unit equipped entirely with aeroplanes, as opposed to any form of airship. At that moment Britain's total strength in military aircraft consisted of two airships and less than a dozen airworthy aeroplanes.

The growing emphasis upon the military use of aeroplanes in various European countries – notably France and, to a lesser extent, Germany – by 1911 inevitably focussed the attention of the British government on the possibility of its own military air service. In August 1911, accordingly, the War Office Committee under the chairmanship of Lord Kitchener presented a report recommending that aeronautics (*sic*) should now be organised in an air corps of the army, separate from the parent Royal Engineers. This recommendation led to the appointment of a Technical Subcommittee of the Committee of Imperial Defence on 18 December 1911, whose terms of reference were to elaborate all the necessary details to give effect to the proposal for establishment of an aviation service. The outcome of all these machinations 'in committee' was a full scheme for the organisation of a new Flying Corps. This scheme received approval from the Committee of Imperial Defence. Royal approval for its intended title

Below: the naval airship *Baby* is pictured (left) with the *Beta* in the background.

Royal Flying Corps (RFC) was granted in March 1912, and it came into existence with effect from 13 May 1912.

Initially, the RFC's organisation included a Military Wing, a Naval Wing, and a Central Flying School for training pilots of both services. In addition there was the Royal Aircraft Factory at Farnborough, entrusted with experimentation and research on all facets of 'aeronautics' likely to be of use or interest to the RFC. The original establishment for the RFC included provision for seven squadrons, each comprising 12 aeroplanes, with two pilots for each aeroplane and a suitable reserve. Total establishment of pilots was given as 364, about half of whom, initially, were intended to be non-commissioned personnel. The CFS was located at Upavon, near Salisbury, Wiltshire, where the erection of buildings began in April 1912. This school was declared open on 19 June that year, and the first course of instruction commenced on 17 August 1912.

Progress was quickly made with the formation of the intended RFC complement of seven complete squadrons of aeroplanes. The original No. 1 Squadron was derived from No. 1 (Airship) Company of the Air Battalion, RE; becoming No. 1 Airship and Kite Squadron in May 1912, but eventually being reformed as No. 1 Squadron, RFC, equipped with aeroplanes only, in May 1914. Similarly, the second unit formed, in May 1912, was No. 3 Squadron, RFC – in effect a retitled No. 2 Company of the defunct Air Battalion, RE. No. 2 Squadron, RFC was formed as an all-aeroplane unit at Farnborough late in May 1912. By August 1914, Nos. 4, 5 and 6 Squadrons, RFC had come into being, while No. 7 Squadron was in embryo form by that month. As the RFC gradually expanded as an adjunct to the army, so the RFC's Naval Wing began to exploit the possibilities for aircraft to aid the Royal Navy. Almost from its inception the RFC's Naval Wing – its official nomenclature initially – tended to regard itself as an entirely individual formation, separate from the military-inclined RFC, and within months of its creation in early 1912 began referring to itself as the Royal Naval Air Service RNAS, a title only officially recognised with effect from 1 July 1914.

This individual attitude applied to all aspects of the Naval Wing's activities, including pilot training. The first RN officers to be taught to fly received their instruction in March-April 1911 at Eastchurch, Isle of Sheppey, which was to become the principal naval air training establishment from December of that year. In December 1912 a second naval air station was established on the Isle of Grain, to be followed by other naval air stations located at

Calshot, Felixstowe and Cromarty in 1913; the early examples of a chain of coastal RNAS establishments created in subsequent years. In 1913 too it was decided to transfer control and organisation of all airship work to the Admiralty, a change which came into effect on 1 January 1914. Accordingly, naval airship stations were brought into being from 1914, the first being Kingsnorth, on the Medway, which was commissioned in April 1914.

The shift of emphasis from airships and balloons to aeroplanes as the prime equipment of the RFC was necessarily and relatively innovative. Though balloons and other non-rigid 'lighter-than-air' vehicles had existed for many decades, the aeroplane had only been truly born in 1903 when the American Wright brothers had made their first, historic hops in powered, man-controlled aircraft. Thus the aeroplanes equipping the first RFC squadrons presented a polymorphous picture. Standardisation in aircraft types for first-line use was, as yet, unknown, and the air and ground crews were forced to cope with a strange, varied blend of aeroplane designs.

Many of the aeroplanes available were of foreign origin, particularly French-designed types such as Deperdussin monoplanes, Blériots, Nieuports, Breguets and Farmans. Intermingled were several British designs, including Bristol monoplanes, Avro biplanes, and the Farnborough-created BE2 series of biplanes. The latter, designed by Geoffrey de Havilland, had first appeared on the scene in 1912 and was generally considered to be the best, all-round type for future equipment of RFC squadrons. Pleasant enough aircraft to fly, the BE2a and BE2b production types were intended primarily for the role of reconnaissance – the duty accepted as the prime purpose of virtually all military aircraft of the period. The other most significant British design in use by 1914 was the Avro two-seat biplane – initially the Avro 500 of 1912 from which was derived the Avro 504; a classic aircraft which was destined to offer invaluable service to the RFC, RNAS and the RAF for at least two decades thereafter. A further type which emerged from Farnborough in early 1913 was the RE1 (Reconnaissance Experimental 1) which in its turn fathered a line of later RE variants which gave doughty service throughout 1914–18 war operations.

The near-complete emphasis on reconnaissance as the foremost operational requirement of military aircraft during the pre-1914 years meant that relatively little attention was paid to defensive or offensive armament for aeroplanes. There were individual exceptions, as always; notably several designs emanating from the Vickers

Below: Sopwith 2F.1 Camel N7136 served aboard HMS *Galatea* in 1918. Note the naval version's armament of an upper-wing Lewis machine-gun and a single Vickers machine-gun.

company from 1912, which incorporated a machine gun fitted in the nacelle nose. Yet in general designers concentrated upon producing stable aircraft, machines needing relatively little attention to control handling in flight, thereby leaving crews fairly free to sketch and observe activities on the ground below. It was a design philosophy which was to alter radically within a year of the 1914–18 war commencing.

The RFC's Naval Wing, later RNAS, depended for its aircraft initially upon a widely varied mixture of British and foreign designs. Unlike the RFC, however, the naval airmen employed a combination of land and seaplanes, necessarily, for their duties of patrolling the coastal waters of the United Kingdom. In Britain the first seaplane fitted with twin floats to fly from water had been a modified Avro biplane, piloted by Commander Oliver Schwann, on 18 November 1911 – the precursor of a host of similarly configured floatplanes to see RNAS and RAF service in subsequent years. The other major form of sea-going aircraft, the flying boat, had been pioneered by the American Glenn Curtiss. As a type of service aircraft its British career began with the Sopwith Bat Boat of 1913, the Franco-British Aviation Company's (FBA's) two-seat biplane 'boat of the same year, the first flying boat design to enter British service use, and similar maritime craft. By the outbreak of war in August 1914, the RNAS possessed one FBA, two Bat Boats, and an impressed Curtiss machine; while by November 1914 two more Curtiss flying boats had been delivered from the USA, and many more were on order. In the iterim such devotees of naval aviation as Charles Rumney Samson and Robert Clark-Hall had pursued various successful trials and experiments with a variety of forms of naval aviation, including armament trials and take-offs from shipborne wooden runways and water surfaces.

Both wings of the RFC depended heavily upon French-designed aero engines for their aircraft in the years preceding the 1914–18 war, and indeed for the early period of operations. The British aeronautical scene was almost exclusively in the hands of private industrial firms – with the notable exception of the Royal Aircraft Factory at Farnborough, a government establishment – and, overall, had yet to be in any sense co-ordinated on a national basis. Nevertheless, such prestigious engineering firms as Rolls-Royce were already pursuing experiments with and construction of powerplants specifically intended for

aircraft. The general need for a self-supporting British aviation industry, though comprehended by the more visionary, had yet to receive the impetus which the imminent conflict was to provide.

The outbreak of war with Germany in August 1914 found the RNAS holding complete responsibility for the aerial defence of the United Kingdom and its coastal waters, while the RFC hastily mobilised its available first-line squadrons and despatched these to France for support of the British Expeditionary Force (BEF). At that fateful moment in history the RNAS possessed a front-line strength of some 50 aeroplanes (including all types of sea-going craft), six airships, 130 officers and 700 non-commissioned personnel; while the RFC could count 63 operational aircraft, served by 146 officers and 1097 'rankers'. The 1914 budgets granted by the government amounted to £1,000,000 for the RFC and £900,000 for the RNAS, double the RFC's 1913 allotment and a 50 per cent increase for the maritime air service.

In terms of specific aircraft for particular roles, both services had yet to categorise their equipment, while airborne armament, virtually non-existent in 1914, was still regarded as secondary to the aeroplane's prime *raison d'être*, reconnaissance. Yet within weeks of the beginning of the war in France there were several

Above: HP V/1500 J1936 'HMA Old Carthusian' bombed Kabul in May 1919 during the Third Afghan War.
Below: Westland-built DH9A F993 was allotted to No. 110 Squadron RAF in 1918 and named 'Hyderabad No. 6'.

16

examples of air crews deliberately seeking offensive action against aerial opponents, the faint beginnings of true aerial warfare. Use of the aeroplane as a bombing vehicle was broadly accepted by most air services from the outset, but the development of the true fighter, via the early single-seat, reconnaissance 'scout' designs, was to be hindered until well into 1915 by the lack of suitable offensive armament installations. It was not until February 1916 that the first RFC squadron to be wholly equipped with a single-seat fighter aircraft (No. 24 Squadron with De Havilland 2s) was sent to France. In the following month two more such units, Nos. 27 and 29 Squadrons, arrived in the fighting zone, equipped with Martinsyde G100 Elephants and DH2s respectively; while a third DH2 squadron, No. 32, entered the lists in May. By mid-1916 these had been supplemented by several other RFC and RNAS fighter squadrons, equipped with such fresh designs as the French Nieuport Scout; while by the end of that year the first examples of the Sopwith Pup had begun to reach operational units of the RNAS in France and the single-seat pusher FE8 type had also been brought into first-line use.

The astonishingly rapid evolution of the fighter aeroplane can be partly judged by the first flights, in prototype forms, of three significant designs during the final three months of 1916: the Bristol F2a, SE5, and Sopwith F1 Camel. All three were eventually to enter first-line use before the summer of 1917 and were to prove themselves as classic fighters by any standards. Meanwhile development of the day or night bomber had shown equally rapid progress. The long outmoded BE series of two-seaters,

virtual mainstay of the 1914–16 reconnaissance and general army co-operation squadrons, had begun to be replaced from mid-1916 by Sopwith 1½ Strutters, and later RE8s, while in March 1917 No. 55 Squadron arrived in France equipped with the new DH4 two-seat day bomber, a design superior to most similar types in use then. For longer-range, night bombing, the mammoth Handley Page 0/100 made its first war sortie in March 1917. In 1918 its improved variant, the HP 0/400, was joined on operations by the DH9 and DH9a two-seaters, while by the Armistice the HP V/1500 development was standing by, ostensibly, to 'bomb Berlin' from its English base.

The RNAS, mainly based in the UK, expanded prodigiously during 1914–18, adding a wealth of varying floatplanes, flying boats, landplanes and airships to its aerial armoury. A continuing series of trials and experiments soon established the earliest forms of shipborne aeroplanes and, significantly, aircraft carriers; ships adapted as seaborne airfields which extended the long arm of naval striking power. Although legally amalgamated with the RFC to form Britain's third Service, the Royal Air Force, on 1 April 1918, the former RNAS continued to regard itself as a separate entity in the context of aerial warfare until the cessation of hostilities with Germany in November 1918. In other fields of RFC/RNAS/RAF activities throughout 1914–18, various distinct forms of use of military and maritime aircraft had their beginnings. In Britain a complete Home Defence organisation evolved as an antidote to German airship and aeroplane bombing attacks against UK targets, including many squadrons designated as 'night fighter' units; a form of aerial warfare

Above right: a Blackburn Perth flying boat pictured at the Marine Aircraft Experimental Establishment, Felixstowe.
Below: His Majesty's Airship R.29.

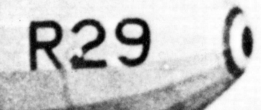

further extended by 1918 when two Sopwith Camel-equipped squadrons were despatched to France for what are now termed 'night intruder' operations. Behind the operational squadrons a vast training organisation was built up, epitomised by the establishment of the School of Special Flying at Gosport which in 1918 helped lay down the rules for all future flying training policy for the RAF.

By the Armistice of November 1918, the recently-created Royal Air Force had become the world's largest, independent (of Army or Navy control) air service. At that date its overall strength stood at 3300 aeroplanes and 103 airships, with a total manpower of 27,333 officers, more than half of whom were trained pilots, and 263,837 non-commissioned personnel. It possessed a total of 675 air stations at home and abroad, with almost 150 operational squadrons, apart from a host of training and other second-line flying units. Throughout the war the somewhat piecemeal British aviation industry had produced slightly more than 55,000 airframes and 41,000 aero engines, apart from purchasing a further 3000 airframes and nearly 17,000 aero engines from other Allied countries. Though loosely co-ordinated by late 1918 in the common war effort, Britain's aviation industry remained primarily in the hands of private enterprise, with the notable exception of the Royal Aircraft Establishment at Farnborough. Nevertheless, the private firms had in effect been responsible in large degree for investigating, testing, experimenting, and generally exploring virtually every known avenue of aeronautical engineering.

The immediate post-war decade brought an inevitable diminution of the RAF as demobilisation of personnel and reduction in material stocks of aircraft were quickly implemented. The remnant then faced an uncertain future, bedevilled by inadequate financing and no little inference from self-seeking members of the military, naval and political hierarchy attempting to dissolve Britain's air service. The RAF's Chief of Air Staff, Hugh Trenchard, patiently fought off all attempts to dismember 'his' Third Service and, within the niggardly annual budgets permitted by the Treasury, slowly built a solid foundation for the RAF's future. His limited funds permitted little allocation for the design or development of new aeroplanes; leaving the few extant squadrons to soldier on with 1918-vintage aircraft and equipment for almost a decade, attempting to control and maintain a tenuous peace in Britain's far-flung empire of that era.

The two decades between the world wars saw a proliferation of fresh aeroplane designs produced by Britain's many private aviation firms; a majority of which were contenders for RAF acceptance and therefore production contracts. Relatively few actually entered service, and these only in modest numbers. The biplane configuration dominated contemporary design philosophy until well into the 1930s in all categories of RAF aircraft. Fighters improved steadily in terms of engine power and

Above: a Hawker Fury I interceptor fighter of No. 1 Squadron based at Tangmere, Sussex, in 1933. The Squadron identification marking was red bars along the side of the fuselage and on the upper wing.
Below: a Hawker Hart (India) photographed at Jhodpur, India, on 14 January 1941.

speed, but clung overlong to the 1918 concept of twin machine gun armament; while 'heavy' bomber designs made little real progress in the context of performance figures, and continued to carry bombs of 1914–18 concept. Occasional aircraft provided jolts to the near-complacency of contemporary thinking, for example, the Fairey Fox biplane bomber of 1925 which could outpace all fighters of its era, yet equipped only one squadron. Indeed, the operational potential of the peacetime RAF was overtly demonstrated on 6 July 1935, when HM King George V reviewed his air service at Mildenhall and Duxford. A total of 37 squadrons (356 aircraft) assembled for his inspections – yet every aeroplane on display was a biplane.

If officialdom appeared glue-footed in modernising the RAF's first-line aircraft, at least the various private aviation firms were attempting to provide up-dated designs by financing their own private venture projects. Most significant of these in terms of operational fighters were the Hawker Hurricane and, slightly later, the Supermarine Spitfire. The Hurricane's origins can be traced to a 1933 design. The prototype first flew in November 1935, the Hurricane was ordered into production and began its RAF service from late 1937; the RAF's and the world's first eight machine-gun fighter capable of speeds in excess of 300 mph. In March 1936 the prototype Spitfire made its initial air test, and production versions entered squadron service from August 1938. On the bomber scene, too, metal monoplanes of advanced conception were on the drawing board from late 1936, when several Air Ministry specificiations were issued calling for truly heavy monoplane bombers; resulting later in the Short Stirling, Handley Page Halifax, Avro Manchester and Avro Lancaster. In the interim many RAF bomber squadrons re-equipped from biplane 'cloth bombers' to twin-engined monoplanes such as the Bristol Blenheim, Armstrong Whitworth Whitley, Handley Page Hampden, and Vickers Wellington. Indeed, the hasty expansion schemes of the mid-1930s, if tardy, at least provided a relatively swift acceleration toward the aim of producing a modern effective RAF, capable, it was hoped, of countering the latent threat of the recently reformed German Luftwaffe.

The ominous warning of the September 1938 Munich Crisis served only to accentuate the RAF's crucial need for quantitative strength, and by 31 August 1939, just three days prior to the outbreak of war with Germany, the service could count a total of 157 squadrons and almost 2000 first-line aircraft, with nearly 8000 more aircraft in reserve. Yet 28 of those squadrons remained equipped with out-moded biplane fighters, bombers or flying boats. Fighter Command, the UK's aerial defence, had 400 Hurricanes and 270 Spitfires on strength, but also included 396 Gloster Gladiators and 111 crudely-converted Blenheim I 'fighters' in its overall stock. Bomber Command could muster nearly 600 Hampdens, Whitleys and Wellingtons, but its greatest quantities were of Blenheims and obsolescent Fairey Battles. Coastal Command presented a curious mixture of modern and out-dated aircraft. Of its total strength of nearly 450 aircraft, 301 were Avro Ansons, 27 were Short Sunderlands, 53 were Lockheed Hudsons, and the remainder were all biplanes. Notwithstanding the overt transitional stage from biplane to monoplane that the RAF found itself in at the outbreak of war with Germany,

modern mass production methods for modern designs had already been set in motion, promising ample quantities of fighters and bombers in the near future; while future four-engined 'heavies' to build Bomber Command's true strategic offensive power were already reaching prototype or production levels.

For the first three years of the European war the RAF was forced to rely heavily upon its pre-war aircraft designs for defence and offense, supplemented in reasonably high numbers by imported American aircraft of many types – not all of which proved operationally effective. Mainstay of Bomber Command was the Wellington, closely supported by Hampdens, Whitleys, and Blenheims. Fighter Command relied almost exclusively on the Hurricane and Spitfire. The first of the truly heavy bombers to enter service, the Stirling, made its operational debut in August 1940, followed by the Manchester and Halifax in February and March 1941 respectively. None of these proved successful initially, while the inferior performance of the Manchester had already led its designers to refashion its basic design to produce a four-

Below: the Miles Master I was powered by a Rolls-Royce Kestrel engine.

engined version which emerged later as the classic Avro Lancaster. Coastal Command, struggling manfully to combat the burgeoning German U-Boat menace to Britain's merchant shipping lifelines, was in sore need of a true long-range aircraft capable of closing the mid-Atlantic aerial gap that could not be covered by land-based planes from the USA or Britain. Hastily converted bombers diverted to maritime roles helped to some degree, but the urgent requirement for a VLR (Very Long Range) submarine hunter/killer was not resolved until the arrival of American Catalina flying boats and, particularly, the Consolidated B-24 Liberator.

Progressive development of the Spitfire as Fighter Command's prime 'sword' continued throughout the war, but fresh fighter designs soon appeared to complement Reginald Mitchell's brain-child. The six-gun, four-cannon pugnacious Beaufighter began to shoulder the responsibility of UK night-fighter defence, while a stablemate to the Hurricane joined operations when the Typhoon made its debut in late 1941. Almost simultaneously the DH Mosquito 'wooden wonder' entered squadron service, an aircraft which was swiftly to impress itself on virtually every form of offensive (and defensive) aerial warfare throughout the conflict. Meanwhile, at RAF Cranwell on 15 May 1941, the relatively small Gloster E.28/39 monoplane made its first full test flight – Britain's first jet-engined aircraft to take to the air, and the herald of a new era in British military and civil aircraft design. In December 1941 the first production

Below: **Gloster Meteor EE528 was one of three Meteor F4s used during training for the RAF's attempts on the World Speed Record in 1946.**

Lancasters were delivered, and the bomber made its first operational sorties in March 1942; the start of a huge and definitive contribution to Bomber Command's part in the ultimate victory over Germany.

Naval aviation, at the outbreak of war, presented a dismal picture in terms of modernity of equipment; the patent outcome of decades of official neglect and even part-indifference in government and Admiralty circles. With the exception of the Skua dive-bomber, the Fleet Air Arm (FAA) in late 1939 was wholly biplane-equipped, and indeed continued to rely heavily upon such obsolescent designs as the faithful Swordfish throughout the war. It was a state the FAA was forced to bear until 1943 when ample quantities of American aircraft became available to re-equip most FAA operational units. Though British-designed aircraft, such as Fulmars, Fireflies and converted RAF aircraft, were introduced at varying stages of the global conflict, the ultimate proud record of the FAA throughout 1939–45 owed much to its American equipment, particularly during the later war years. By 1945, however, the prime importance of naval air power had, at last, come to be acknowledged; a recognition exemplified by the wide and rapid expansion of the Navy's aircraft-carrying vessels of many types.

By late 1944 Bomber, Coastal and Fighter Commands had established aerial superiority in their respective areas of action, albeit in the face of steadily dwindling Luftwaffe opposition. In that year too the RAF's first-ever

operational jet fighter, the Meteor, made its initial war sorties. In May 1945 Germany was defeated, while in August 1945 Japan capitulated. On the brink of its latest era of peace, the RAF stood second only to the USAAF among the world's air forces in the contexts of technical and numerical strengths. On overall RAF charge was a gross total of 55,469 aircraft, of which some 9200 were considered to be in first-line use. By August 1945 the FAA could boast of 11,300 aircraft, though little more than one tenth of these were actually in first-line operational use.

The immediate post-1945 era witnessed significant changes in British military aircraft; the age of the jet had begun. The principal jet aircraft was the Gloster Meteor in its progressively developed versions, which by mid-1952 equipped no less than 29 of Fighter Command's 45 squadrons, and a further seven squadrons based overseas. Partnering the Meteor was the De Havilland Vampire jet fighter which was also to be developed and employed for many years. By 1951 jet fighters had also been introduced to the FAA, when No. 800 Squadron FAA received Attackers in August of that year. Rapid run-down of surplus aircraft in the immediate post-war period was inevitable, and the RAF's first-line strength for the year 1950 was officially promulgated as 4510 aircraft. Two years later this figure had risen to 6338 aircraft, the service's peak numerical strength from 1946 to the present day. If Fighter Command had wasted little time in converting to the jet age, Bomber Command lagged dolefully behind

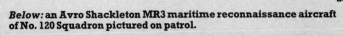

Below: an Avro Shackleton MR3 maritime reconnaissance aircraft of No. 120 Squadron pictured on patrol.

with its piston-engined Lincolns and borrowed American-designed Washingtons until the gradual introduction of the Canberra jet bomber from 1951. Coastal Command fared little better, relying on ageing Lancasters and their development, the Shackleton; the latter stalwart continuing in the maritime role until very recent years before giving way to the Nimrod hunter/killer anti-submarine jet.

In 1954 the superb Hawker Hunter entered squadron use, along with the ill-starred Swift fighter, both intended to replace the interim American Sabre swept-wing jet fighters purchased and used from 1953–56. While the Canberra fulfilled the immediate needs of Bomber Command in the 1950s, plans had already been finalised and progressed towards the intended V-bomber force whereby the three V-bomber designs, Valiant, Victor and Vulcan would eventually become Britain's nuclear deterrent strategic strike force. Beginning with the Valiant in 1955, all three entered RAF service by 1957; a year which saw the notorious Sandys' Defence White Paper revise the whole future policy for Britain's defence by advocating the demise of manned aircraft and a wider reliance on unmanned guided missiles as the country's future defence. As such, this policy virtually condemned any progress in fighters particularly. This was reinforced in 1958 by

another government White Paper announcing a decision to buy Thor IRBMs (intermediate range ballistic missiles) for Bomber Command, and by the acceptance into service that year of the first Bloodhound surface-to-air missiles with Fighter Command. The false philosophy of the Sandys' Paper was soon apparent, and the RAF continued to receive up-dated new manned aircraft to undertake varied roles.

The lessons of the various 'peace-time' emergencies – the Berlin Airlift, Malaya, Korea, and the Suez Crisis among others – were fully appreciated in terms of future planning and equipment; particularly the RAF's need for very-long-range transport aircraft for swift reinforcement of 'hot spots' overseas and other tasks. This latter need was successively filled by the introduction of the Comet, Britannia, Belfast and other mammoth transport designs in subsequent years. In the fighter field the delta-winged Javelin all-weather jet interceptor entered squadron use in 1956, while four years later the RAF accepted the first examples of its first true supersonic fighter, the Lightning, capable of twice the performance of the excellent Hunter. In keeping with the all-jet RAF envisaged in the mid-1940s, flying training had been converted to include *ab initio* training jet designs; while the ubiquitous helicopter

Above: a Hawker Sea Hawk naval fighter is positioned on HMS
Ark Royal's steam catapult in October 1955.
Below: a pair of Gloster Javelin FAW7 fighters of No. 23 Squadron
carry DH Firestreak air-to-air missiles.

became a vital adjunct to RAF, Army and Royal Navy operational strength.

Development and future production plans for such designs as the TSR2 low-level strategic strike-bomber, the P.1154 V/STOL (Vertical/Short Take-Off and Landing) supersonic interceptor and HS 681 V/STOL transport were abruptly cancelled from early 1965. All were intended to be replaced by purchase of American Phantom and Hercules aircraft, and the controversial American F-111K 'swing-wing' fighter. From 1962 the nuclear deterrent responsibility was passed to the Royal Navy from the RAF;

while on 1 April 1964 the three service Ministries were amalgamated under a newly-created Ministry of Defence, each Service having merely its own Department within this bureaucratic monopoly. Since its peak in numerical aircraft strength in 1952, the RAF had steadily, inexorably declined in strength, until in 1968, the 50th anniversary of the RAF's initial formation, the Third Service possessed a total of 2526 aircraft, of which only 1902 were classified as first-line.

Continuing paring of Britain's aerial strength saw the order for the swing-wing F-111Ks cancelled in 1968, though

Below: a Supermarine Swift FR5 fighter reconnaissance aircraft pictured in the markings of No. 2 Squadron.

that year saw the first Phantom aircraft arrive in Britain. They entered squadron service the next year. In 1969 too the first VTOL Harrier squadron was equipped, and the first RAF Buccaneer squadron was formed; the latter design being an ex-FAA type transferred to the RAF as a stop-gap equipment for low-level strike operations. In 1970 the government announced a decision to equip four squadrons with the Anglo-French SEPECAT Jaguar tactical strike fighter; meanwhile Coastal Command had begun to receive the Nimrod submarine-hunter to replace its 20-years' old Shackleton in squadrons.

The astronomical production and development costs of any modern military aircraft meant early agreement between the various Western partners of NATO in planning mutual projects for future designs; the most significant of such 'inter-Allied' aircraft today being the Panavia Tornado multi-role combat design. Destined to replace the RAF's Vulcans, Buccaneers and, in certain aspects, even Jaguars in their various roles, the Tornado will be the key combat aircraft of the 1980s. It will serve with the air forces of Britain, West Germany and Italy.

Part One

1912

1918

Below: a Bristol F2b of No. 139 Squadron RAF based at Villa Verla, Italy, 1918.

D·8084

Above: an AW FK3 'Little Ack' of the School of Air Fighting, Doon, 1917.

Armstrong Whitworth FK3

Type: reconnaissance; bomber; trainer.
Crew: two.
Power plant: 90hp RAF 1a; 105 hp RAF 1b.
Dimensions: span 40 ft 0⅝ in; length 20 ft; height 11 ft 10¾ in.
Weights (RAF 1a): empty 1386 lb; loaded 2056 lb.
Performance (RAF 1a): maximum speed 87 mph at ground level; climb to 10,000 ft, 48 mins 56 secs; service ceiling 12,000 ft; endurance at 8000 ft, 3 hrs.
Armament: trainer, nil; reconnaissance, bomber, one 0.303 in Lewis machine gun and up to 224 lb of bombs.

First produced in 1915 as a supplement to the standard BE2c, the AW FK3 saw limited service in Middle East war zones from 1916–18 as a general reconnaissance and bombing aircraft. Its main RFC use was as a trainer in the UK, 1916–18, where it was unofficially dubbed 'Little Ack' (to distinguish from the AW FK8 'Big Ack'); while the RNAS in Britain used a few for coastal patrols. Of some 500 FK3s eventually ordered, 62 were still on RAF charge on 31 October 1918, and several survived on the Civil Register after the war.

Armstrong Whitworth FK8

Type: reconnaissance; bomber.
Crew: two.
Power plant: 120 hp Beardmore; 160 hp Beardmore.
Dimensions: span 43 ft 6 in; length 31 ft (160 hp Beardmore); height 11 ft (160 hp Beardmore).
Weights (160 hp Beardmore): empty 1916 lb; loaded 2811 lb.
Performance (160 hp Beardmore): maximum speed 98.4 mph at ground level; climb to 10,000 ft, 27 mins 50 secs; service ceiling 13,000 ft; endurance 3 hrs.
Armament: one or two 0.303 in Lewis machine guns in rear cockpit; one 0.303 in Vickers machine gun forward; approximately 300 lb of bombs on external racks.

The prototype FK8 first flew in May 1916, and the first RFC unit fully equipped, No.35 Squadron, crossed to France in January 1917. Robust in

Right: this AW FK8 was at Risalpur, India, in 1919 on the strength of No. 31 Squadron.

structure, the 'Big Ack' was popular with its crews, and saw plentiful active service until November 1918, in France and in the Middle East. Two of the 19 Victoria Crosses awarded to airmen in WW1 went to AW FK8 pilots. Total production is unknown precisely but on 31 October 1918 the RAF still had 694 FK8s in service.

Avro 504

Type: trainer.
Crew: two.
Power plant: various 80 hp Gnome, Le Rhône, Gnome Monosoupape rotary engines; 100 hp, 110 hp, 130 hp engines fitted in individual machines.
Dimensions: span 36 ft; length 29 ft 5 in; height 10 ft 5 in.
Weights (production model): empty 924 lb; loaded 1574 lb.
Performance (504K, Le Rhône): maximum speed 95 mph at ground level; climb to 10,000 ft, 16 min; service ceiling 16,000 ft; endurance 3 hrs.
Armament: trainer, nil; home defence, one 0.303 Lewis machine gun above upper wing; bomber 4 x 20 lb Hales bombs.

Derived from the 1912 Avro 500, the 504 made its debut in September 1913. As such it was the forerunner of a total of 8340 504s to be produced in World War I alone, and the start of two decades of RFC/RNAS/RAF use of the basic type. Though used briefly as a bomber by the RNAS and RFC in the early weeks of the war, the 504 is best remembered as a basic trainer, in particular the 504J variants used by the Gosport School of Special Flying, and the 504K versions which provided most initial instruction in the post-1918 RAF, until superseded by yet another variant, the 504N Lynx from 1927–33. During 1918 five squadrons in the UK were equipped with armed, single-seat converted 504Ks for Home Defence duties. Numerous trial installations of a wide variety of power plants were made during the 504's long life, though none produced any truly significant' improvement over the original rotary-engined design. Six 504Ns of the Central Flying School, Wittering pioneered blind flying (instrument flying) from September 1931, while the aerobatic qualities of the 504 were epitomised in the early 1930s at the

Right: an Avro 504K pictured in flight.
Below right: an Avro 504K preserved at the Old Rhinebeck Museum, United States.

annual Hendon Displays. In 1933 the 504N was gradually replaced in service by a stablemate design, the Avro Tutor.

BE2 Series

Type: reconnaissance.
Crew: two.
Power plant: 70 hp Renault (BE2, 2a, 2b); 90 hp RAF 1a, 105 hp RAF 1b, 150 hp Hispano-Suiza (BE2c); 90 hp RAF 1a (BE2e).
Dimensions: span 38 ft 7½ in (BE2, 2a, 2b); 37 ft (2c); 36 ft 10 in (2d); 40 ft 9 in (2e).
Weights: empty 1274 lb (BE2a), 1370 lb (BE2c, RAF 1a), 1431 lb (2e); loaded 1600 lb (2a), 2142 (2c, RAF 1a), 2100 lb (2e).
Performance: maximum speeds, 70 mph at ground level (BE2a), 72 mph at 6500 ft (BE2c), 90 mph at ground level (BE2e); climb to 3000 ft, 9 mins (BE2a), climb to 3500 ft, 6 mins 30 secs (BE2c), climb to 6000 ft, 20 mins 30 secs (BE2e); service ceiling, 10,000 ft (BE2a, 2c), 7000 ft (BE2e); endurance 3 hrs (BE 2a), 3¼ hrs (BE2c), 4 hrs (BE2e).

Stemming from the BE1 designed in 1911 at Farnborough by Geoffrey de Havilland and F M Green, the BE2 first emerged in 1912, becoming the BE2a and then BE2b in production forms. Intended solely for air reconnaissance and general army co-operation, the BE was for its day and purpose an excellent design, and by 1914 represented a major type in squadron use by the RFC. With the outbreak of war a number of BEs were taken to France, and the first-ever award of a Victoria Cross to an airman went to a BE2b pilot, Lieutenant W B Rhodes Moorhouse of No.2 Squadron RFC in April 1915. A development, the BE2c, first appeared in June 1914 and was ordered in quantity for the RFC and RNAS, and the first unit to arrive in France wholly equipped with BE2cs was No.8 Squadron RFC in April 1915. Though remarkably stable in flight, and thus ideal for its designed role, the BE2c quickly proved to be virtually helpless when aerial combat became widespread along the Western Front in the latter months of 1915; a defect well marked in the mounting losses among BE crews. In the UK, however, many BE2cs were allotted to Home Defence against marauding Zeppelins by night, and BE2c crews claimed the destruction of five German airships in all. Attempts either to protect, arm or enhance the performance of BEs proved in the main of little avail, though one variant, the single-bay BE2e of 1916, was built in greater quantity than any other BE version. BEs saw active service on

Above: **BE2c 2574 'Central Argentine Railway Aeroplane' was built by the Daimler Company of Coventry.**

virtually every war front and even as far afield as India, until the end of the war, though by 1918 a majority were employed in training duties in Britain. A single-seat, re-engined variant, the BE12 was produced from mid-1916 in several versions and fully equipped two RFC squadrons, Nos. 19 and 21, in France, but these were quickly withdrawn from operations after heavy losses. Though never designed for combat, the BEs and their courageous crews gave dogged service from the first to the final day of the war.

Below: **BE2e serial number 6669.**

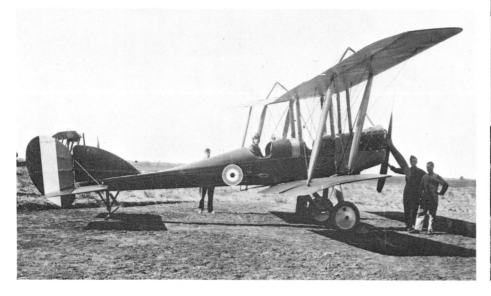

Blackburn Kangaroo

Type: bomber.
Crew: two (normal) or three.
Power plants: two 250 hp Rolls-Royce Falcon.
Dimensions: span (upper) 74 ft 10¼ in, (lower) 52 ft 10½ in; length 46 ft; height 16 ft 10 in.
Weights: empty 5284 lb; loaded 8017 lb.
Performance: maximum speed 100 mph at ground level; climb to 5000 ft, 12 mins 30 secs; service ceiling 10,500 ft; endurance 8 hrs.
Armament: one 0.303 in Lewis machine gun in nose cockpit; one 0.303 in Lewis machine gun in rear cockpit; four 230 lb bombs carried internally in fuselage; additional under-fuselage racks for four bombs.

Developed from the Blackburn GP and SP seaplanes, the lanky Kangaroo appeared on the operational scene in the spring of 1918 and equipped just one squadron, No.264 at Seaton Carew. Only 20 Kangaroos were built and at least 10 of these were used by 264 Squadron for anti-submarine and other forms of coastal patrol between May and November 1918, one (B9972) being part-responsible for the destruction of the German submarine *UC.10* on 28 August 1918. After the war all remaining Kangaroos were civilianised, and several individual aircraft undertook lengthy commercial work with a few surviving until 1929.

Bristol Scouts

Type: reconnaissance.
Crew: one.
Power plant: 80 hp Gnome/Le Rhône/Clerget; 110 hp Clerget.
Dimensions (Scout C): span 24 ft 7 in; length 20 ft 8 in; height 8 ft 6 in.
Weights (Scout C, 80 hp Le Rhône): empty 757 lb; loaded 1195 lb.
Performance (Scout C, 80 hp Le Rhône): maximum speed 92.7 mph at ground level; climb to 10,000 ft, 21 mins 20 secs; service ceiling 15,500 ft; endurance 2½ hrs.

Designed by F Barnwell, the first Bristol Scout A emerged in February 1914, and two more machines (Scout B) were delivered to the RFC by the outbreak of war. In November 1914 production of Scout C versions began, totalling 211 ultimately; while the fourth variant, the Scout D, appeared in late 1915, with a total of 80 being built in all. Individual Scouts, mainly Scout Cs, were attached to various units in France during 1914–16, and were often adapted locally to carry weapons. One such, fitted with a machine gun, was used in combat by Captain L G Hawker, DSO, resulting in Hawker's award of a VC; while several other RFC aces, including Albert Ball, VC, received their initial baptism of single-seat fighting experience in Bristol Scouts. From 1916–18 Bristol Scouts were mainly relegated to training roles and were often coveted as 'personal' machines by more senior pilots

Left: **20 Blackburn Kangaroos were built.**
Below: **a Bristol Scout D is re-rigged in the Middle East, 1918.**

due to their delightful flying qualities. One Bristol Scout C, No.1255, piloted by Flight Lieutenant Fowler, achieved an historic first on 3 November 1915 by taking off from the forward deck of HMS *Vindex* while under way; the first, wheeled-undercarriage take-off from a naval ship during the war.

Bristol F2A/F2B

Type: reconnaissance; fighter.
Crew: two.
Power plant: 190/200 hp Rolls Royce Falcon I/II; 275 hp RR Falcon III; 200 hp Sunbeam Arab; 200 hp Hispano-Suiza; 230 hp Siddeley Puma; 200 hp Wolseley Viper; 290 hp Liberty 8; 400 hp Liberty 12.
Dimensions: span 39 ft 3 in; length 25 ft 10 in (F2B, Falcon); height 9 ft 4 in (F2B, Falcon I).
Weights (F2B, Falcon I): empty 1700 lb; loaded 2650 lb.
Performance (F2B, Falcon III): maximum speed 123 mph at 4000 ft; climb to 10,000 ft, 11 mins 15 secs; service ceiling 21,500 ft; endurance 3 hrs.
Armament: one fixed 0.303 in Vickers machine gun forward; one/two 0.303 in Lewis machine guns in rear cockpit; up to 12 25 lb Cooper bombs under lower wings.

This type, commonly known as the Bristol Fighter, first appeared as the F2A in late 1916, and entered RFC service with No.48 Squadron in France in March 1917. Early combat experience led within months to the modified F2B variant, and F2Bs eventually equipped many units in France, Italy and Palestine and in the UK as home defence fighters. The F2B quickly established itself as possibly the best two-seat fighter in France during 1917–18, and in the

Below: **a Bristol F2b of No. 208 Squadron RAF flies over Ismailia, Egypt, in 1925.**

post-1918 RAF continued in first-line service as a general duties recconnaissance-cum-bombing and army co-operation aircraft in the UK, Middle East and India until early 1932. Total production of F2Bs during World War I amounted to 3101, while further examples were produced in small batches in the 1920s. The only flying example still in existence is D8096, belonging to the Shuttleworth Collection at Old Warden, Bedfordshire, which saw active service originally with No.208 Squadron RAF.

Bristol M.1

Type: fighter.
Crew: one.
Power plant: 110 hp Clerget (1A/1B); 130 hp Clerget (1B); 150 hp AR1 (1B); 110 hp Le Rhône (1C).
Dimensions: span 30 ft 9 in; length 20 ft 4 in; height 7 ft 10 in.
Weights: empty 900 lb; loaded 1350 lb.
Performance: maximum speed 132 mph (1A), 125 mph (1B), 130 mph (1C); service ceiling 17,000 ft (1A), 15,000 ft (1B), 20,000 ft (1C); endurance $2\frac{3}{4}$ hrs (1A), $1\frac{3}{4}$ hrs (1C).
Armament: one 0.303 in Vickers machine gun fixed on forward fuselage.

It is not often realised that a British-designed monoplane operational fighter was in service from as early as September 1917, in which month first production examples of the Bristol M.1 were delivered to the RFC. The M.1A, a private venture design, first flew on 14 July 1916, and immediately achieved the then astonishing speed of 132 mph. Bought by the War Office for evaluation, the M.1A was re-engined and armed with a Vickers machine gun, in which form it became titled M.1B, and was tested by the RFC in late 1916. A lingering prejudice against monoplanes, combined with the 'fast' landing speed

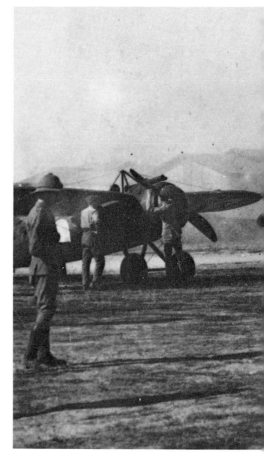

Above: **Bristol M.1 Scouts of No. 72 Sqn, 1918.**

of some 49 mph, precluded official approval for use operationally in France, but production examples (M.1Cs) were despatched to the Mediterranean zone, where they partly equipped five squadrons during 1918. The bulk of the 130 aircraft built – 125 of which were M.1Cs – were relegated as unarmed trainers to UK RAF stations. A handful survived as civil aircraft after 1918; while one M.1C, re-engined, remains today as a memorial at Minlaton, South Australia.

De Havilland 2

Type: fighter.
Crew: one.
Power plant: 100 hp Gnome Monosoupape; 110 hp Le Rhône 9J rotary.
Dimensions: span 28 ft 3 in; length 25 ft 2½ in; height 9 ft 6½ in.
Weights: empty 943 lb; loaded 1441 lb.
Performance: maximum speed 93 mph at ground level; climb to 10,000 ft, 24 mins 45 secs; service ceiling, 14,000 ft; endurance 2¾ hrs.
Armament: one 0.303 in Lewis machine gun forward.

First designed in early 1915 by Geoffrey de Havilland, the DH2 first equipped No.24 Squadron RFC in late 1915, and in February 1916 this unit went to France to commence operations. Total production amounted to 400, and the DH2 equipped three RFC squadrons in France, apart from serving in small numbers in various zones of the Middle East. Until June 1917, when it was finally superseded on active service in France, the DH2 was used to good effect against admittedly superior enemy fighters. Major Lionel Rees, commanding officer of 32 Squadron, was awarded a Victoria Cross for a particularly outstanding combat against high odds in DH2 No. 6015.

De Havilland 4

Type: day bomber.
Crew: two.
Power plant: 230 hp BHP; 230 hp Siddeley Puma; 250 hp Rolls-Royce Eagle III; 275 hp Rolls-Royce Eagle VI/VII; 375 hp Rolls-Royce Eagle VIII; 400 hp Liberty 12.
Dimensions: span 42 ft 4⅝ in; length 30 ft 8 in (RR and Puma engines); height 10 ft 5 in (RR Eagle III).
Weights: empty 2387 lb (RR Eagle VIII); loaded 3472 lb (RR Eagle VIII).
Performance (RR Eagle VIII): maximum speed 143 mph at ground level; climb to 10,000 ft, 9 mins; service ceiling 22,000 ft; endurance 6¾ hrs (max).
Armament: one fixed 0.303 in Vickers machine gun forward; one/two 0.303 in Lewis machine gun in rear cockpit; up to 500 lb bombs on underwing racks.

The first British aircraft specifically designed for day-bombing duties, the DH4 arrived in France with No.55 Squadron in March 1917 and continued on operations until the end of the war. In all-round performance the DH4 outclassed virtually all contemporaries of its type, and was often faster than enemy fighters encountered during operations. The DH4 also entered wide service with the RNAS in early 1917, both in France and in Britain, undertaking bombing, home defence, reconnaissance and anti-submarine roles. One DH4 from Great Yarmouth air station was responsible for shooting down the Zeppelin L.70 on 5 August 1918, while seven days later four DH4s from No.217 Squadron claimed the destruction of the submarine *UB.12*. From October 1917 DH4s helped pioneer long range bombing of strategic targets in Germany, and continued in this role with the Independent

Below: **a DH2 of No. 32 Sqn RFC, France, 1916.**

Above: De Havilland 4 day bombers photographed in 1917.

Force, RAF until the Armistice. American interest in the DH4 resulted in production contracts for a total of 9500 machines, to be fitted with the American Liberty 12 engine, and by the Armistice some 1885 US-built DH4s had been despatched to France, where they helped equip 12 USAS squadrons. British DH4 production totalled 1449 machines. After the war DH4s helped pioneer civil passenger and freight businesses in the UK, while in the USA several hundred American-built and modified DH4s were used for many years by the US air services, postal departments and other bodies.

De Havilland 5

Type: fighter.
Crew: one.
Power plant: 110 hp Le Rhône 9J rotary.
Dimensions: span 25 ft 8 in; length 22 ft; height 9 ft 1½ in.
Weights: empty 1010 lb; loaded 1492 lb.
Performance: maximum speed 102 mph at 10,000 ft; climb to 10,000 ft, 12 mins 25 secs; service ceiling 16,000 ft; endurance 2¾ hrs.
Armament: one 0.303 in Vickers machine gun forward.

The 'back-stagger' DH5 design was an attempt by Geoffrey de Havilland to combine the excellent pilot's field of vision of the pusher-

Below: DH5 A9393 was serving at Sedgeford in 1918.

type DH2 and the superior flying qualities of a tractor-type fighter. Introduced to operations in France in early 1917, the DH5 equipped five RFC squadrons in all, but was not considered a great success in its intended combat role, because of poor performance at heights above 10,000 feet. As a low-level ground-attack aircraft, however, it excelled during the summer of 1917, though at high cost in casualties. By February 1918 DH5s had been replaced in all first-line squadrons, and by the close of 1918 none remained in service.

De Havilland 6

Type: trainer.
Crew: two.
Power plant: 90 hp RAF 1a; 90 hp Curtiss OX-5; 80 hp Renault.
Dimensions: span 35 ft 11⅛ in; length 27 ft 3½ in; height 10 ft 9½ in.
Weights (RAF 1a): empty 1460 lb; loaded 2027 lb.
Performance: maximum speed 66 mph at 6500 ft (RAF 1a); climb to 6500 ft, 29 mins (RAF 1a); service ceiling approx 6000 ft; endurance 2 hrs.
Armament: nil (trainer); up to 100 lb of bombs (anti-submarine role).

Virtually viceless and almost unspinnable, the DH6 was produced from early 1917 as a training machine, and a total of 2282 were ultimately completed. Its near foolproof flying qualities earned the DH6 many cynical or comical nicknames, chief amongst these being 'The Clutching Hand', 'Sky Hook', and 'Clockwork Mouse'.

In March 1918 nearly 200 DH6s, superseded in RFC use, were offered to the RNAS for anti-submarine patrol duties around Britain's coastal waters. These were fitted to carry up to 100 pounds of Cooper bombs, and were usually flown by a pilot alone, because of the aircraft's inability to cope with the weight of both observer and bomb load.

De Havilland 9

Type: day bomber.
Crew: two.
Power plant: 230 hp BHP; 230 hp Siddeley Puma; 290 hp Siddeley Puma; 250 hp Fiat A-12; 430 hp Napier Lion; 400 hp Liberty 12-A.
Dimensions: span 42 ft 4⅝ in; length 30 ft 6 in (Puma); height 11 ft 2 in.
Weights (230 hp): empty 2203 lb; loaded 3669 lb.
Performance: maximum speed 111.5 mph at 10,000 ft (230 hp BHP Siddeley); climb to 10,000 ft, 20 mins 5 secs (230 hp BHP Siddeley); service ceiling 17,500 ft (absolute); endurance 4½ hrs.
Armament: one fixed 0.303 in Vickers machine gun forward; one/two 0.303 in Lewis machine guns in rear cockpit; up to 500 lb of bombs on underwing racks.

Above: **Fairey F.22 Campania at Calshot.**

Fairey Campania

Type: patrol seaplane.
Crew: two.
Power plant: 250 hp Rolls-Royce Mk IV (F. 16); 275 hp Rolls-Royce Eagle V (F. 17); 250 hp Sunbeam Maori (F. 22); 345 hp Rolls-Royce Eagle VIII.
Dimensions: span (upper) 61 ft 7½ in; length 43 ft 0⅝ in (F. 17 and F. 22); height 15 ft 1 in.
Weights (F.22, Maori Mk II): empty 3672 lb; loaded 5329 lb.
Performance (F. 22, Maori II): maximum speed 85 mph at sea level; climb to 5000 ft, 18 mins; service ceiling 6000 ft; endurance 4½ hrs.
Armament: one 0.303 in Lewis machine gun in rear cockpit; up to 250 lb of bombs on under-fuselage racks.

The Campania, named after its intended parent vessel HM Seaplane Carrier *Campania*, was the second aircraft designed and built by the Fairey Aviation Company. Designed in 1916, the first (F.16) version flew in February 1917. It was followed by several F.17 variants, and eventually by the Maori-engined F.22 improved type. Of the total of 220 Campanias contracted for production, only 62 were actually built, and these gave steady but unspectacular service at

Above: **DH6 C6833 served with a training squadron in the United Kingdom, 1918.**

Intended initially as a longer-range replacement for the DH4, the DH9 was first produced in late 1917, and began reaching RFC squadrons in France early in 1918. In practice, however, the DH9's unreliable BHP engine offered poor performance, being unable to hold height with a full war load at 15,000 feet, and seldom able to operate above 13,000 feet; figures below those of the DH4. On operations with the Independent Force RAF, DH9 crews were thus fated to run a constant gauntlet of enemy fighters and anti-aircraft fire during their forays by day into German territory, and suffered appalling casualties. Despite succinct objections by the IF commander, Hugh Trenchard, DH9s continued to be produced and issued for operations until the end of the war; even replacing the superior DH4 in some units. The RAF continued using DH9s in the 1919–20 support campaign in Russia, but most were withdrawn in favour of its successor, the DH9A, by 1921.

Right: **the de Havilland 9 day bomber suffered high losses in combat.**

sea and from shore-based stations during the latter part of World War I and in the 1919–20 Russian support campaign.

Fairey Hamble Baby

Type: seaplane scout.
Crew: one.
Power plant: 110 hp Clerget; 130 hp Clerget rotaries.
Dimensions: span 27 ft 9¼ in; length 23 ft 4 in; height 9 ft 6 in.
Weights: empty 1386 lb; loaded 1946 lb.
Performance: maximum speed at 2000 ft, 90 mph; climb to 2000 ft, 5 min 30 secs; service ceiling 7600 ft; endurance 2 hrs.
Armament: one fixed forward 0.303 in Lewis machine gun; two 65 lb bombs under fuselage.

Though basically a variant of the Sopwith Baby (itself derived from the Sopwith Tabloid and Schneider), the Hamble Baby was in many ways a fresh design, fitted with adjustable trailing-edge flaps for increased lift on take-off or landing; the Fairey Patent Camber Gear. A total of 180 were eventually built, 50 by the parent company and the rest by Parnall & Sons of Bristol, and many appeared with wheel under-carriages in place of floats for land-based naval air units. A number gave useful service with Royal Navy ships in the Mediterranean zones of operations, while the majority were based in Britain for coastal patrol work or training duties.

Below: a Fairey Hamble Baby Scout pictured at Calshot, 20 September 1917.

FE2b/2d

Type: fighter; reconnaissance; bomber.
Crew: two.
Power plant: 120/160 hp Beardmores; RAF 5; 250 hp Rolls-Royce Mk I (FE2d); 250 hp Rolls-Royce Mk III (FE2d).
Dimensions: span 47 ft 9 in; length 32 ft 3 in; height 12 ft 7½ in.
Weights: empty 2061 lb (FE2b, Beardmore), 2401 lb (FE2d, RR); loaded 3037 lb (FE2b, Beardmore), 3549 lb (FE2d, RR).
Performance: maximum speed 91.5 mph at ground level (FE2b, Beardmore), 92 mph at ground level (FE2d, Rolls-Royce); climb to 10,000 ft, 39 mins 44 secs (FE2b, Beardmore), 32 mins 30 secs (FE2d, Rolls-Royce); service ceiling 11,000 ft (FE2b, Beardmore), 17,000 ft (FE2d, Rolls-Royce); endurance 3 hrs (FE2b, Beardmore), 3¼ hrs (FE2d, RR).
Armament: one or two 0.303 in Lewis machine guns in forward cockpit; up to 300 lb of bombs on external racks.

Tracing its origins to the Farnborough-designed FE2 of 1912, via the FE2a of 1914–15, the FE2b was first produced in late 1915, and several examples were on charge to No.6 and No.12 Squadrons, RFC in France by February 1916. The first fully-equipped FE2b unit was No.20 Squadron RFC which arrived in France in January 1916, to be followed by three more FE squadrons by April 1. Initially powered by the 120 hp Beardmore, most FE2bs were soon uprated by installation of 160 hp Beardmores in the spring of 1916. Though relatively slow and

lumbering in flight, the FE2b soon proved its combat worth against the contemporary Fokker *Eindecker* scouts, and on 18 June an FE2b crew from No.25 Squadron was credited with shooting down the *Eindecker* ace Max Immelmann. Further attempts to improve the performance of the FE2b led to the FE2d version; basically a re-engined FE2b with a Rolls-Royce engine. The prototype FE2d first flew in April 1916, and by July FE2ds were arriving in France for operations. This 'improved' version proved only marginally superior to the FE2b, but its crews continued to uphold the doughty fighting reputation of its predecessor. Particularly notable was Flight Sergeant T Mottershead, DCM of 20 Squadron RFC, who sacrificed his own life in his burning FE2d to save his observer, and was awarded a posthumous VC. By mid-1917, however, both versions were clearly outclassed by German opponents, and the type was relegated to night-fighting, bombing and general reconnaissance roles in France and in the UK. Nevertheless, night-bomber FEs were still flying operationally along the Western Front until almost the end of the war. One interim variant, the FE2c, reversed pilot and observer locations, and was used as a pure bomber in 1918 in small numbers. Total production of the FE2a and FE2b amounted to 1939, while at least 248 FE2ds are known to have been issued to the RFC. A patient, if plodding work-horse, the cumbersome FE gave splendid service in many roles for almost three years of the war.

Right: a FE2b with modified undercarriage.

Right: a Darracq-built FE8 fighter.
Below right: a US-built FE8 replica.

FE8

Type: fighter.
Crew: one.
Power plant: 100 hp Gnome Monosoupape;
110 hp Le Rhône; 110 hp Clerget.
Dimensions: span 31 ft 6 in; length 23 ft 8 in;
height 9 ft 2 in.
Weights (Gnome Monosoupape): empty 895 lb;
loaded 1346 lb.
Performance (Gnome Monosoupape):
maximum speed 94 mph at ground level; climb
to 10,000 ft, 17 mins 30 secs; service ceiling
14,500 ft; endurance 2½ hrs.
Armament: one 0.303 in Lewis machine gun
forward.

Designed at the Royal Aircraft Factory, Farnborough, the FE8 was first flown in October
1915. Testing and other delays prevented initial
production machines appearing before May
1916, and No. 40 Squadron RFC, the first to be
fully equipped, did not reach France until
August 1916. The second FE8 unit, No.41
Squadron RFC, joined operations in October
1916 and was to continue using the type until
June 1917. Though a total of 297 FE8s was
eventually ordered for production, only 182
were delivered to the RFC. Mainly out-classed
by contemporary German fighters, the FE8
became the last pusher-configuration fighter
used by the RFC.

Felixstowe F2A

Type: patrol flying boat.
Crew: four.
Power plant: two 345 hp Rolls-Royce Eagle VIII.
Dimensions: span 95 ft 7½ in (upper), 68 ft 5 in
(lower); length 46 ft 3 in; height 17 ft 6 in.
Weights: empty 7549 lb; loaded 10,978 lb.
Performance: maximum speed 95.5 mph at
2000 ft; climb to 2000 ft, 3 mins 50 secs; service
ceiling 9600 ft; endurance 6 hrs.
Armament: four 0.303 in Lewis machine guns;
two 230 lb bombs on underwing racks.

Above: **Felixstowe F2a 'Old Blackeye' served at Killingholme in 1918.**

The doughty Felixstowe series of World War I flying boats had their origins in the original designs of the American pioneer Glenn Curtiss, and an early Curtiss flying boat design used by the RNAS in 1915 was modified and improved by Squadron Commander J C Porte of RNAS Felixstowe, resulting in the Felixstowe F.1, No.3580. Encouraged by his various experiments in hull modification with the F.1, Porte commenced work on larger hulls and, by marrying the hull of his Porte Baby three-engined flying boat design to the wing structure of a Curtiss H.12, he produced the Felixstowe F.2. With appropriate refinements, this design went into production as the F.2A, and deliveries to RNAS units commenced in November 1917. From early 1918 until the close of 1918 the 'Large Americas' – a soubriquet loosely applied to virtually all Porte-designed flying boats – gave splendid active service. Sea patrols, anti-Zeppelin combat, aerial fights with German seaplanes, experiments, reconnaissance – all were grist to the F2A crews' mills. Though produced to a standard configuration, F2As were subjected to a host of local and individual modifications and refinements at unit level. Nearly 170 F2As were ordered, though little more than 100 appear to have been built; many original contracts being amended to include production of F.3 and F.5 developments in 1918. On 31 October 1918 53 F2As remained on RAF charge.

Handley Page 0/100 & 0/400

Type: night bomber.
Crew: four.
Power plants: 0/100 – two 250 hp Rolls-Royce Mk II; two 320 hp Sunbeam Cossack. 0/400 – two 250 hp Rolls-Royce Mk IV; two 360 hp Rolls-Royce Eagle VIII; two 275 hp Sunbeam Maori; two 350 hp Liberty 12-N.
Dimensions: span 100 ft (upper), 70 ft (lower); length 62 ft 10¼ in; height 22 ft.
Weights (0/400, Eagle VIII): empty 8502 lb; loaded 13,360 lb.
Performance (0/400, Eagle VIII): maximum speed 97.5 mph at ground level; climb to 6500 ft, 27 mins 10 secs; service ceiling 8500 ft; endurance 8 hrs.
Armament: two 0.303 in Lewis machine guns in rear cockpit; one or two 0.303 in Lewis machine guns in nose cockpit; up to 16 112 lb bombs, or one 1650 lb SN bomb; one 0.303 in Lewis machine gun firing through floor of rear cockpit.

Built to an Admiralty specification of December 1914, the prototype 0/100 first flew in December 1915. Incorporating fold-back wings for hangarage, the design also accommodated its bomb load within the fuselage. Beginning in September 1916 a total of 40 0/100s were delivered to RNAS units, and by April 1917 were flown on operations in France. Development of the 0/100 design in 1917 resulted in the 0/400 variant, distinguishable externally by the removal of the fuel tanks from behind the engine nacelles, and internally by a completely revised fuel system. Production 0/400s began to reach operational units in significant numbers in the spring of 1918, and formed the heavy night bomber elements of that year's Independent Force RAF tasked with strategic bombing of Germany's war industry. During September-November 1918 0/400s occasionally carried single 1650 lb SN bombs to their targets – the largest bombs used by the Allies during World War I. A total of 46 HP 0/100s and 554 HP 0/400s were actually built and

Right: **HP 0/100 3128 served with No. 214 Squadron at Dunkirk, 1 June 1918.**
Below: **an HP 0/400 of No. 207 Squadron flying over Germany in May 1919.**

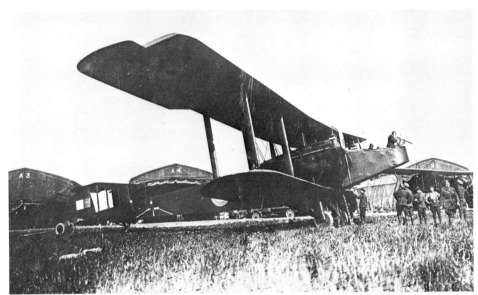

Though produced too late for operations in World War I, the HP V/1500 is included here as Britain's first true strategic bomber, and the first British four-engined bomber to go into production. Built to an Air Ministry requirement for a bomber capable of bombing Berlin and similar long-range objectives from East Anglian bases, the V/1500 first flew in May 1918, and by the Armistice 255 V/1500s had been contracted for production. Of these only three were ready for use in November 1918, and the type was not accepted for the postwar RAF. Had the war lasted into 1919 at least eight squadrons of English-based V/1500s were envisaged as an element of an expanded Independent Force RAF for strategic attacks on Germany.

Martinsyde G.100/G.102 Elephant

Type: fighter (originally); bomber.
Crew: one.
Power plant: 120 hp Beardmore (G.100); 160 hp Beardmore (G.102).
Dimensions: span 38 ft; length 26 ft 6 in (G.100), 27 ft (G.102); height 9 ft 8 in.
Weights: empty 1759 lb (G.100), 1793 lb (G.102); loaded 2424 lb (G.100), 2370 lb (G.102).
Performance (G.102): maximum speed 104 mph at 2000 ft; climb to 10,000 ft, 15 mins 55 secs; service ceiling 16,000 ft; endurance 4½ hrs.
Armament: one 0.303 in Lewis machine gun on upper-wing mounting; one 0.303 in Lewis machine gun on cockpit mounting; up to 250 lb of bombs under wings and/or fuselage.

The Martinsyde Elephant G.100 prototype was first tested in September 1915, and entered operational service on 1 March 1916 when No.27 Squadron arrived in France wholly equipped with the type. Though initially intended to be a long-range fighting scout, the Elephant's lack of

delivered in the UK; while production orders for American-built 0/400s totalled 1500 officially, though only 107 were recorded as delivered. On 31 October 1918 the RAF had a total of 258 HP 0/400s still on charge, some of which continued in service as transport and communications aircraft in the RAF, while others were converted to civil airliners. The latter were further modified to become the basis for HP 0/7, 0/10 and 0/11 civil airliners.

Handley Page V/1500

Type: strategic night bomber.
Crew: six or seven (original requirement of nine).
Power plants: four 375 hp Rolls-Royce Eagle VIII; four 500 hp Galloway Adriatic; four 450 hp Napier Lion; four 400 hp Liberty 12.
Dimensions: span 126 ft; length 62 ft; height 23 ft.
Weights: empty 17,602 lb; loaded 24,080 lb.
Performance: maximum speed 90.5 mph at 6500 ft; climb to 6500 ft, 21 mins 5 secs; service ceiling 11,000 ft; endurance (with 5318 lb fuel) 14 hrs.
Armament: single 0.303 in Lewis machine gun in nose, dorsal, ventral and tail cockpits; bomb load up to 30 250 lb bombs.

Below: **the HP V/1500 was fitted with folding wings.**

Below: **Martinsyde G.102 Elephant A6297 photographed at Brooklands in 1916.**

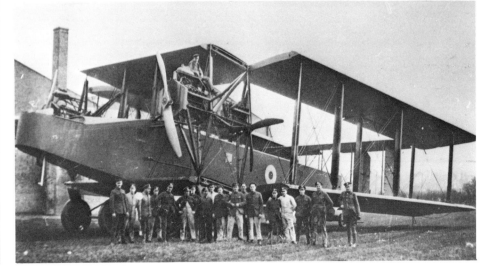

combat agility and good load-carrying qualities quickly led to its major employment as a bomber and general reconnaissance machine. Conversion from G.100 to G.102 standard was basically a matter of installing the more powerful 160 hp Beardmore engine, and such conversions were often undertaken in the field. Though several squadrons received Elephants, occasionally enough to equip complete flights, 27 Squadron remained the sole unit to be wholly equipped with the type; a fact perpetuated in the present 27 Squadron's official badge motif of an elephant. The design saw active service in France until the end of 1917, and in Palestine and Mesopotamia (Iraq) until the end of the war. In all 270 Elephants were produced.

Nieuport Scouts 17, 24 & 27

Type: fighter.
Crew: one.
Power plant: 110 hp Le Rhône 9Ja (17C.1); 120 hp Le Rhône 9Jb (24/27); 130 hp Le Rhône 9Jb (24/27).
Dimensions: span 26 ft 9 in (upper), 25 ft 7 in (lower) – 17C.1; 26 ft 11 in (upper), 25 ft 8 in (lower) – 24/27; length 19 ft (17), 19 ft 3 in (24/27); height 7 ft 10 in (all).
Weights: empty 825 lb (17), 783 lb (24); loaded 1232 lb (17), 1206 lb (24), 1179 lb (27).
Performance: maximum speed 103 mph at ground level (17), 106 mph at ground level (24), 107 mph at ground level (27); climb to 6560 ft, 6 mins 50 secs (17), 5 mins 40 secs (24/27); service ceiling 15,744 ft (17), 22,640 ft (24), 22,500 ft (27); endurance 1¾ hrs (17), 2¼ hrs (24/27).
Armament: one 0.303 in Lewis machine gun mounted above upper wing (17), one 0.303 in Vickers machine gun fixed on forward fuselage (24/27); eight Le Prieur rockets attached to wing struts if required.

The tiny Nieuport series of single-seat fighting scouts began service with the RNAS in January 1916 when Nieuport 11 scouts were supplied by France. Nieuport 16s followed later in the same year and were issued in small numbers to both RNAS and RFC squadrons. It was on a Nieuport 16 that the great British fighting ace Albert Ball, VC, really commenced his unique combat career. From July 1916 a further variant, the Nieuport 17, began to reach RFC squadrons.

Below: **this Nieuport 27 Scout, serial number B3650, was used operationally by No. 29 Squadron and No. 60 Squadron of the RFC in 1917.**

Though originally delivered fitted with a synchronised fixed Vickers machine gun forward, RFC Nieuport 17s were modified to replace these with a Lewis machine gun on an upper-wing Foster mounting as standard. The 17 was, for its day, very successful, and its designers proceeded to refine and modify it. Two later versions used widely by the British and Allied air services were the Nieuport 24 and 27. Essentially these were refined variants of the Nieuport 17 differing mainly in having altered tail unit configurations and modified wing sections. Of these two versions, the 24 found only limited operational use by the RFC but the 27 was still in squadron use in France until April 1918; while a small number continued in RAF service until late 1918. In 1916–17, Nieuport Scouts were flown by many RNAS and RFC pilots who achieved great distinction as fighter pilots, including Albert Ball and W A Bishop – both recipients of Victoria Cross awards – Edward 'Mick' Mannock (later to receive the Victoria Cross), R Dallas and many other British and Empire airmen of equal prowess.

Norman Thompson NT2b

Type: flying boat trainer.
Crew: two.
Power plant: 160 hp Beardmore; 200 hp Sunbeam Arab; 150 hp Hispano-Suiza; 200 hp Hispano-Suiza.
Dimensions: span 48 ft 4¾ in (upper), 27 ft 6¾ in (lower); length 27 ft 4½ in; height 10 ft 8 in.
Weights (Sunbeam Arab): empty 2321 lb; loaded 3169 lb.
Performance (Sunbeam Arab): maximum speed 85 mph at 2000 ft; climb to 2000 ft, 4 mins 10 secs; service ceiling 11,400 ft; endurance 2 hrs.
Armament: nil.

From 1917 until the Armistice the NT2b – nicknamed 'Ruptured Duck' by its RNAS/RAF crews – became the standard flying boat basic trainer. More than 150 examples were built but few survived the war in service.

Below: **a Norman Thompson NT2b 'unsticks'.**

RE7

Type: reconnaissance; bomber.
Crew: two.
Power plant: 120 hp Beardmore; 160 hp Beardmore; 150 hp RAF 1a; 190 hp Rolls-Royce Falcon; 250 hp Rolls-Royce Mk III; 200 hp RAF 3a; 225 hp Sunbeam.
Dimensions: span 57 ft (upper), 42 ft (lower); length 31 ft 10½ in; height 12 ft 7 in.
Weights (160 hp Beardmore): empty 2285 lb; loaded 3290 lb.
Performance: maximum speed 91.3 mph at ground level (160 hp Beardmore); climb to 10,000 ft, 31 mins 50 secs (160 hp Beardmore); service ceiling 7000 ft; endurance 6 hrs.
Armament: one 336 lb, or two 112 lb bombs; one 0.303 in Lewis machine gun on unofficial mounting on occasion.

Developed from the RE5 of Farnborough design, the RE7 was intended to lift an increased war load, and production machines began to emerge from late 1915. In January 1916 the sole fully-equipped unit, No.21 Squadron RFC, arrived in France. In a brief operational career, the RE7 proved useful as a bomber during the 1916

Somme battles, but it was soon replaced by higher performance designs. Approximately 250 RE7s were built, of which total 224 were delivered to RFC units; latterly for training and target-towing duties.

RE8

Type: reconnaissance and artillery-spotter; bomber.
Crew: two.
Power plant: 150 hp RAF 4a.
Dimensions: span 42 ft 7 in (upper), 32 ft 7½ in (lower); length 27 ft 10½ in; height 11 ft 4½ in.
Weights: empty 1803 lb; loaded (2 112 lb bombs) 2869 lb.
Performance: maximum speed 103 mph at 5000 ft; climb to 5000 ft, 8 mins 10 secs; service ceiling 13,500 ft (minus bombs), 11,000 ft (bombs); endurance 4¼ hrs (minus bombs).
Armament: one fixed 0.303 in Vickers machine gun forward; one or two 0.303 in Lewis machine guns in rear cockpit; up to 250 lb of bombs in under-wing racks.

Above: RE7 2415 was built by the Siddeley-Deasey Company in 1916.

Known universally as the 'Harry Tate' (after a contemporary music hall performer), the RE8 was a Farnborough design of early 1916. In the early production examples a tendency to spin led to an unfavourable reputation, but eventual modifications redeemed the design to some extent. The first all-RE8 unit to go to France was No.52 Squadron RFC in November 1916 and some 25 squadrons were ultimately part- or fully-equipped with the type. Its poor performance, lack of combat manoeuvrability, and general obsolescence in terms of operational use meant that, like the earlier BE2c crews, RE8 crews suffered high casualties. Nonetheless the design remained in service in France and in the Middle East zones until the Armistice. A total of 4077 RE8s were built, though only 45 of these were actually constructed at Farnborough, with the bulk being sub-contracted.

Below: an RE8 of No. 15 Squadron RAF, 1918.

SE5 & SE5a

Type: fighter.
Crew: one.
Power plant: 150 hp Hispano-Suiza; 200 hp Hispano-Suiza; 200 hp Wolseley Viper.
Dimensions: span 27 ft 11 in (originally), later 26 ft 7.4 in; length 20 ft 11 in; height 9 ft 6 in.
Weights: empty 1280 lb (150 hp H-S), 1400 lb (200 hp H-S); loaded 1827 lb (150 hp H-S), 1953 lb (200 hp H-S).
Performance: maximum speed 128.5 mph at ground level (150 hp H-S), 126 mph at 10,000 ft (200 hp H-S); climb to 10,000 ft, 12 mins 25 secs (150 hp H-S), 13 mins 15 secs (200 hp H-S); service ceiling 19,000 ft (150 hp H-S), 17,000 ft (200 hp H-S); endurance 2½ hrs (150 hp H-S), 2¼ hrs (200 hp H-S).
Armament: one 0.303 in Lewis machine gun on upper-wing mounting; one fixed 0.303 in Vickers machine gun on forward fuselage; four 25 lb Cooper bombs racked under fuselage.

Designed by Farnborough specifically to utilise the Hispano-Suiza engine, the prototype SE5 first flew on 22 November 1916. Production contracts were issued by the end of December 1916 and the first fully-equipped SE5 unit, No.56 Squadron, flew to France in April 1917. Modifications soon led to the SE5a version, the first production contract for which was dated February 1917. Eventually the 200 hp Hispano-Suiza engine was standardised for the SE5a, despite numerous minor technical difficulties in operational spheres. Later still the Wolseley Viper was specified for all 1918 contracts. By 1918 the SE5a had come to be recognised as one of the best fighters on operations, being strong, aerobatic and a steady gun platform. As such it was the mount of many leading Allied fighter pilots such as Mannock, McCudden, Ball, Beauchamp-Proctor (all VCs) and others of equally high prowess. By the Armistice of November 1918 a total of 24 RAF squadrons were SE5a-equipped. Total production of the type amounted to 5205, of which 2973 were distributed to service units by 31 October 1918. After the war the SE5a disappeared quickly from RAF use, but several examples continued in civilian guise for almost a decade.

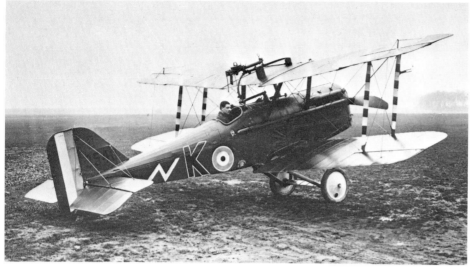

Above: **SE5a D3540 served with No. 40 Squadron. The zig-zag marking identified the squadron and the interplane struts were doped in black and white.**

Short 184

Type: patrol seaplane; torpedo bomber.
Crew: two.
Power plant: 225 hp Sunbeam; 240 hp Sunbeam; 260 hp Sunbeam; 275 hp Sunbeam Maori III; 250 hp Rolls-Royce (Eagle); 240 hp Renault.
Dimensions: span 63 ft 6¼ in; length 40 ft 7½ in; height 13 ft 6 in.
Weights (260 hp Sunbeam): empty 3703 lb; loaded 5363 lb.
Performance (260 hp Sunbeam): maximum speed 88.5 mph at 2000 ft; climb to 2000 ft, 8 mins 35 secs; service ceiling 9000 ft; endurance 2¾ hrs.
Armament: one 0.303 in Lewis machine gun in rear cockpit; one 14-inch torpedo slung between floats or up to 500 lb of bombs.

Of the many Short designs to see service with the RNAS and RAF during World War I, the Short 184 was the most outstanding in both quantity and quality of services. At least 650 were built, and it became the standard patrol seaplane in use. In August 1915 two Short 184s sank enemy vessels with torpedoes; the world's first such successes. However, the major part of its distinguished war record concerned its many bombing raids, gun-spotting sorties and wide patrol duties from 1915 to 1918 in several war theatres.

Short 320

Type: patrol seaplane; torpedo bomber.
Crew: two.
Power plant: 310 hp Sunbeam Cossack; 320 hp Sunbeam Cossack.
Dimensions: span 75 ft (upper), 46 ft 9½ in (lower); length 45 ft 9 in; height 17 ft 6 in.
Weights (320 hp Sunbeam): empty 4891 lb; loaded (two 230 lb bombs) 7021 lb.
Performance (320 hp Sunbeam, with bombs): maximum speed 79 mph at 2000 ft; climb to 2000 ft, 8 mins 35 secs; service ceiling 5500 ft; endurance 6 hrs.
Armament: one 0.303 in Lewis machine gun in front cockpit; one 18-inch Mk IX torpedo (1000 lb) beneath fuselage, or two 230 lb bombs.

The partner to the standard Short 184 for maritime roles, the Short 320 was produced from 1916, and differed from the 184 in many respects including having its pilot's cockpit at the rear. At least 137 examples were contracted for production and these saw service at various UK naval air stations and in the Middle East. Primarily designed as a torpedo bomber, the Short 320 was another forerunner of future naval air striking power.

Right: **Short 320 N4393 taxies away from Calshot beach on 19 February 1918 for a torpedo trial.**
Below right: **a Short Bomber (right) pictured with a Sopwith 1½ Strutter, both built by Mann Egerton of Norwich in 1916.**
Below: **a Short 184 seaplane.**

Short Bomber

Type: night bomber.
Crew: two.
Power plant: 225 hp Sunbeam; 250 hp Rolls-Royce Eagle.
Dimensions: span 84 ft; length 36 ft 6 in, later 45 ft; height 15 ft.
Weights: empty 5000 lb; loaded 6800 lb.
Performance (Rolls-Royce): maximum speed 77.5 mph at 6500 ft; climb to 6500 ft, 21 min 25 secs; service ceiling 9500 ft; endurance 6 hrs.
Armament: one 0.303 in Lewis machine gun on pillar mounting above upper wing, originally, then on normal rear cockpit ring mounting; four 230 lb, or eight 112 lb bombs.

Essentially a stop-gap design until the promised Handley Page 0/100 heavy bomber was available, the Short Bomber of 1916 was initially a Short 184 seaplane fuselage and engine fitted with new wings and a wheeled undercarriage. Modifications after trials produced a bigger

span, longer fuselage machine, and an eventual total of 83 was produced. Short Bombers were first in action in November 1916 with No.7 Squadron RNAS near Dunkirk, and later were used by No.5 Wing RNAS in early 1917. Fifteen aircraft were sent to the newly-formed No.3 Wing RNAS to help implement that unit's *raison d'etre*, strategic bombing, but were transferred to the RFC in mid-1916. The arrival of the first HP 0/100s in November nullified further necessity for the Short Bomber, and by mid 1917 all had been withdrawn from operations.

Sopwith Tabloid

Type: scout.
Crew: one.
Power plant: 80 hp Gnome rotary.
Dimensions: span 25 ft 6 in; length 20 ft 4 in; height 8 ft 5 in.
Weights: empty 730 lb; loaded 1120 lb.
Performance: maximum speed 92 mph at ground level; climb to 1200 ft, 1 min; endurance 3½ hrs.
Armament: one 0.303 in Lewis machine gun fitted in various forward positions; up to four 20 lb Hales bombs could be carried under fuselage.

The first single-seat scout to achieve production status, the Tabloid derived from a two-seat prototype of late 1913. Production began in early 1914 for the RFC, but in the early weeks of the war the type was also used by the RNAS units in France; two of the latter being responsible for a bombing raid on German airship sheds at Cologne and Dusseldorf on 7 October 1914 in which Zeppelin Z.IX was destroyed. Though the Tabloid achieved little operationally, it was the father of a successful line of Sopwith single-seat fighters throughout World War I. One Tabloid, refitted with twin floats, won the Schneider Trophy Contest at Monaco in April 1914, and became inadvertently the precursor of the Sopwith Baby line of naval air scouts.

Below: a Sopwith Tabloid fitted with the original form of undercarriage.

Sopwith Schneider & Baby

Type: maritime patrol scout.
Crew: one.
Power plant: 110 hp Clerget; 130 hp Clerget.
Dimensions: span 25 ft 8 in; length 22 ft 10 in; height 10 ft.
Weights (130 hp Clerget): empty 1226 lb; loaded 1715 lb.
Performance (130 hp Clerget): maximum speed 100 mph at sea level; climb to 10,000 ft 35 mins; endurance 2¼ hrs.
Armament: one 0.303 in Lewis machine gun firing forward; two 65 lb bombs under fuselage (Baby).

Totals of 136 Schneiders and 286 Babys were ultimately built, all having derived initially from the Tabloid-conversion machine which won the 1914 Schneider Trophy Race. Production Schneiders began reaching naval air stations in Britain early in 1915 where they were used for coastal patrols, while several examples went to sea aboard naval vessels. Initially powered by a 100 hp Gnome Monosoupape rotary engine, by 1916 Schneiders were being fitted with the 110 hp Clerget and thereafter were more usually titled Baby. Modified variants were produced by the Fairey and Blackburn companies and many of these remained in service until the end of the war, serving with naval air units in the Mediterranean and Aegean zones, as well as with units of the Grand Fleet.

Sopwith 1½ Strutter

Type: day bomber.
Crew: two.
Power plant: 110 hp Clerget 9Z; 130 hp Clerget 9Bc; 135 hp Clerget 9Ba; 110 hp Le Rhône 9J; 130 hp Le Rhône 9Jby; 80 hp Le Rhône 9C.
Dimensions: span 33 ft 6 in; length 25 ft 3 in; height 10 ft 3 in.
Weights: empty 1259 lb (110 hp Clerget), 1305 lb (130 hp Clerget); loaded 2149 lb (110 hp Clerget), 2150 lb (130 hp Clerget).
Performance (110 hp Clerget): maximum speed 106 mph at ground level; climb to 10,000 ft, 20 mins 25 secs; service ceiling 15,000 ft; endurance 4¼ hrs.
Armament: one fixed 0.303 in Vickers machine gun forward; one 0.303 in Lewis machine gun in rear cockpit; up to 230 lb of bombs.

Above: **Sopwith Pup B1807 served with a training unit in the UK in 1918.**

Built to an Admiralty contract and officially known as the Sopwith Type 9400, the Sopwith 1½ Strutter was Britain's first true tractor two-seater to carry a synchronised forward-firing machine gun on operations. Initial deliveries to the RNAS began in February 1916, while a single-seat bomber version (Admiralty designation Type 9700) was also brought into service in France. Contracts for 1½ Strutters for the RFC were also placed early in 1916 and No.70 Squadron was the first unit so equipped, with two flights participating in the opening phase of the 1916 Somme battle. In RFC use the type was superseded by late 1917, but the RNAS made considerable use of its 1½ Strutters as bombers, fighters, and shipborne scouts, as well as for numerous trials and experiments in naval air war. At least 1500 1½ Strutters were built for RFC and RNAS use and contemporary documentation indicates that the French Government contracted production of some 4500 machines for the use of its air services; while other countries to use the type included Belgium, Russia and the USA. In Britain, in 1917–18, at least 60 1½ Strutters were allotted to home defence squadrons where they were subjected to a variety of local armament modifications.

Sopwith Pup

Type: fighter.
Crew: one.
Power plant: 80 hp Le Rhône; 80 hp Gnome; 80 hp Clerget; 100 hp Gnome Monosoupape.
Dimensions: span 26 ft 6 in; length 19 ft 3¾ in; height 9 ft 5 in.
Weights (Le Rhône): empty 787 lb; loaded 1225 lb.
Performance (Le Rhône): maximum speed 111.5 mph at ground level; climb to 10,000 ft, 14 mins; service ceiling 17,500 ft; endurance 3 hrs.
Armament: one 0.303 in Vickers machine gun forward (standard), or one 0.303 in Lewis machine gun firing through or above centre section of upper wing; four 20 lb Hales bombs could be carried under fuselage.

Often described as the perfect flying machine, the delightful Sopwith Pup first appeared in prototype form in the spring of 1916, and first production examples began to reach RNAS units in France by October of that year. The first

Below: **a Sopwith 1½ Strutter serving with No. 5 (N) Squadron RNAS at Dunkirk, 1917.**

Above: a rebuilt Sopwith Pup flying at Old Warden, Bedfordshire.

RFC Pup unit was No.54 Squadron which arrived in France on Christmas Eve 1916. Only two other first-line RFC squadrons, Nos.46 & 66, were Pup-equipped. The RNAS, however, used Pups widely, not only in France where seven squadrons flew the type, but aboard many ships of the Grand Fleet, where they were responsible for many pioneering trials of shipborne aircraft techniques. Beardmore-built variants of the Pup, titled Beardmore WB IIIs, incorporated folding wings for shipborne stowage. A total of 1770 Pups were built, and though replaced in the main by Sopwith 2F.1 Camels and other types for front-line use by 1918, on 31 October 1918 the RAF still had 888 Pups in service, mainly in training units.

Sopwith Triplane

Type: fighter.
Crew: one.
Power plant: 110 hp Clerget; 130 hp Clerget.
Dimensions: span 26 ft 6 in; length 18 ft 10 in; height 10 ft 6 in.
Weights (130 hp Clerget): empty 1101 lb; loaded 1541 lb.
Performance: maximum speed 117 mph at 5000 ft; climb to 5,000 ft, 4 mins 35 secs; service ceiling 20,500 ft; endurance 2¾ hrs.
Armament: one fixed 0.303 in Vickers machine gun forward.

The unorthodox Sopwith Triplane first appeared in France in June 1916 when the prototype was sent to 'A' Squadron RNAS for operational evaluation. Production Triplanes were first

Right: Sopwith Triplane N5350 was one of 152 manufactured.

Above: **Sopwith Triplane N5912 is preserved at the RAF Museum, Hendon.**

issued in late 1916 and were employed almost exclusively by RNAS squadrons in France. The design's excellent combat manoeuvrability, high rate of climb, and strong structure led to a deserved reputation as a formidable fighter; exemplified by the successes of No.10 Squadron RNAS's B Flight, led by the Canadian ace Ray Collishaw, which accounted for at least 87 enemy aircraft in May–July 1917. By November 1917 virtually all Triplanes in France had been withdrawn in favour of Sopwith Camels, but the Triplane's fighting record guaranteed the design a permanent niche in the combat annals of the British air services. A total of 152 Triplanes was built.

Sopwith Camel

Type: fighter.
Crew: one.
Power plant: 110 hp Clerget; 130 hp Clerget; 110 hp Le Rhône; 150 hp BR1; 100 hp Gnome Monosoupape.
Dimensions: span 28 ft (F.1); 26 ft 11 in (2F.1); length 18 ft 9 in (F.1, Clerget), 18 ft 6 in (2F.1, Clerget); height 8 ft 6 in (F.1, Clerget), 9 ft 1 in (2F.1).
Weights: empty 929 lb (F.1, 130 hp Clerget), 956 lb (2F.1, 130 hp Clerget); loaded 1453 lb (F.1, 130 hp Clerget), 1523 lb (2F.1, 130 hp Clerget).
Performance: maximum speed 113 mph at 10,000 ft (F.1, 130 hp Clerget), 114 mph at 10,000 ft (2F.1, 130 hp Clerget); climb to 10,000 ft, 10 mins 35 secs (F.1, 130 hp Clerget), 11 mins 40 secs (2F.1, 130 hp Clerget); service ceiling 19,000 ft (F.1, 130 hp Clerget), 19,000 ft (2F.1, 130 hp Clerget).
Armament: two fixed 0.303 in Vickers machine guns forward (F.1 & 2F.1) or one 0.303 in Vickers machine gun forward and one 0.303 in Lewis machine gun above upper wing (2F.1); two 0.303 in Lewis machine guns above upper wing (home defence F.1); four 25 lb Cooper bombs under fuselage if required.

The Sopwith Camel was the most successful fighter produced by any nation during World War I; its pilots claiming almost 3000 combat victories. The prototype first flew in December 1916, and the first combats took place in early June 1917 by pilots of No.4 Squadron RNAS based near Dunkirk. In the same month No.70 Squadron became the first RFC unit to be equipped with Camels. The first British fighter designed from the outset to incorporate the classic twin forward-firing machine gun installation, the Camel also possessed astonishing manoeuvrability and general aerobatic qualities; ideal characteristics for the contemporary conditions of aerial combat. Re-equipment of first-line squadrons in France with Camels steadily mounted until, by the end of February 1918, no less than 13 Camel squadrons were operational along the Western Front, while three more had already been sent to the Italian war zone. By August 1918 there were 19 Camel squadrons available for operations on the French front. In Britain several home defence squadrons began to receive Camels from mid-1917, and many machines had their standard twin-Vickers gun armament changed to include

Below: **this Sopwith F1 Camel is displayed in the RAF Museum at Hendon.**

Left: a cutaway artwork of a Sopwith F1
Camel carrying the markings of No. 203 Sqn.
Above left: Camel D3332 served with four
operational squadrons and is pictured in
No. 210 Squadron markings carrying the
monogram of Capt AW Carter.
Above: Sopwith F1 Camel H7000 served with
No. 209 Squadron in 1918.

one or two upward-firing Lewis machine guns.
The use of Camels for night fighting was
extended to the formation of two squadrons,
Nos.151 and 152, tasked with night intruder
roles along the Western Front from June 1918.
A naval version of the Camel, the 2F.1, or Ships'
Camel as it was officially titled, commenced
production in late 1917, and 2F.1s gradually
replaced Pups and other shipborne fighters in
1918. Sea-going 2F.1s achieved several operational successes, but the most significant were
the occasions when a 2F.1, piloted by Lieutenant
S D Culley, took off from a towed wood platform
and destroyed the Zeppelin L.53 on 10 August
1918; while on 18 July six 2F.1s took off from the
forward deck of HMS *Furious* and successfully
bombed airship sheds at Tondern, destroying
Zeppelins L.54 and L.60 in the process – the first
occasion of a land target being successfully
attacked by carrier-borne aircraft. A total of
5597 F.1s and 317 2F.1s were eventually
ordered, though it is not known if 200 of these
were actually built.

Sopwith Dolphin

Type: fighter.
Crew: one.
Power plant: 200 hp Hispano-Suiza (Mk 1);
300 hp Hispano-Suiza (Mk II); 200 hp direct-drive
Hispano-Suiza (Mk III).
Dimensions: span 32 ft 6 in; length 22 ft 3 in;
height 8 ft 6 in.
Weights (Mk 1, with two Vickers): empty
1436 lb; loaded 1911 lb.
Performance (Mk 1, two Vickers): maximum
speed 128 mph at 10,000 ft; climb to 10,000 ft, 11
mins; service ceiling 21,000 ft; endurance 2 hrs.
Armament: two fixed 0.303 in Vickers machine
guns forward, plus if required, one or two 0.303
in Lewis machine guns on upper wing
mountings; four 25 lb Cooper bombs if required.

The Sopwith 5F.1 Dolphin prototype was first
tested in June 1917, and production aircraft
began to be delivered to the RFC before the end
of the year. Only four squadrons, Nos. 19, 79, 23
and 87 (in order of re-equipment) were issued
with Dolphins and they continued using the type
until the close of hostilities. Though designed to
carry four machine guns, the armament in
combat was usually restricted to the twin
Vickers installation. Although highly manoeuvrable, with an excellent high altitude performance, the Dolphin suffered from unreliable
engines, apart from somewhat biased views of
its 'backward stagger' wings by pilots. Attempts
to improve engine power resulted in Mk II and
III versions, but the engine reliability problems
remained. In combat Dolphins proved formidable fighters, particularly at altitude, and in the
latter months of the war were often used as top
cover elements of various multi-squadron
attacks against German airfields and installations. A total of 1532 Dolphins was eventually
produced but few survived to see postwar
service, although several examples were sold
to Poland and the USA in 1918–20. Dolphins also
formed the initial equipment of No.1 Squadron,
Canadian Air Force in 1918, though this unit saw
no operational service before the Armistice.

Right: a line-up of Sopwith 5F.1 Dolphin
fighters of No. 1 Squadron, Canadian Air
Force, pictured in England during
November 1918.
Below: sideviews of Sopwith aircraft include
the ground-attack Salamander.

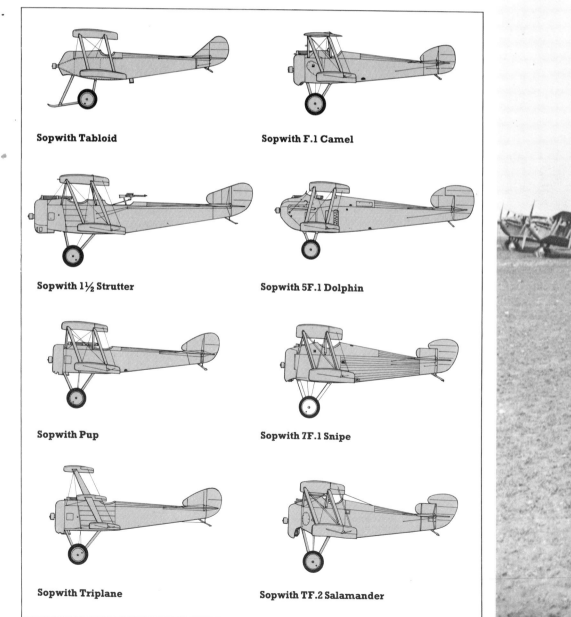

Sopwith Tabloid

Sopwith F.1 Camel

Sopwith 1½ Strutter

Sopwith 5F.1 Dolphin

Sopwith Pup

Sopwith 7F.1 Snipe

Sopwith Triplane

Sopwith TF.2 Salamander

M.816.R

Above: a Sopwith 7F.1 Snipe in 1918.

Sopwith Snipe

Type: fighter.
Crew: one.
Power plant: 150 hp BR1; 230 hp BR2; 320 hp ABC Dragonfly.
Dimensions: span 31 ft 1 in (upper wing with balanced ailerons); length 19 ft 10 in; height 9 ft 6 in.
Weights: empty 1312 lb; loaded 2020 lb.
Performance: maximum speed 121 mph at 10,000 ft; climb to 10,000 ft, 9 mins 25 secs; service ceiling 19,500 ft; endurance 3 hrs.
Armament: two fixed 0.303 in Vickers machine guns forward; four 25 lb Cooper bombs under fuselage if required.

The Sopwith 7F.1 Snipe first appeared in prototype form in mid-1917, intended as a replacement for its stablemate the Camel. In the event it was to be almost a year later before production Snipes became available for issue to the RAF; consequently relatively few Snipes, less than 100 by November 1918, saw operational war service. First to use the type were pilots of No.43 Squadron, from late September 1918, to be followed in re-equipment from Camels by No.4 Squadron Australian Flying Corps and No.208 Squadron RAF. One Snipe, E8102, gained lasting fame as the Snipe in which Major W G Barker, DSO, MC gained a Victoria Cross for a single-handed combat against great odds on 27 October 1918. Although just 497 Snipes had been built by the Armistice, production continued after the war when the type

became a standard RAF fighter. Final production amounted to 2103 Snipes. In post-1918 years the Snipe's aerobatic qualities were fully exploited at displays to the public, and it remained in service until 1927.

Sopwith Cuckoo

Type: torpedo bomber.
Crew: one.
Power plant: 200 hp Hispano-Suiza; 200 hp Sunbeam Arab; 200 hp Wolseley W4A Viper; 275 hp Rolls-Royce Falcon III.
Dimensions: span 46 ft 9 in; length 28 ft 6 in (Arab engine); height 11 ft.
Weights (Arab): empty 2199 lb; loaded 3883 lb.
Performance (Arab): maximum speed 103.5 mph at 2000 ft; climb to 2000 ft, 4 mins; service ceiling 12,100 ft; endurance 4 hrs.
Armament: one 18-inch Mk IX, 1000 lb torpedo.

Like the Handley Page V/1500 and others, the Cuckoo was designed and produced prior to the Armistice but saw no operational service during World War I. It was, nevertheless, the first torpedo bomber to be in full squadron equipment aboard an aircraft carrier, when in October 1918 No.185 Squadron RAF was embarked on HMS *Argus*. The Cuckoo remained in RAF service until 1923, while six examples taken to Japan virtually formed the basis for Japan's development of torpedo bombers, which were used to deadly effect in World War II.

Below: a Sopwith Cuckoo releases its torpedo.

Above: a Spad S7 in RFC markings, 1918.

Spad 7

Type: fighter.
Crew: one.
Power plant: 140 hp Hispano-Suiza; 150 hp Hispano-Suiza.
Dimensions: span 25 ft 8 in; length 20 ft 3½ in; height 7 ft.
Weights: loaded 1632 lb.
Performance: maximum speed 119 mph at 6500 ft; service ceiling 17,500 ft; endurance 2¼ hrs.
Armament: one fixed 0.303 in Vickers machine gun forward.

One of the classic French-designed fighters of World War I, a single Spad 7 entered RFC service with No.60 Squadron in September 1916. The type then re-equipped No.19 Squadron between October 1916 and February 1917. By April 1917 a second unit, No.23 Squadron RFC, had also been fully equipped with Spads. Though these were the only wholly-equipped units, several Spads were flown in the Middle East by Nos.30, 63 and 72 Squadrons RFC. Strong in construction and with good manoeuvrability, the Spad 7 proved to be a worthy opponent to its German counterparts. They remained in first-line RFC service until late 1918.

Vickers FB5

Type: fighter; reconnaissance.
Crew: two.
Power plant: 100 hp Gnome Monosoupape; 110 hp Clerget.
Dimensions: span 36 ft 6 in; length 27 ft 2 in; height 11 ft.
Weights: empty 1220 lb; loaded 2050 lb.
Performance: maximum speed 70 mph at 5000 ft; climb to 5000 ft, 16 mins; service ceiling 9,000 ft; endurance 4½ hrs.
Armament: one 0.303 in Lewis machine gun in forward cockpit.

Evolved from a line of experimental gun-carrying pusher biplanes which commenced with the 1913 Vickers Type 18 Destroyer, the FB5 first appeared in July 1914 and was given a production contract in the following month. By February 1915 a few examples were in France and on 25 July 1915 the first, fully-equipped unit, No.11 Squadron RFC, arrived in France; the first-ever squadron equipped throughout with a single type of aircraft and specifically allocated

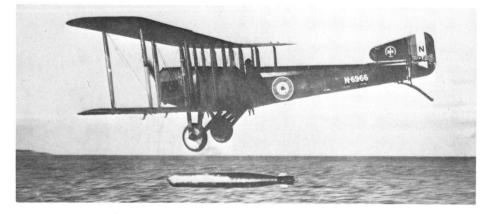

to 'fighting duties'. Several other squadrons received one or two examples that year, but by the spring of 1916 the FB5 was withdrawn from first-line duties and allotted to training roles in Britain. One FB5 pilot, Lieutenant G S M Insall of No.11 Squadron, received a Victoria Cross for his determination in combat on 7 November 1915. An improved variant, the FB9, was produced in late 1915, but few saw operational service; being mainly employed as training machines. Though entirely unofficial, the FB5 in particular was often referred to as the Vickers 'Gunbus'.

Below: a Vickers FB5 is armed with a Lewis machine gun mounted in the front cockpit.

Wight 'Converted' Seaplane

Type: patrol seaplane; trainer.
Crew: two.
Power plant: 275 hp Rolls-Royce Mk II; 265 hp Sunbeam Maori.
Dimensions: span 65 ft 6 in (upper), 55 ft (lower); length 44 ft 8½ in; height 16 ft.
Weights (Rolls-Royce): empty 3758 lb; loaded 5556 lb.
Performance (Rolls-Royce): maximum speed 84.5 mph at 2000 ft; climb to 2000 ft, 4 mins 20 secs; service ceiling 9600 ft; endurance 3½ hrs.
Armament: one 0.303 in Lewis machine gun in rear cockpit; up to 500 lb of bombs under fuselage.

Above: a Wight 'Converted' Seaplane, powered by a Rolls-Royce Eagle engine, takes off from Calshot on 10 January 1919. The Wight designation derived from the J. Samuel White Company's location on the Isle of Wight.

Derived from a 1916 bomber designed for the Admiralty by the Wight (J S White & Co.) firm, the Wight 'Converted' was basically an improved bomber fitted with floats and (mainly) the same power plant, the 275 hp Rolls-Royce Mk II. Though only 37 examples were actually built, these gave sturdy service in 1917–18 first as patrol bombers in UK coastal waters, and latterly as useful seaplane trainers.

Part Two
1918

1939

Above: a Fairey IIIF of No. 202 Squadron RAF pictured during a sortie from Malta in 1933.

Armstrong Whitworth Atlas

Type: army co-operation.
Crew: two.
Power plant: 400 hp Jaguar IVC.
Dimensions: span 39 ft 7 in; length 28 ft 7 in; height 10 ft 6 in.
Weights: empty 2550 lb; loaded 4020 lb.
Performance: maximum speed 142 mph at sea level; climb to 15,000 ft, 28 mins; service ceiling 16,800 ft; endurance 3¼ hrs.
Armament: one fixed 0.303 in Vickers machine gun forward; one 0.303 in Lewis machine gun in rear cockpit; four 120 lb bombs on racks under lower wings.

Designed from the outset as an army co-operation aircraft, the Atlas entered RAF service in early 1927, and fully equipped No.26 Squadron by November that year. In the years 1927–30 it also equipped five other squadrons. Of all-metal structure with, mainly, fabric covering, the Atlas could carry wireless, photographic and message pick-up equipment. A total of 478 Atlases was produced, and the type remained in RAF service until 1933, latterly as a training aircraft. At least 16 examples went to the RCAF, several of which continued in service until 1941.

Armstrong Whitworth Siskin III & IIIA

Type: fighter.
Crew: one.
Power plant: 325 hp Jaguar III (Mk III); 385 hp Jaguar IV (Mk IIIA).
Dimensions: span 33 ft 1 in (Mk III), 33 ft 2 in (Mk IIIA); length 23 ft (Mk III), 25 ft 4 in (Mk IIIA); height 9 ft 9 in (both Mks).
Weights: empty 1830 lb (Mk III), 2061 lb (Mk IIIA); loaded 2735 lb (Mk III), 3012 lb (Mk IIIA).
Performance: (Mk IIIA): maximum speed 153 mph at 10,000 ft; climb to 10,000 ft, 6 mins 35 secs; service ceiling 27,100 ft; endurance 1.2 hrs (full throttle).
Armament: two fixed 0.303 in Vickers machine guns forward; four 20 or 25 lb bombs on underwing racks.

Introduced into RAF service in May 1924 in the Mark III version, the Siskin's genesis lay in the 1918 Siddeley Siskin SR2, which had been slowly developed in the interim. In all 63 were built for RAF use, including 47 two-seat variants. Siskin III, J7001, was converted to act as a prototype Mark IIIA, powered by the more powerful Jaguar IV engine which gave a far better performance range. First Mark IIIAs went to

Above: **a trio of AW Atlas army co-operation aircraft of No. 26 Squadron fly from Catterick in 1933.**

No.111 Squadron RAF in September 1926 and eventually equipped ten other squadrons. A total of almost 350 Mark IIIAs was built, mostly for the RAF. The type began to be phased out of first-line use in 1933; though a batch sent to the RCAF continued in use until 1939. Highly aerobatic and pleasant to fly, the angular Siskin was liked by most of its pilots, and marked an advance in general fighter design by being the RAF's first all-metal structure fighter to achieve quantity production status.

Below: **an Armstrong Whitworth Siskin IIIa carries No. 43 Squadron markings.**

Avro 504N

Type: trainer.
Crew: two.
Power plant: 160 hp AS Lynx IV; 180 hp AS Lynx IV; 215 hp AS Lynx IVC.
Dimensions: span 36 ft; length 28 ft 6 in; height 10 ft 11 in.
Weights: empty 1584 lb; loaded 2240 lb.
Performance: maximum speed 100 mph at ground level; climb to 2000 ft, 3 mins; service ceiling 14,600 ft; endurance 3 hrs.
Armament: nil.

Usually referred to as the Lynx (from its engine), the 504N was a radial-engined variant of the legendary Avro 504K, with revised wings and undercarriage designs. Production versions began to be built in 1925, totalling ultimately 598 machines by 1933. It replaced the 504K as the RAF's standard *ab initio* trainer in those years, and became the RAF's first instrument flying (blind flying) trainer. The 504N's aerobatic qualities were displayed to good effect at the annual Hendon Air Displays until 1933, the year the type was replaced in RAF service. It also saw useful service with the Auxiliary Air Force and the University Air Squadrons. From 1933 many 504Ns were used by various civil firms, and in 1940 seven civil 504Ns were impressed for RAF service again as glider-tugs with the Christchurch Special Duties Flight; while three others were in use at the Royal Aircraft Establishment, Farnborough, Hampshire.

Below: **Avro 504N trainers from No. 4 Flying Training School, Abu Sueir, Egypt, practice line-abreast formation flying.**

Above: **an Avro Bison of No. 423 Flight, FAA.**

Avro Bison

Type: maritime reconnaissance.
Crew: three or four.
Power plant: 480 hp Napier Lion II.
Dimensions: span 46 ft; length 36 ft; height 14 ft 2 in (Mk II).
Weights: empty 4116 lb; loaded 6132 lb.
Performance: maximum speed 110 mph at sea level (Mk I); climb to 10,000 ft, 24 mins; service ceiling 14,000 ft (Mk I), 12,000 ft (Mk II); range 360 miles (Mk II).
Armament: one fixed 0.303 in Vickers machine gun forward; one 0.303 in Lewis machine gun in dorsal cockpit.

The Bison was designed to naval requirements for a deck-landing reconnaissance and gun-spotting biplane. The prototype first appeared in 1921, and production Mark IIs entered RAF service with No.3 Squadron at Gosport in 1922. The Fleet Air Arm began receiving Bisons in 1923 and the type served at various shore stations and aboard aircraft carriers both with the Home and Mediterranean Fleets until its eventual replacement by Fairey IIIFs in 1929. The gross fuselage was deliberately designed to offer ample accommodation for naval observers and their impedimenta, while the open cockpit for the pilot was necessarily located high ahead of the upper wing to give a clear field of vision for deck landings. A total of 53 Bisons was produced.

Avro Tutor

Type: trainer.
Crew: two.
Power plant: 180 hp Armstrong Siddeley Lynx IV; 240 hp AS Lynx IVC.
Dimensions: span 34 ft; length 26 ft 4½ in; height 9 ft 7 in.
Weights: empty 1844 lb; loaded 2493 lb.
Performance: maximum speed 120 mph at sea level; climb to 5000 ft, 5.9 mins; service ceiling 16,000 ft; endurance 2¾ hrs.
Armament: nil.

The type was first introduced to the RAF in 1930 as the Avro 621 Trainer with uncowled Mongoose engine. It was adopted as the standard RAF trainer, replacing the Avro 504N, from 1932, and of the total of 795 Tutors built, 394 were delivered to the RAF. Fully aerobatic and easy to fly, the Tutor continued the pattern of instrument flying technique pioneered by its predecessor. Its aerobatic qualities were demonstrated by the Tutors of Central Flying School at each annual Hendon Air Display. The Tutor remained in RAF service until 1939. A batch of 14 Tutors was modified to accept twin floats to

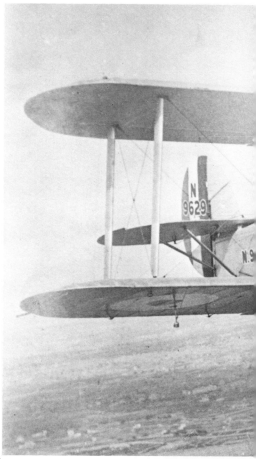

Above: **Avro Tutor K3215 is preserved in flying condition by the Shuttleworth Trust at Old Warden, Bedfordshire.**

become Sea Tutors and these served mainly at RAF Calshot as trainers for future maritime RAF crews. Today the only flying Tutor in existence is held by the Shuttleworth Collection at Old Warden, Bedfordshire; K3215, formerly civil-registered as G-AHSA.

Avro Anson

Type: maritime reconnaissance; bomber; trainer; communications aircraft.
Crew: three or four.
Power plant: two 335 hp Armstrong Siddeley Cheetah IX (Mk I); two 395 hp AS Cheetah XIX (Mk I); two 450 hp Pratt & Whitney Wasp Junior (Mk V & VI).
Dimensions: span 56 ft 6 in; length 42 ft 3 in; height 13 ft 1 in.
Weights (Mk I): empty 5375 lb; loaded 8000 lb.
Performance (Mk I): maximum speed 188 mph at 7000 ft; initial climb rate 750 ft per min; service ceiling 19,500 ft; range 660 miles.
Armament: one fixed 0.303 in Browning machine gun in nose; one 0.303 in Vickers K Gas Operated machine gun in dorsal turret.

Below: **Avro Ansons of No. 220 Sqn, 1939.**

Included in this section because of its initial wide service in the RAF prior to World War II, the Avro Anson – 'Faithful Annie' – served with distinction throughout 1939–45, and continued in first-line RAF use until eventual official retirement in June 1968. More than 11,000 Ansons were built, and some 7000 of them wore RAF livery at some stage of the type's 32 years' service life. A military development of the Avro 652 civil passenger monoplane of 1935, the Anson I entered RAF service with No.48 Squadron in March 1936 as a coastal patrol and reconnaissance aircraft. It thus became the RAF's first monoplane with a retractable undercarriage in first-line use. By September 1939 and the outbreak of war with Germany RAF Coastal Command possessed 301 Ansons; some 60 per cent of that Command's operational aircraft strength at that time. The Anson saw wide if unspectacular active service in its initial role until being superseded before the close of 1941; after which a number continued to be employed on vital air search and rescue duties for a further two years. In 1940–41, however, the Anson commenced a long career as a trainer and, slightly later, a general communications aircraft. Training variants began their service in

1939, but the widest use in this role came in World War II and the immediate postwar years; particularly in connection with the Empire Air Training Scheme's schools in Canada, Australia, Rhodesia, South Africa and New Zealand. The ultimate Anson variant was the Mark T22. At some period in its extended career the 'Annie' undertook virtually every possible role, in every RAF Command, and in every theatre of operations; a record almost unmatched in RAF annals.

Above: a Blackburn Blackburn torpedo spotter reconnaissance aircraft photographed in flight.

Blackburn Blackburn

Type: maritime reconnaissance.
Crew: three.
Power plant: 450 hp Napier Lion IIB (Mk I); 465 hp Napier Lion V (Mk II).
Dimensions: span 45 ft 6½ in; length 36 ft 2 in; height 12 ft 6 in (Mk I), 14 ft 4½ in (Mk II).
Weights: empty 5330 lb; loaded 6662 lb.
Performance (Mk II): maximum speed 122 mph at 3000 ft; initial climb rate 690 ft per min; service ceiling 13,000 ft; range 440 miles.
Armament: one 0.303 in Lewis machine gun in dorsal cockpit; one fixed 0.303 in Vickers machine gun forward.

Possibly one of the ugliest aeroplanes ever used operationally by the British air services, the Blackburn was produced to the same naval requirements which spawned the equally unlovely Avro Bison. Totals of 33 Mark Is and 29 Mark IIs were produced, and these saw Fleet Air Arm service from 1922–31 before being replaced by more modern designs. Despite its elephantine appearance the Blackburn handled well and fulfilled its designed role admirably, albeit at the expense of good performance.

Blackburn Dart

Type: torpedo bomber.
Crew: one.
Power plant: 450 hp Napier Lion IIB; 465 hp Napier Lion V.
Dimensions: span 45 ft 5¾ in; length 35 ft 4½ in; height 12 ft 11 in.
Weights: empty 3599 lb; loaded 6383 lb (with Mk IX torpedo).
Performance: maximum speed 107 mph at 3000 ft (with dummy torpedo); initial climb rate 600 ft per min; service ceiling 12,700 ft; endurance 3 hrs.
Armament: one Mk VIII or Mk IX 18-inch torpedo; alternative load up to 520 lb of bombs under wings.

Above: a Blackburn Dart torpedo bomber.

The Dart was developed from the Blackburn Swift torpedo bomber of 1920. It was first flown as a prototype in October 1921, and deliveries of production machines began in March 1922. Despite its size for a single-seat bomber, the Dart handled well and remained in service for 10 years, seeing extensive use aboard aircraft carriers in the Home and Mediterranean Fleets. In July 1926 Darts helped pioneer deck-landing techniques by night; while Dart crews in general achieved high success rates in regular bombing and torpedo exercises. Total production of Darts amounted to 117 aircraft.

Below: an Avro Anson C.19 VIP transport.

Blackburn Ripon II/IIA

Type: torpedo bomber.
Crew: two.
Power plant: 570 hp Napier Lion.
Dimensions: span 44 ft 8½ in (upper), 45 ft 6½ in (lower) – Mk II; length 36 ft 9 in; height 13 ft 4¼ in.
Weights: empty 4132 lb; loaded 8014 lb (Mk II).
Performance (Mk II): maximum speed 132 mph at sea level; initial climb rate 800 ft per min; service ceiling 13,000 ft; range 1060 miles (reconnaissance) or 815 miles (carrying a torpedo).
Armament: one fixed 0.303 in Vickers machine gun forward; one 0.303 in Lewis machine gun in rear cockpit; one Mk VII or Mk IX 18-inch torpedo; alternative bomb load up to three 520 lb bombs.

Intended as a replacement for the Dart in Fleet Air Arm service, the prototype Ripon first flew in April 1926, but was modified to a more refined external appearance, particularly in regard to engine housing, before going into production. Stressed for catapulting, and designed for interchangeability of float or wheeled undercarriage, the Ripon II first entered FAA service in August 1929. The main production version, the Mark IIA, was in use by 1931. Overall production of Ripons (all Marks and prototypes) amounted to 96 aircraft, but the design was gradually superseded by its stablemate the Baffin from 1934.

Above: **Blackburn Baffins of No. 811 Squadron FAA fly over the Firth of Forth during a naval-air exercise.**

Blackburn Baffin

Type: torpedo bomber.
Crew: two.
Power plant: 565 hp Bristol Pegasus IM3.
Dimensions: span 44 ft 10 in (upper), 45 ft 6½ in (lower); length 38 ft 3¾ in; height 12 ft 10 in.
Weights: empty 3184 lb; loaded 7610 lb.
Performance: maximum speed 136 mph at 6500 ft; initial rate of climb 480 ft per min; service ceiling 15,000 ft; endurance 4½ hrs (at 5000 ft).
Armament: one fixed 0.303 in Vickers machine gun forward; one 0.303 in Lewis machine gun in rear cockpit; one Mk VIII or IX 18-inch torpedo (1576 lb), or alternative bomb loads up to 2000 lb.

Virtually a re-engined Ripon – the prototypes were initially titled Ripon V – the Baffin introduced air-cooled radial engines to its makers' designs, and began superseding Ripons in FAA service from January 1934. Only 29 Baffins were produced as such, though at least 68 Ripons were converted to Baffins in addition. The Baffin equipped just three FAA squadrons but, its performance being only marginally better than that of the Ripon, it was in turn replaced as first-line equipment from 1936. In the following year a total of 29 Baffins were sold to New Zealand, where they formed three Territorial squadrons for coastal defence, and all three units were operational until 1941.

Blackburn Iris & Perth

Type: flying boat, long-range reconnaissance.
Crew: five (normal).
Power plants: three 650 hp Rolls-Royce Condor III (Iris I); three 675 hp Rolls-Royce Condor IIIA (Iris II); three 675 hp Rolls-Royce Condor IIIB (Iris III); three 825 hp Rolls-Royce Buzzard IIMS (Perth).
Dimensions: span 95 ft 6 in (Iris I, II, IV), 97 ft (Iris III, Perth); length 66 ft 6⅛ in (Iris I, II, IV), 67 ft 4¾ in (Iris III), 70 ft (Perth); height 24 ft 6½ in (Iris I, II, IV), 25 ft 6 in (Iris III), 26 ft 5½ in (Perth).
Weights: empty 19,096 lb (Iris I), 18,930 lb (Iris II), 19,048 lb (Iris III), 17,500 lb (Iris IV), 20,927 lb (Perth); loaded 27,608 lb (Iris I), 27,358 lb (Iris II), 29,489 lb (Iris III), 30,250 lb (Iris IV), 32,500 lb (Perth).
Performance: maximum speed 130 mph at sea level (Iris IV), 132 mph at sea level (Perth); initial rate of climb 665 ft per min (Iris IV), 800 ft per min (Perth); service ceiling 11,850 ft (Iris I), 11,500 ft (Perth).

Initially designed to a 1924 Air Ministry Specification R.14/24, the first Iris (wood-hull) was launched in June 1926. Modified for a metal hull and other items, it re-emerged as the Iris II. It was relaunched in August 1927 and flew extensively in RAF livery. An 'improved' version, the Iris III, was then ordered to equip No.209 Squadron RAF, which unit reformed in

Right: **Blackburn Iris S1263 was serving with No. 209 Squadron in May 1932.**

January 1930. The prototype Iris III was launched in November 1929 and, with three other Iris IIIs became the largest aircraft in RAF service until then. Four further Iris variants were built; Iris IV (Iris II, N185 converted) and three Iris Vs (with higher power engines and other new features). The third production Iris V, S1593, with a 37mm Coventry Ordnance Works (COW) cannon in the front cockpit, became the prototype of the Perth (sometimes titled Iris VI). Only four Perths were built, three of these going to 209 Squadron. The Perth was the largest biplane flying boat ever used by the RAF, and was superseded in squadron use by the Short Singapore by 1937–38.

Blackburn Shark

Type: torpedo bomber; reconnaissance.
Crew: two.
Power plant: 700 hp Armstrong Siddeley Tiger IV; 760 hp AS Tiger VI; 800 hp Bristol Pegasus III; 840 hp Bristol Pegasus IX.
Dimensions: span 46 ft (upper), 36 ft (lower); length 35 ft 3 in (landplane), 38 ft 5 in (seaplane); height 12 ft 1 in (landplane), 14 ft 3 in (seaplane).
Weights (Mk II landplane): empty 4039 lb; loaded 8050 lb (with torpedo).
Performance (Mk II landplane, Tiger VI): maximum speed 157 mph at sea level; initial rate of climb 895 ft per min; service ceiling 16,000 ft; range 625 miles (with torpedo), 1130 miles with 150-gallon overload tank for reconnaissance.
Armament: one fixed 0.303 in Vickers machine gun forward; one ring-mounted 0.303 in Vickers-Berthier or Lewis machine gun in rear cockpit; one 1500 lb torpedo or equivalent bomb load.

Last of the Blackburn biplane torpedo bombers to enter FAA service, the Shark was of particularly rugged construction and was specially fitted with numerous refinements for ease of deck handling and operation. Designed to operate as either a land- or seaplane, the type began its FAA service officially in May 1935 and was replaced in first-line FAA squadrons in 1938. Thereafter Sharks continued to offer valuable second-line service as target-tugs,

Above: **a Blackburn Shark crashes into its parent carrier's island.**

trainers and in other duties throughout World War II. In all, 238 Sharks were produced, 26 of which (seven built by Blackburn, 19 by Boeing of Canada) saw extensive service with the RCAF from October 1936 until 1944. The only Sharks known to have flown actual war operations against an enemy were several flown in Malaya during the 1941 Japanese invasion.

Boulton & Paul Sidestrand

Type: day bomber.
Crew: three (normal).
Power plants: two 460 hp Bristol Jupiter VIIIF.
Dimensions: span 71 ft 11 in; length 46 ft; height 14 ft 9½ in.
Weights: empty 6010 lb; loaded 10,200 lb.
Performance: maximum speed 140 mph at 10,000 ft; climb to 15,000 ft, 19 mins; service ceiling 24,000 ft; range 500 miles.
Armament: three 0.303 in Lewis machine guns in nose, dorsal and ventral positions; up to 1050 lb of bombs.

Below: **a Boulton & Paul Sidestrand.**

The Sidestrand was the RAF's first twin-engined day bomber in service since the De Havilland 10 of 1918, and first flew in prototype form in 1926. Highly manoeuvrable and a rock-steady gun and bomb platform, the Sidestrand only equipped one squadron, No.101, from April 1928 until 1934 when its successor, the Overstrand, replaced it. Total production was 18 aircraft, several of which were later converted to Overstrands with more powerful engines and power-operated turret.

Boulton & Paul Overstrand

Type: medium day bomber.
Crew: three (normal) to five.
Power plants: two 580 hp Bristol Pegasus IIM3.
Dimensions: span 72 ft; length 46 ft; height 15 ft 6 in.
Weights: empty 7936 lb; loaded 12,000 lb.
Performance: maximum speed 153 mph at 6500 ft; initial rate of climb 1100 ft per min; service ceiling 22,500 ft; range (normal) 545 miles.
Armament: one 0.303 in Lewis machine gun in power-operated nose turret; two 0.303 in Lewis machine guns in dorsal and ventral locations; up to 1600 lb of bombs.

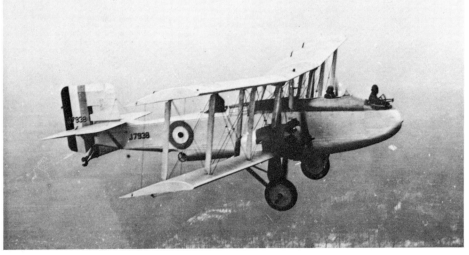

Above: a Boulton & Paul Overstrand.

A replacement for the Sidestrand, the Overstrand was the first RAF bomber equipped with a totally-enclosed, power operated (pneumatic) gun turret. First flown in 1933, Overstrands superseded Sidestrands in No.101 Squadron from December 1934, the only squadron fully equipped, though four Overstrands were used by No.144 Squadron briefly. They continued in first-line use until 1937, but were still employed in secondary roles as late as 1941. Fully aerobatic, the Overstrand offered greater performance range than the Sidestrand. No.101 Squadron's unique equipment with turreted Overstrands is permanently commemorated by a castle with turrets as the unit's official badge motif.

Bristol Bulldog IIA

Type: fighter.
Crew: one.
Power plant: 440 hp Bristol Jupiter VIIF.
Dimensions: span 33 ft 10 in; length 25 ft 2 in; height 8 ft 9 in.
Weights: empty 2222 lb; loaded 3530 lb.
Performance: maximum speed 178 mph at 10,000 ft; climb to 20,000 ft, 14 mins; service ceiling 29,300 ft.
Armament: two fixed 0.303 in Vickers machine guns forward; four 20 or 25 lb bombs if required.

Developed from a private venture prototype of 1927, the Bulldog entered squadron service initially as the Mark II in May 1929. Its superb aerobatic qualities, strength of construction, and, for its day, excellent performance envelope endeared it to most pilots, and the Bulldog eventually equipped a total of 10 RAF squadrons. At least 87 two-seat Bulldog versions were later produced as trainers. The last 17 Bulldogs built were sold to Finland in 1934, and these saw active service in the 1939–40 Winter War against the USSR. The final Bulldogs in RAF squadron use were replaced by the end of 1937, but their aerobatic displays at Hendon remain a vivid memory to contemporaries.

De Havilland 9A

Type: day bomber.
Crew: two.
Power plant: 375 hp Rolls-Royce Eagle VIII; 400 hp Liberty 12; 450 hp Napier Lion.
Dimensions: span 45 ft 11⅜ in; length 30 ft 3 in; height 11 ft 4 in.
Weights (Liberty 12): empty 2800 lb; loaded 4645 lb.
Performance (Liberty 12): maximum speed 123 mph at ground level; climb to 10,000 ft, 15 mins 45 secs; service ceiling 16,750 ft; endurance 5¼ hrs.
Armament: one fixed 0.303 in Vickers machine gun forward; one 0.303 in Lewis machine gun in rear cockpit; up to 660 lb of bombs on underwing racks.

The DH9A – or 'Ninak' as it is remembered by its crews – evolved from a promise of mass-produced, American-designed and built Liberty 12 engines, and an urgent need for an improved version of the DH9 for operations in France. Production of the DH9A began early in 1918, and the first operational unit equipped was No.110 Squadron which moved to France on 31 August 1918 and flew its first sorties on 14 September. Three other RAF units – Nos.99, 18 and 205 Squadrons – received some DH9As by November 1918, but only a handful of No.99 Squadron's aircraft undertook any operations before the Armistice. The only other DH9As to see active war service that year were part of a batch of at least 53 Ninaks supplied to the US Marine Corps Northern Bombing Group, a few of which flew sorties in October-November. By January 1919 a total of 885 DH9As had been built, and for the

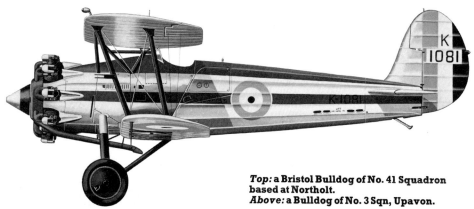

Top: a Bristol Bulldog of No. 41 Squadron based at Northolt.
Above: a Bulldog of No. 3 Sqn, Upavon.

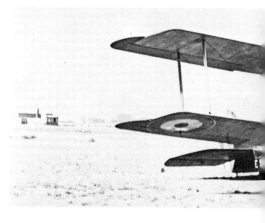

Above: a DH9A of No. 4 FTS, Abu Sueir.

next decade Ninaks gave doughty service to the RAF as a 'general purpose' aircraft; mainly maintaining an uneasy peace in the various mandated or Empire countries of the Middle East and India. In the UK Ninaks were the initial equipment for several freshly-created Auxiliary Air Force units in 1925; while individual DH9As became test vehicles for a wide variety of experimental trials and installations, including a small batch fitted with the Napier Lion engine. By 1930, however, no DH9A remained in a first-line squadron and, like any good soldier, the Ninak gently faded away from RAF use.

De Havilland 10

Type: bomber.
Crew: three.
Power plants: two 360 hp Rolls-Royce Eagle VIII (Mk II); two 400 hp Liberty 12 (Mks III, IIIa); two 375 hp Rolls-Royce Eagle VIII (Mk IIIc).
Dimensions: span 62 ft 9 in (Mks I, II), 65 ft 6 in (Mks III, IIIa); length 38 ft 10$\frac{1}{8}$ in (Mks I, II), 39 ft 7$\frac{7}{8}$ in (Mk III); height 14 ft 6 in.
Weights (Mk I): empty 5004 lb; loaded 6950 lb.
Performance (Mk I): maximum speed 109 mph at ground level; climb to 10,000 ft, 20 mins 55 secs; service ceiling 15,000 ft; endurance 3$\frac{1}{2}$ hrs.
Armament: one 0.303 in Lewis machine gun in each of nose and rear cockpits; up to 900 lb of bombs carried internally.

Below: a DH10a of No. 99 Squadron at Risalpur, India, 1919.

First flown in March 1918, the DH 10 was ordered into production for strategic bombing of Germany but was too late to see wartime operations apart from three or four examples sent to France in November 1918. Postwar, DH 10s part-equipped No.120 Squadron for air mail duties to Germany; while a few were used in northern India by No.97 Squadron (retitled No.60 Squadron from 1 April 1920) for operations in the North-west Frontier Province. These last remained on operations until early 1923, but 60 Squadron's crews had no great opinion of the type; reflected in an extract from a unit song:

Most every day we have a crash or two
That's why we are so short of men
So if you want to take a trip to Heaven quick
You've only got to fly a D.H.10.

Other examples were used from 1921–23 in the Middle East, mainly as freight and mail carriers.

Fairey IIID

Type: general purpose.
Crew: two or three.
Power plant: 450 hp Napier Lion IIB/V/Va.
Dimensions: span 46 ft 1 in; length 31 ft 5 in (landplane), 36 ft 1 in (seaplane); height 12 ft (landplane, 13 ft (seaplane).
Weights: empty 3430 lb (landplane), 3990 lb (seaplane); loaded 5050 lb (landplane), 5050 lb (seaplane).
Performance: maximum speed 120 mph at sea level (landplane); climb to 10,000 ft, 12$\frac{1}{2}$ mins; service ceiling 20,000 ft; endurance 6 hrs.
Armament: one fixed 0.303 in Vickers machine gun forward; one 0.303 in Lewis machine gun in rear cockpit; four 20 or 25 lb bombs.

A total of 227 Fairey IIIDs was produced, all but 20 of these intended for the RAF and FAA, and the type served from 1924–30. Designed for land- or seaplane configuration, the IIID was probably Fairey's most successful aircraft for several decades. Tough, reliable, and highly adaptable to the myriad roles imposed upon it, it served in home waters and in the Middle and Far East, as well as participating in various route-proving and endurance flights. Its strength of construction was exemplified by its pioneering role in trials of catapult take-offs from ships at sea from 1925.

Fairey Fawn

Type: day bomber; reconnaissance.
Crew: two.
Power plant: 470 hp Napier Lion II.
Dimensions: span 49 ft 11 in; length 32 ft 1 in; height 11 ft 11 in.
Weights: empty 3481 lb; loaded 5834 lb.
Performance: maximum speed 114 mph at ground level; climb to 5000 ft, 6 mins 30 secs; service ceiling 13,850 ft; endurance 5 hrs.
Armament: one fixed 0.303 in Vickers machine gun forward; one 0.303 in Lewis machine gun in rear cockpit; up to 460 lb of bombs.

Below: a Fairey IIID from RAF Calshot.

Above: a Fairey Fawn of No. 12(B) Sqn based at Northolt in 1926.

A development of the cumbersome Fairey Pintail amphibian, the bulky Fawn was the first post-1918 type of light day bomber to enter RAF service, and was initially intended as a replacement for the DH9A in the army co-operation role. Only 70 production Fawns were built and these served with five RAF and AAF squadrons from 1924–27. Though pleasant to fly, its distinctly utilitarian lines hardly lived up to its given title.

Fairey Flycatcher

Type: naval fighter.
Crew: one.
Power plant: 400 hp Armstrong Siddeley Jaguar IV.
Dimensions: span 29 ft; length 23 ft (landplane), 29 ft (seaplane); height 12 ft (landplane), 13 ft 4 in (seaplane).
Weights: empty 2039 lb; loaded 3028 lb (landplane), 3531 lb (seaplane).
Performance: maximum speed 134 mph at sea level (landplane), 126 mph (seaplane); climb to 10,000 ft, 8 mins 38 secs (landplane), 14 mins (seaplane); service ceiling 20,600 ft (landplane), 14,000 ft (seaplane); endurance (at max speed) 1.82 hrs (both types).
Armament: two fixed 0.303 in Vickers machine guns forward; provision for four 20 or 25 lb bombs.

Though by no means a thing of beauty, the tiny Flycatcher was probably more popular with its crews than any other aircraft of its period. Moreover, for most of its Service life, from 1923–34, the Flycatcher reigned supreme as the only FAA fighter type in active use. Superbly aerobatic, a pleasure to fly, and possessing a unique 'blue note' engine sound when dived at full speed, the Flycatcher first entered FAA service in 1923, and by September 1924 all FAA fighter flights were equipped with the type. Production of the ultimate total of 196 Flycatchers (including all prototypes and variants) lasted from 1923–30. In service the Flycatcher served with every aircraft carrier, at home, in the Mediterranean, and as far afield as China. It performed equally well as fighter, dive-bomber, float-plane or amphibian – even retaining its aerobatic qualities when fitted with floats. It was the first FAA fighter to be stressed for catapulting, though its normal short take-off run needed no additional boost aboard carriers; while at least one Flycatcher floatplane was used in trials of landing-on a carrier deck in this configuration. An improved variant, the Flycatcher II with different engine and all-metal wings, was tested in 1928 but was not adopted by the FAA, despite the Mark II's considerably improved performance range.

Below: **Fairey Flycatcher N9662 photographed during a flight from Hal Far, Malta.**

Fairey Fox

Type: day bomber.
Crew: two.
Power plant: 480 hp Curtiss D-12 Felix.
Dimensions: span 37 ft 8 in; length 28 ft 3 in; height 10 ft 8 in.
Weights: empty 2609 lb; loaded 4170 lb.
Performance: maximum speed 156 mph at sea level; climb to 15,000 ft, 21½ mins; service ceiling 17,000 ft; range 500 miles at 130 mph.
Armament: one fixed 0.303 in Vickers machine gun forward; one 0.303 in Lewis machine gun in rear cockpit; up to 460 lb of bombs.

Only 28 Foxes were ever built, yet their introduction to RAF service created a minor legend. Built to the same basic official requirements which had resulted in the cumbersome Fawn bomber, the Fox was deliberately designed to demonstrate what could be achieved without official restrictions. With an American Curtiss

D-12 engine, the production Fox showed a clear 50 mph advantage over any Fawn and could readily outpace every contemporary RAF fighter. Yet only one squadron, No.12, was equipped, receiving its first examples in June 1926; an event permanently celebrated by the fox's mask motif of that unit's official badge. No.12 Squadron retained the Fox until 1931, during which time it reaped a crop of bombing awards in annual RAF competitions, and was even given certain restrictions in performance during annual air exercises – to give the fighters a chance. It's main test pilot Norman Macmillan has recorded, 'The Fox was the most stable aeroplane I have ever flown. . . . it flew both hands and feet off through really turbulent air . . . I have never known another aircraft with such positive anti-spin characteristics.'

Below: a Fairey Fox of No. 12(B) Sqn displaying the unit's fox's mask badge on the fin.

Above: Fairey IIIFs of the FAA fly over the carriers *Eagle* and *Courageous.*

Fairey IIIF

Type: naval reconnaissance.
Crew: two or three.
Power plant: 570 hp Napier Lion XI.
Dimensions: span 45 ft 9 in; length 36 ft 9 in (landplane), 35 ft 6 in (seaplane); height 14 ft 2 in (landplane), 12 ft 7 in (seaplane).
Weights: empty 3945 lb; loaded 5300 lb (Mk II seaplane), 5874 lb (Mk IIIM landplane), 6041 lb (Mk IVM/A landplane).
Performance: maximum speed 135 mph (Mk II seaplane), 120 mph at 10,000 ft (Mk IVM/A landplane); climb to 5000 ft, 6.42 min (Mk IIIM/B seaplane), 6 min (Mk IVM/A landplane); service ceiling 20,000 ft; endurance 3½ hrs.
Armament: one fixed 0.303 in Vickers machine gun forward; one 0.303 in Lewis machine gun in rear cockpit; up to 500 lb of bombs.

A cleaned-up development of the IIID, the IIIF was the last of the so-designated 'III' series from Fairey to see RAF service. The IIIF entered RAF service in 1927, then saw FAA use in the following year. It remained widely employed by both services until 1932–33, serving with eight RAF squadrons and virtually every FAA flying unit – the most widely-used FAA aircraft of the inter-war era. A total of 622 IIIFs was eventually built (including 25 export models), and though officially superseded by 1933, some individual IIIFs continued in secondary roles until at least 1941. At least three were converted to become Fairey Queens – auto-pilot controlled, radio-equipped gunnery targets.

Fairey Gordon & Seal

Type: day bomber; naval reconnaissance.
Crew: two or three.
Power plant: 525 hp Armstrong Siddeley Panther IIA.
Dimensions: span 45 ft 9 in; length 36 ft 9 in (Gordon), 35 ft 4 in (Seal, seaplane); height 14 ft 2 in (Gordon), 14 ft 6 in (Seal seaplane).
Weights: empty 3500 lb; loaded 5906 lb (Gordon), 6400 lb (Seal, seaplane).
Performance: maximum speed 145 mph at 3000 ft (Gordon), 129 mph (Seal, seaplane); initial climb rate 1000 ft per min (Gordon); service ceiling 22,000 ft (Gordon), 13,900 ft (Seal, seaplane); range 600 miles (Gordon).
Armament: one fixed 0.303 in Vickers machine gun forward; one 0.303 in Lewis machine gun in rear cockpit; up to 460 lb of bombs.

Below: a Fairey Seal from RAF Calshot.
Bottom: a Fairey Gordon of No. 6 Sqn alongside a Bristol F2b, Ismailia, Egypt.
Bottom left: the floatplane version of the Fairey Flycatcher.

The Gordon and Seal were originally projected as the Fairey IIIF Mark V and Mark VI respectively, but fresh power plants and other refinements made fresh designations necessary. The Gordon entered RAF service in April 1931, while its FAA equivalent, the Seal, made its Service debut in 1933. In all seven RAF bomber squadrons were equipped with Gordons which continued in service until 1938–39, while Seals equipped six FAA squadrons and other units.

Fairey Hendon

Type: heavy night bomber.
Crew: four to six.
Power plants: two 600 hp Rolls-Royce Kestrel VI.
Dimensions: span 101 ft 9 in; length 60 ft 9 in; height 18 ft 9 in.
Weights: empty 12,773 lb; loaded 20,000 lb.
Performance: maximum speed 155 mph at 15,000 ft; initial rate of climb 940 ft per min; service ceiling 21,400 ft; range 1360 miles.
Armament: three 0.303 in Lewis machine guns in nose, dorsal and tail positions; up to 1660 lb of bombs.

As the first cantilever monoplane heavy bomber to be built in Britain, the Fairey Night Bomber – it was only named Hendon in October 1934 – first flew in prototype form in November 1931; yet was not to enter RAF service until November 1936, and then only to equip fully one squadron, No.38, by which time it was already obsolete. Its bomb load was carried internally, while inside the fuselage was a catwalk whereby crew members could move from nose to tail cockpits. Only 14 Hendons were produced, and No.38 Squadron began replacing their Hendons with Vickers Wellingtons from November 1938.

Below: **Fairey Hendon K5085 was the first production aircraft.**

Felixstowe F5

Type: patrol flying boat.
Crew: three or four.
Power plants: two 375 hp Rolls-Royce Eagle VII.
Dimensions: span 103 ft 8 in; length 49 ft 3 in; height 18 ft 9 in.
Weights: empty 9100 lb; loaded 12,682 lb.
Performance: maximum speed 88 mph at 2000 ft; climb to 6500 ft, 30 mins; service ceiling 6800 ft; endurance 7 hrs.
Armament: four 0.303 in Lewis machine guns in nose and midship locations; up to 920 lb of bombs.

Designed and initially produced in 1918, the F5 arrived too late for operations prior to the Armistice, but became the RAF's standard flying boat from 1918 to 1925, after which it was replaced by the Supermarine Southampton. Though of no better performance than its predecessor, the F3, the F5 proved to be a dependable design and successfully completed several long-range cruises in service. In 1924 one F5 (N.177) was built with an all-metal hull; the world's first such military flying boat. A number of Canadian-built F5s for the USA's use were fitted with 400 hp Liberty engines and titled F.5L and these gave many years of service with US Navy coastal air units. The F5 formed the equipment of eight RAF squadrons and some Coastal Reconnaissance Flights.

Below: **a Felixstowe F5 flying boat is moored at RAF Calshot in 1920.**

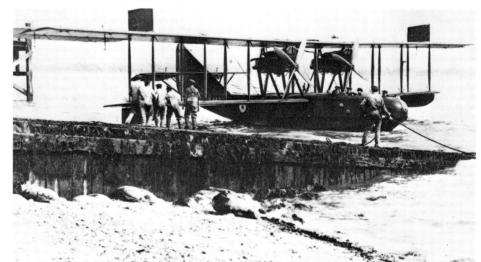

Above: **Gloster Grebes of No. 25 Sqn.**

Gloster Grebe

Type: fighter.
Crew: one.
Power plant: 400 hp Armstrong Siddeley Jaguar IV.
Dimensions: span 29 ft 4 in; length 20 ft 3 in; height 9 ft 3 in.
Weights: empty 1695 lb; loaded 2538 lb.
Performance: maximum speed 162 mph at sea level; climb to 20,000 ft, 24 mins; service ceiling 23,500 ft; endurance 3 hrs at 20,000 ft.
Armament: two fixed 0.303 in Vickers machine guns forward.

The first Gloster aeroplane to be produced in large quantity for the RAF, the Grebe and its contemporary the AW Siskin were the first fighters of the post-1918 era to equip RAF squadrons. The Grebe entered RAF service with No.111 Squadron in October 1923 at flight strength, then fully equipped five other squadrons. Its light, sensitive controls appealed to fighter pilots of the day, but the type had a tendency to wing flutter and experienced several problems with its Jaguar engine fuel systems. Various modifications included a thinner centre-section in the upper wing for improved pilot vision, and wing strengthening to offset the flutter problems. Two Grebes, J7400 and J7385, were specially modified in 1926 for air-launching experiments from the rigid airship R.33. Grebes remained in first-line squadron use with the RAF until mid-1928 and three Grebes purchased by the New Zealand government saw service with the New Zealand Permanent Air Force (later retitled RNZAF) until 1938. An overall total of 133 Grebes was built, including prototypes and several two-seat variants.

Gloster Gamecock

Type: fighter.
Crew: one.
Power plant: 425 hp Bristol Jupiter VII.
Dimensions: span 30 ft 1 in (upper), 26 ft 4½ in (lower); length 19 ft 10½ in; height 9 ft 11 in.
Weights: empty 2050 lb; loaded 3082 lb.
Performance: maximum speed 157 mph at 5000 ft; climb to 15,000 ft, 13.3 mins; service ceiling 21,600 ft; endurance 2 hrs at 15,000 ft.
Armament: two fixed 0.303 in Vickers machine guns forward.

The problems with the Grebe's recalcitrant power plant led to a re-engined development, the Gamecock, which appeared in prototype form in February 1925. Delivery of production Gamecocks commenced in May 1926 when No.23 Squadron received its first examples. Four more squadrons, Nos.3, 17, 32 and 43, re-equipped later. Delightful to fly, and remembered for its aerobatic displays, the Gamecock nevertheless had inherited several faults from its predecessor the Grebe, and during its first 19 months of RAF service no less than 22 Gamecocks crashed, killing eight pilots. The Gamecock remained in squadron service until July 1931, and was the last RAF fighter of 'wooden wall' construction, but it's memory led to No.43 Squadron's nickname of 'The Fighting Cocks', and the unit's adoption of a Gamecock as the motif for its official badge.

Below: **a Gloster Gamecock of No. 43(F) Squadron.**

Gloster Gauntlet

Type: fighter.
Crew: one.
Power plant: 640 hp Bristol Mercury VIS2.
Dimensions: span 32 ft 9½ in; length 26 ft 2 in (Mk I), 26 ft 5 in (Mk II); height 10 ft 3 in.
Weights: empty 2755 lb (Mk I), 2770 lb (Mk II); loaded 3950 lb (Mk I), 3970 lb (Mk II).
Performance: maximum speed 230 mph at 15,800 ft; climb to 20,000 ft, 9 mins; service ceiling 33,500 ft.
Armament: two fixed 0.303 in Vickers machine guns forward.

Developed from the Gloster SS18 of 1927, the prototype Gauntlet first flew in 1933 and displayed a 40 mph margin over the Bristol Bulldog's maximum speed. It was to be the last RAF fighter with an open cockpit, but was the first Folland-designed Gloster fighter of all-metal construction to enter service. Production Gauntlet Is commenced squadron re-equipment in May 1935 with No.19 Squadron, and by May 1937 were being flown by 14 RAF first-line squadrons. In its silver finish embellished by the colourful peacetime unit markings, the Gauntlet quickly achieved fame for its public displays of aerobatic formations and its efficiency in internal RAF competitions for gunnery and fighting tactics. Indeed, many Gauntlet pilots of the period cut their tactical teeth on the type before gaining great distinction as fighting leaders in

Below: **a Gloster Gauntlet of No. 46 Sqn.**

World War II. During 1934 the Hawker Aircraft company completed its takeover of the Gloster firm, and an improved Mark II Gauntlet produced was constructed to Hawker ideas. By 1939 Gauntlets had nearly all been replaced in first-line squadrons, but soldiered on in secondary roles both at home and overseas until early 1943. In November 1936 three Gauntlets (K7797, K7799 and K7800) of No.32 Squadron achieved an historic first by being directed by radar from Bawdsey Manor to complete a successful interception of an inbound civil transport aircraft; the world's first such interception. From 1929–37 the Gloster company produced a total of 229 Gauntlets – one prototype, 24 Mark Is and 204 Mark IIs. A further 17 were built in Denmark during 1936–38; while 25 Gauntlet IIs were sent to Finland in early 1940 to boost Finnish air strength against the Russian invasion.

Handley Page Hyderabad

Type: heavy bomber.
Crew: four.
Power plants: two 450 hp Napier Lion IIB/V.
Dimensions: span 75 ft; length 59 ft 2 in; height 16 ft 9 in.
Weights: empty 8900 lb; loaded 13,600 lb.
Performance: maximum speed 109 mph at ground level; initial rate of climb 800 ft per min; service ceiling 14,000 ft; range 500 miles.
Armament: three 0.303 in Lewis machine guns in nose, dorsal and ventral locations; 1100 lb of bombs.

Originally titled HP W.8d in response to a 1922 Air Ministry specification for a replacement for the DH 10 and Vickers Vimy, the Hyderabad prototype first flew in October 1923, and production versions went to No.99 Squadron in December 1925. Two years later a second unit, No.10 Squadron, equipped with the type, and in the following year two Auxiliary Air Force cadre squadrons also received Hyderabads. Its performance was superior to the Virginia III and Avro Aldershot, and its remarkable safety record – no Hyderabad crash ever caused a fatal casualty – spoke well for its wooden construction. It was the last wooden-built heavy bomber to be used by the RAF. The Hyderabad was superseded in RAF squadrons by early 1931, and in the AAF by 1934.

Below: **Handley Page Hyderabad J9031 served with No. 99 Squadron.**

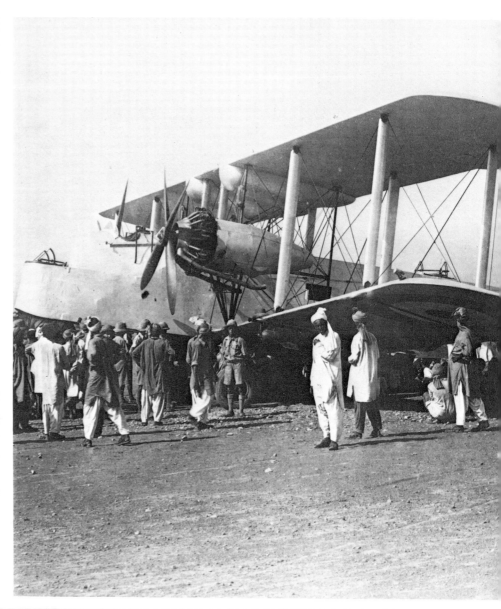

Above: the Handley Page Hinaidi prototype **J7745 was a re-engined Hyderabad. It served with the RAF Heavy Transport Flight, Lahore, India and is pictured here at Peshawar in January 1929 during the Kabul Airlift operation.**

Handley Page Hinaidi

Type: heavy bomber.
Crew: four.
Power plants: two 450 hp Bristol Jupiter VIII or VIIIF.
Dimensions: span 75 ft; length 59 ft 3 in; height 16 ft 9 in.
Weights: empty 8040 lb; loaded 14,500 lb.
Performance: maximum speed 122 mph; initial rate of climb 400 ft per min; service ceiling 14,500 ft; range 850 miles.
Armament: three 0.303 in Lewis machine guns in nose, dorsal and ventral locations; maximum bomb load 1450 lb.

The Hinaidi was a re-engined development of the Hyderabad, with later production Hinaidis being of metal construction. The lighter weight Jupiter engines made it necessary for the Hinaidi's wings to be slightly swept by some 2½ degrees. Replacing Hyderabads in four squadrons from late 1929, the Hinaidi served until 1934

before gradually being replaced. A wood-constructed troop carrier version, initially titled Chitral but later named Clive, was first flown in February 1928, and one example gave several years' service in India.

Handley Page Heyford

Type: heavy bomber.
Crew: four.
Power plants: two 575 hp Rolls-Royce Kestrel IIIS (Mk I); 640 hp RR Kestrel VI (Mks II and III).
Dimensions: span 75 ft; length 58 ft; height 17 ft 6 in.
Weights: empty 9200 lb (Mk I), 10,200 lb (Mks II and III); loaded (maximum) 16,750 lb (Mk I), 17,000 lb (Mks II and III).
Performance: maximum speed 138 mph (Mk I), 154 mph (Mks II and III); service ceiling 21,000 ft; range 920 miles.
Armament: three 0.303 in Lewis machine guns in nose, dorsal and ventral locations; maximum bomb load 1660 lb (Mk I), 3500 lb (Mks II & III).

Remembered chiefly as the last RAF biplane heavy 'cloth' bomber, the elegant Heyford prototype first flew in May 1930 but production Heyfords did not begin to equip RAF squadrons until November 1933. They eventually formed the equipment of 11 RAF squadrons. Mark II and Mark III developments were mainly improved in engine power and rating enabling heavier bomb loads to be lifted, but the basic configuration remained almost identical to the Mark I. Deliveries of Heyfords to the RAF totalled 124

Above: a Handley Page Heyford of No. 99 Squadron pictured in 1937.

machines (all Marks) and though withdrawn from first-line roles by 1939, a number were used 1939–41 as glider-tug trainers. In squadron service the 'gentle giant' was easy to maintain and service, while its agility for such a large design was clearly demonstrated during the 1935 RAF Display at Hendon when a Heyford of No. 102 Squadron was serenely looped. Its bomb load was carried on the strengthened lower centre-section between the wheels, thereby enabling armourers to re-arm a Heyford in less than 30 minutes.

Handley Page Harrow

Type: bomber; transport.
Crew: four.
Power plants: two 925 hp Bristol Pegasus XX.
Dimensions: span 88 ft 5 in; length 82 ft; height 19 ft 5 in.
Weights: empty 13,600 lb; loaded (maximum) 23,000 lb.
Performance: maximum speed 200 mph at 10,000 ft; initial rate of climb 700 ft per min; service ceiling 23,000 ft; range 1250 miles.
Armament: two 0.303 in VGO 'K' machine guns in FN14 (nose) turret; two 0.303 in VGO 'K' machine guns in FN15 (tail) turret; one 0.303 in VGO 'K' machine gun in dorsal cupola; up to 3000 lb of bombs stowed internally.

Below: a Handley Page Harrow.

Built to a 1935 Air Ministry Specification, the monoplane Harrow bomber initially entered RAF first-line use with No. 214 Squadron at Scampton in January 1937, followed respectively by Nos.37, 115, 75 and 215 Squadrons. Production, which ceased in December 1937, totalled 100 aircraft. Though all Harrows had been relegated from first-line use by early 1940, many stored aircraft were converted to become unarmed transports, widely nicknamed 'Sparrows', and in this guise the type continued on highly active service in Europe and the Middle East until the end of World War II. Others gave useful service as bombing and gunnery instruction vehicles, while five aircraft of No.420 Flight (later, No.93 Squadron) were equipped to carry 'Long Aerial Mines' (LAM) on Operation Mutton in which parachute-suspended explosive charges trailing 2000 feet of piano wire were to be dropped across the flight path of raiding Luftwaffe bombers by night, during the 1940–41 Blitz.

Above: **Hawker Horsleys of No. 504 Sqn AAF.**

Hawker Woodcock II

Type: fighter (night and day).
Crew: one.
Power plant: 380 hp Bristol Jupiter IV.
Dimensions: span 32 ft 6 in; length 26 ft 2 in; height 9 ft 11 in.
Weights: empty 2014 lb; loaded 2979 lb.
Performance: maximum speed 141 mph at ground level; climb to 10,000 ft, 8 mins 18 secs; service ceiling 22,500 ft; endurance 2¾ hrs.
Armament: two fixed 0.303 in Vickers machine guns forward.

Designed initially to meet a 1922 Air Ministry Specification for a night fighter, the prototype was first flown in 1923, but proved a disappointment. Re-designed with a fresh engine, the Mark II flew in prototype form in 1924, and production Woodcocks began to reach No.3 Squadron at Upavon in May 1925. Only one other unit was equipped, No.17 Squadron based at Hawkinge, and a total of 61 Woodcock IIs was eventually delivered for RAF use. In 1928 both Woodcock squadrons were re-equipped with Gloster Gamecocks, but the Woodcock should be remembered as the very first single-seat fighter produced by the Hawker Company which had been established in November 1920 and therefore as the progenitor of a distinguished line of future Hawker fighters.

Below: **the Hawker Woodcock II prototype J6988 had single-bay wings and helmets fitted over the engine cylinder heads.**

Hawker Horsley

Type: bomber; torpedo bomber.
Crew: two.
Power plant: 665 hp Rolls-Royce Condor IIIA.
Dimensions: span 56 ft 5¾ in; length 38 ft 10 in; height 13 ft 8 in.
Weights: empty 4760 lb; loaded 9270 lb.
Performance: maximum speed 125 mph at 6000 ft (bomber), 118 mph at 5000 ft (torpedo bomber); climb to 10,000 ft, 14 mins 20 secs; service ceiling 14,000 ft; endurance 9½–10 hrs.
Armament: one fixed 0.303 in Vickers machine gun forward; one 0.303 in Lewis machine gun in rear cockpit; up to 1500 lb of bombs, or one 2150 lb torpedo.

The Horsley was the Hawker Company's last wooden-constructed aircraft. Designed initially to an Air Ministry Specification of 1923 for a medium day bomber, but later modified to meet a 1925 specification for increased bomb loads and/or carriage of a standard torpedo. First unit to receive Horsleys was No.11 (Bomber) Squadron at Netheravon from January 1927; followed shortly after by No.100 Squadron at Spittlegate near Grantham. By 1928 two more units, Nos.33 and 15, had been Horsley-equipped. In June 1928 No.36 Squadron at Donibristle began receiving the torpedo-carrying version of the

Horsley and was soon sent to Singapore as the first land-based RAF torpedo squadron to see overseas service. By February 1934 all UK-based Horsley units had been re-equipped. Two modified Horsleys (J8607 and J8608) attempted to secure new world long-distance flight records in 1927; one of these succeeding briefly.

Hawker Hart

Type: light day bomber.
Crew: two.
Power plant: 525 hp Rolls-Royce Kestrel IB.
Dimensions: span 37 ft 3 in; length 29 ft 4 in; height 10 ft 5 in.
Weights: empty 2530 lb; loaded 4554 lb.
Performance: maximum speed 184 mph at 5000 ft; climb to 10,000 ft, 8 mins 20 secs; service ceiling 21,350 ft; endurance 3 hrs.
Armament: one fixed 0.303 in Vickers machine gun forward; one 0.303 in Lewis machine gun in rear cockpit; up to 520 lb of bombs.

Of all the pre-1939 Hawker designs, the Hart can be truly regarded as a classic aircraft, and proved to be one of the most adaptable biplanes ever used by the RAF by providing the basic

Right: **Hawker Hart Is of No. 12(B) Sqn.**
Below: **a Hawker Hart I of No. 24 Sqn converted to accommodate a passenger in the rear seat.**

Hawker Fury I & II

Type: fighter.
Crew: one.
Power plant: 525 hp Rolls-Royce Kestrel IIS (Mk I); 640 hp Rolls-Royce Kestrel VI (Mk II).
Dimensions: span 30 ft (Mks I and II); length 26 ft 8 in (Mk I), 26 ft 9 in (Mk II); height 10 ft 2 in (Mks I and II).
Weights: empty 2623 lb (Mk I), 2734 lb (Mk II); loaded 3490 lb (Mk I), 3609 lb (Mk II).
Performance: maximum speed 207 mph at 14,000 ft (Mk I), 223 mph at 16,500 ft (Mk II); climb to 10,000 ft, 4 mins 25 secs (Mk I), 3 mins 50 secs (Mk II); service ceiling 28,000 ft (Mk I), 29,500 ft (Mk II).
Armament: two fixed 0.303 in Vickers Mk III machine guns (Mk I), Mk V (II), forward; provision for light bomb racks under wings if required.

The Fury was the RAF's first-ever operational fighter to exceed 200 mph in level flight. It was also probably the RAF's most aesthetically pleasing biplane fighter of all time; its elegance being equalled by its superb aerobatic qualities and highly sensitive controls. The first produc-

configuration for numerous variants and developments. The Hart first equipped No.33 Squadron at Eastchurch in January 1930 (resulting in a Hart's Head becoming 33's official badge motif), and a year later the second Hart unit was No.12 Squadron at Kenley. The Hart's superior performance to contemporary RAF fighters created something of a furore, while the obvious development potential opened possibilities of other roles. One of the first variants was the Hart (India), built for operational duties along India's North-west Frontier Province, and 30 Hart (India) aircraft were shipped to India at the end of 1931 to re-equip Nos.11 and 39 Squadrons. By January 1933 a total of 126 Harts had been built, and the RAF possessed nine Hart squadrons. Fully equipped dual-control Hart Trainers were then built, while most RAF stations were soon issued with individual Harts as fast communications aircraft. By 1936 Harts were beginning to be replaced in first-line use (by Hawker Hinds) but not before a total of 20 RAF and AAF squadrons had employed them. Nevertheless, Harts continued in operational use in India and the Middle East zones until well into World War II, and many were exported to South Africa and other air forces. A total of 1042 Harts was built.

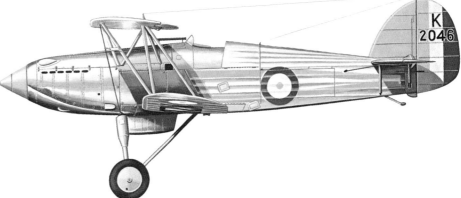

Above: a Hawker Fury I of No. 1 (F) Squadron.
Left: a formation of Hawker Fury IIs of No. 25(F) Squadron, 1937.

tion Fury I made its maiden flight on 25 March 1931, and in May that year No.43 Squadron became first to receive the type. Part of the Fury's Service needs was fast interception of bombers and the design's initial climb rate of almost 2400 feet per minute fulfilled this requirement. By May 1932 Nos.1 and 25 Squadrons had also been equipped with Fury fighters. The Fury was further modified to produce the Fury II which showed a 20 per cent increase in power, a greater rate of climb, and a higher top speed. Five squadrons received Fury IIs in 1936–37. Several foreign countries ordered Furies for first-line use in their air forces, including three ordered in 1935 which eventually participated in the Spanish Civil War. With a cantilever undercarriage, this Spanish Fury variant could achieve a maximum speed of 242 mph – the fastest of all production Furies. By 1939 all squadron Furies had been replaced by Gloster Gladiators, Hawker Hurricanes or other designs.

Below: the first prototype Hawker Nimrod pictured after full modification to the standards of Specification 16/30.

Hawker Nimrod

Type: naval fighter.
Crew: one.
Power plant: 477 hp Rolls-Royce Kestrel IIS; 608 hp RR Kestrel VFP.
Dimensions: span 33 ft 6¾ in; length 26 ft 6½ in; height 9 ft 10 in.
Weights: empty 3115 lb; loaded 4059 lb.
Performance: maximum speed 196 mph at 12,000 ft (Kestrel IIS), 193 mph at 14,000 ft (Kestrel VFP); climb to 10,000 ft, 6 mins 8 secs (Kestrel IIS), 5 mins (Kestrel VFP); service ceiling 26,900 ft (Kestrel IIS), 28,800 ft (Kestrel VFP).
Armament: two fixed 0.303 in Vickers Mk III machine guns forward; provision for four 20 or 25 lb bombs if required.

Bearing an obvious resemblance to its stable-mate the Fury, the Nimrod – initially titled Norn – was in fact of distinctly different lineage, being a private venture design of 1929–30, around which Air Ministry Specification 16/30 was drafted. The first production Nimrod (S1577) was first flown in October 1931, and commenced re-equipment of No.408 Flight FAA in the autumn of 1932. Production Mark IIs were first delivered in March 1934, incorporating arrester gear; while from early 1935 Kestrel II engines were gradual-

ly replaced by Kestrel Vs, with accompanying up-rating of performance. All Nimrods were designed for interchangeability of wheel or float undercarriage. Nimrods remained in first-line FAA use until May 1939, but were replaced before the outbreak of war by (mainly) Sea Gladiators and Blackburn Skuas. A total of 87 Nimrods of all marks was built.

Hawker Demon

Type: fighter.
Crew: two.
Power plant: 485 hp Rolls-Royce Kestrel IIS; 584 hp Kestrel VDR in turret fighter.
Dimensions: span 37 ft 2 in; length 29 ft 7 in; height 10 ft 5 in.
Weights: empty 3067 lb, 3336 lb (turret fighter); loaded 4464 lb, 4668 lb (turret fighter).
Performance (Kestrel IIS): maximum speed 182 mph at 13,000 ft; climb to 10,000 ft, 7 mins 25 secs; service ceiling 24,500 ft.
Armament: two fixed 0.303 in Vickers Mk III machine guns forward; one 0.303 in Lewis machine gun in rear cockpit usually on gun ring No.15, some with Frazer-Nash powered turret.

The superior speed of the Hawker Hart over contemporary RAF fighters upon its service debut quickly led to the conception of a Hart Fighter (its original title) – or as its designer Sydney Camm expressed it, 'A Hart to catch a Hart'. Air Ministry Specification 15/30 was issued for this purpose, and Hart J9933 was suitably modified and then tested in this context. A small batch of production Hart Fighters was issued to No.23 Squadron in early 1931 for evaluation, and in early 1932 further production was undertaken; the design being retitled Demon in July of that year. Thus the RAF's first two-seat fighter since 1918 entered full squadron service. By late 1934 the prototype Hart Fighter, J9933 (which had been the first production Hart originally) had been further modified to accept the first Frazer-Nash hydraulic-operated gun turret in its rear cockpit, incorporating a 'turtle-back' folding shield for the air gunner. From mid-1936 all Boulton & Paul-built Demons featured this type of turret. Demons eventually equipped 12 RAF and AAF squadrons in Britain and the Middle East, and though declared obsolete by September 1939, several Demons continued to serve in minor roles until 1943–44. Total production of 298 Demons included 64 sent to Australia from March 1935, the first 18 of which equipped No.1 Squadron RAAF, replacing the unit's Westland Wapitis.

Below: a Hawker Hart Fighter serving with No. 23(F) Squadron.

Hawker Osprey

Type: fleet spotter; reconnaissance; interceptor.
Crew: two.
Power plant: 630 hp Rolls-Royce Kestrel II MS.
Dimensions: span 37 ft; length 29 ft 4 in, 31 ft 10¼ in (floats); height 10 ft 5 in, 12 ft 5 in (floats).
Weights: empty 3405 lb; loaded 4950 lb (landplane), 5570 lb (floats).
Performance (landplane): maximum speed 168 mph at 5000 ft; climb to 10,000 ft, 7 mins 40 secs; service ceiling 23,500 ft.
Armament: one fixed 0.303 in Vickers Mk III machine gun forward; one 0.303 in Lewis machine gun in rear cockpit; eight 20 or 25 lb bombs, or two 112 lb bombs under wings.

With folding wings, flotation gear, arrester gear, and interchangeable wheel or float undercarriage, the Osprey was in effect a navalised Hart; indeed, the prototype Osprey was Hart J9052 duly modified, and refashioned to the requirements of Air Ministry Specification 0.22/26. Production Ospreys first appeared in 1932, and by 1933 the type had been adopted by most ships and units of the Royal Navy involved with the FAA. Several FAA squadrons flew a mixture of Ospreys and Nimrods, or were wholly Osprey-equipped. A final production version, the Mark IV, in 1935 was fitted with the Kestrel V engine and mainly used in the Mediterranean area. By 1938 Ospreys were being withdrawn from units of the Home Fleet, and were finally declared obsolete in 1940.

Above: a Hawker Osprey mounted on the catapult-launcher at RAF Leuchars.

Hawker Audax

Type: army co-operation.
Crew: two.
Power plant: 530 hp Rolls-Royce Kestrel IB.
Dimensions: span 37 ft 3 in; length 29 ft 7 in; height 10 ft 5 in.
Weights: empty 2938 lb; loaded 4386 lb.
Performance: maximum speed 170 mph at 2400 ft; climb to 10,000 ft, 8.65 mins; service ceiling 21,500 ft; endurance 3½ hrs.
Armament: one fixed 0.303 in Vickers machine gun forward; one 0.303 in Lewis machine gun in rear cockpit; four 20 or 25 lb, or two 112 lb bombs under wings.

The Hart's obvious potential for adaptation to various roles led to the Audax army co-operation design, intended to replace the ageing Armstrong Whitworth Atlas in squadron use. The first production Audax, K1995, flew in December 1931, and apart from extended exhaust manifolds and such impedimenta as a message pick-up hook, was otherwise a near-standard Hart. First squadron to receive the Audax was No.4 (AC) in February 1932, and a further eight squadrons in Britain, India and the Middle East were later equipped with the type. Of the ultimate total of 618 Audaxes built, 34 were exported to Iraq and 56 to Persia; both versions being fitted with various radial engines. Production of the Audax ceased in 1937, but the type saw active service on a small scale in the Middle East theatre during 1939–41.

Hawker Hardy

Type: general purpose (tropical).
Crew: two.
Power plant: 530 hp Rolls-Royce Kestrel IB; 581 hp RR Kestrel X.
Dimensions: span 37 ft 3 in; length 29 ft 7 in; height 10 ft 7 in.
Weights: empty 3195 lb; loaded 5005 lb.
Performance: maximum speed 161 mph at ground level; climb to 10,000 ft, 10.2 mins; service ceiling 17,000 ft; endurance 3 hrs.
Armament: one fixed 0.303 in Vickers machine gun forward; one 0.303 in Lewis machine gun in rear cockpit; provision for four 20 or 25 lb bombs.

Another Hart variant, the Hardy closely resembled the Audax in appearance but was modified to carry a wider variety of external equipment for its general purpose role. Again,

Below: **a Hawker Audax pictured in service with No. 11 FTS, Wittering.**

Above: **Hawker Hardys of No. 30 Squadron based at Mosul, Iraq. Hardy K4051 later served with No. 6 Squadron.**

the prototype was a modified Hart, K3013, which first flew in September 1934. Total Hardy production amounted to 47 aircraft – all built by the Gloster Aircraft Company at Hucclecote – and in October 1934 the first issues were shipped to No.30 Squadron at Mosul, Iraq. Four years later, on receipt of its Blenheim replacements, No.30 Squadron sent its Hardys to No.6 Squadron in Palestine. On the outbreak of war No.6 Squadron in turn handed over its Hardys to No.237 (Rhodesia) Squadron (already flying Audaxes) and this unit saw active operations against Italian forces in Italian Somaliland and Eritrea in 1940.

Hawker Hind

Type: bomber.
Crew: two.
Power plant: 640 hp Rolls-Royce Kestrel V.
Dimensions: span 37 ft 3 in; length 29 ft 3 in; height 10 ft 7 in.
Weights: empty 3251 lb; loaded 5298 lb.
Performance: maximum speed 186 mph at 16,400 ft; climb to 10,000 ft, 8.1 mins; service ceiling 26,400 ft.
Armament: one fixed 0.303 in Vickers machine gun forward; one 0.303 in Lewis machine gun in rear cockpit; up to 520 lb of bombs.

As the RAF's last biplane light bomber, the Hind was produced as an interim to bridge the gap between existing obsolescent biplane bombers and the monoplane designs promised from the RAF expansion programmes of the mid-1930s. Though derived from the Hart, the Hind differed in many respects, including a more powerful engine, revised gunner's cockpit, tail wheel (instead of traditional skid), 'ram-horn' exhaust manifolds and other modifications. The prototype, K2915, first flew in September 1934, and total production, including all exported machines, amounted to 592 aircraft. The Hind began its RAF service with No.21 Squadron in December 1935; the first of an eventual 42 RAF and AAF squadrons to fly the type as part or whole equipment. In late 1937 many Hinds began to be modified, either at the manufacturer's or by RAF units, to become bomber trainers, and it can be said that the vast bulk of embryo RAF bomber crews of the 1938–40 period received their advanced instruction in Hinds. By late 1939 all Hinds had been replaced in squadron use.

Hawker Hector

Type: army co-operation.
Crew: two.
Power plant: 805 hp Napier Dagger III MS.
Dimensions: span 36 ft 11½ in; length 29 ft 9¾ in; height 10 ft 5 in.
Weights: empty 3389 lb; loaded 4910 lb.
Performance: maximum speed 187 mph at 6560 ft; climb to 10,000 ft, 5 mins 40 secs; service ceiling 24,000 ft; endurance 2½ hrs.
Armament: one fixed 0.303 in Vickers machine gun forward; one 0.303 in Lewis machine gun in rear cockpit; up to 250 lb bombs.

To obviate the great demand for Rolls-Royce Kestrel engines necessitated by large production of the Hind, the Hector – intended to replace Audaxes in army co-operation units – was fitted with the Dagger engine. The prototype Hector, K3719, first flew in February 1936, and production machines entered service with No.4 (AC)

Above: Hawker Hinds of No. 50 Squadron.
Right: the Hawker Hector prototype K3719
was converted from an Audax I.

Squadron at Odiham in February 1937. Another
11 squadrons of the RAF and AAF were equipped by mid-1939. The only Hectors to see first-
line operations during World War II were six
aircraft from No.613 Squadron AAF, based at
Hawkinge in May 1940, which carried out dive-
bombing attacks on German gun positions near
Calais and dropped supplies to the beleaguered
Calais garrison. By mid-1940 a total of 72 Hectors
were still on RAF charge, all as trainers, target-
tugs or in other secondary duties. An overall
total of 179 Hectors was built.

Parnall Panther

Type: carrier-borne reconnaissance.
Crew: two.
Power plant: 230 hp Bentley BR2 rotary.
Dimensions: span 29 ft 6 in; length 24 ft 11 in;
height 10 ft 6 in.
Weights (prototype): empty 1328 lb; loaded
2595 lb.
Performance: maximum speed 108.5 mph at
6500 ft; climb to 10,000 ft, 17 mins 5 secs; service
ceiling 14,500 ft; endurance 4½ hrs.
Armament: one fixed 0.303 in Vickers machine
gun forward (prototype only); one 0.303 in
Lewis machine gun in rear cockpit.

Above: **the Parnall Panther carrier-borne reconnaissance aircraft was one of the aeroplanes which were used to pioneer deck-landing techniques in the Royal Navy.**

Designed in 1918 – the prototype first flew in May 1918 – the Panther was designed from the outset as an aircraft carrier-borne fleet reconnaissance aircraft; the first such specific type in Britain. Six prototypes and 168 production Panthers were built, of which 150 were intended for the RAF. Entering FAA service in 1924, the Panther was one of the aircraft used to pioneer deck-landing techniques. Though recorded by a Panther pilot as 'a delightful aeroplane to fly with none of the vices common to other aeroplanes fitted with big rotary motors', the design's performance range remained unspectacular, due partly to problems with the BR2 engine. The Panther remained in service until 1926. Twelve Panthers ordered for the Japanese Navy in 1921 became co-founders of the Japanese Naval Air Service.

Saro Cloud

Type: amphibian maritime trainer.
Crew: two (and up to eight passengers).
Power plants: two 340 hp Armstrong Siddeley Serval III or V.
Dimensions: span 64 ft; length 50 ft 1½ in; height 16 ft 5 in.
Weights: empty 6800 lb; loaded 9500 lb.
Performance: maximum speed 118 mph at sea level; initial rate of climb 750 ft per min; service ceiling 14,000 ft; endurance 4 hrs.
Armament: two 0.303 in Lewis machine guns in dorsal locations; up to 200 lb bombs under wings if required.

Introduced to RAF service in August 1933 at RAF Calshot, the Cloud provided advanced maritime instruction to embryo flying boat crews. A scaled-up version of the civil Saro Cutty Sark,

Below: **Saro Cloud K2898 served with the Seaplane Training Squadron at RAF Calshot in 1933.**

the Cloud provided full navigational and wireless instruction facilities for pupils, and a total of 17 Clouds was produced for the RAF. Its novelty as an amphibian was enhanced by the degree of crew and passenger comfort provided, epitomised by the totally enclosed cockpit for its two pilots. The Cloud remained in service until early 1939.

Saro London II

Type: reconnaissance and general purpose flying boat.
Crew: five.
Power plants: two 920 hp Bristol Pegasus X.
Dimensions: span 80 ft; length 56 ft 9½ in; height 18 ft 9 in.
Weights: empty 11,100 lb; loaded 18,400 lb.
Performance: maximum speed 142 mph at sea level; initial rate of climb 1180 ft per min; service ceiling 19,900 ft; endurance 5 hrs.
Armament: one 0.303 in Lewis machine gun in nose cockpit; two 0.303 in Lewis machine guns in dorsal cockpits; up to 2000 lb of bombs.

Above: **a Saro London moored at RAF Mount Batten, Plymouth in 1937.**

Only 49 Londons were produced, but the type entered service in October 1936 and saw active operations until 1941. At the outbreak of war 17 Londons were on the strength of Coastal Command, and they continued to serve until the early months of 1941 with No. 202 Squadron at Gibraltar.

Short Singapore III

Type: general reconnaissance flying boat.
Crew: five or six.
Power plants: four tractor/pusher Rolls-Royce 730 hp Kestrel VIII or IX.
Dimensions: span 90 ft; length 64 ft 2 in; height 23 ft 7 in.
Weights: empty 18,420 lb; loaded 31,500 lb.
Performance: maximum speed 145 mph at 2000 ft; initial rate of climb 700 ft per min; service ceiling 15,000 ft; range 1000 miles.
Armament: one 0.303 in Lewis machine gun in nose cockpit; one 0.303 in Lewis machine gun in tail cockpit; one 0.303 in Lewis machine gun in dorsal cockpit; up to 2000 lb of bombs.

Below: **Short Singapore III K6916, pictured serving with No. 230 Squadron, was later transfered to the RNZAF.**

After protracted and progressive development in different forms, the Singapore III first entered RAF service in December 1935, and remained in squadron use until 1941, albeit in small numbers. Only 37 Singapore IIIs were produced. During its service life the Singapore had a virtually accident-free career, providing many thousands of trouble-free flying hours over several seas and oceans. On relinquishing its final Singapore IIIs in mid-1941, No.205 Squadron despatched four aircraft to Fiji, where they continued in first-line use with the RNZAF until the end of the war.

Supermarine Southampton

Type: general reconnaissance flying boat.
Crew: five.
Power plants: two 470 hp Napier Lion V (Mk I); two 502 hp Napier Lion VA (Mk II).
Dimensions: span 75 ft; length 51 ft 1½ in; height 22 ft 4½ in.
Weights (Mk II): empty 9,000 lb; loaded 15,200 lb.
Performance: maximum speed 108 mph at sea level; initial rate of climb 610 ft per min; service ceiling 14,000 ft; endurance 9 hrs (11 hrs with overload fuel).
Armament: three 0.303 in Lewis machine guns in nose and mid-fuselage locations; up to 1100 lb of bombs if required.

Introduced to RAF service in August 1925, the Southampton was the first post-1918 design of flying boat to reach squadrons, replacing wartime Felixstowe F3s and F5s. Only 78 Southamptons (all Marks) were ever produced, yet the RAF quota provided some 10 years faithful service, finally retiring in 1936. Mark I Southamptons were initially wooden-hulled, but the Mk II had a metal hull, thereby eliminating the penalty weight of some 400 pounds sea water soakage incurred by the wood-constructed variant. The Southampton was noted

for its dependability, epitomised by the historic four-aircraft Far East Flight of 1927–28 which completed a 24,000-miles cruise to Singapore without mishap and virtually on planned schedule on each leg of the flight. Nicknamed 'Old Faithful' by its crews, the Southampton provided a basic pattern and a foundation of hard experience for subsequent RAF flying boats and their crews.

Supermarine Scapa

Type: general reconnaissance flying boat.
Crew: five.
Power plants: two 525 hp Rolls-Royce Kestrel IIIMS.
Dimensions: span 75 ft; length 53 ft; height 21 ft.
Weights: empty 10,010 lb; loaded 16,040 lb.
Performance: maximum speed 141.5 mph at 3380 ft; climb to 10,000 ft, 20 mins 30 secs; service ceiling 15,500 ft; endurance 8 hrs.
Armament: three 0.303 in Lewis machine guns in nose and dorsal locations; up to 1000 lb of bombs if required.

Initially titled the Southampton Mark IV, the Scapa was basically a re-engined, all-metal version of its parent design which entered RAF squadron use in mid-1935. The type remained in service until 1938, and 14 were built for the RAF.

Supermarine Stranraer

Type: general reconnaissance flying boat.
Crew: five or six.
Power plants: two 920 hp Bristol Pegasus X.
Dimensions: span 85 ft; length 54 ft 10 in; height 21 ft 9 in.
Weights: empty 11,250 lb; loaded 19,000 lb.
Performance: maximum speed 165 mph at 6000 ft; service ceiling 18,500 ft; endurance 9 hrs 36 mins.
Armament: three 0.303 in Lewis machine guns in nose, dorsal and tail locations.

The final development of the Southampton, the Stranraer was also the ultimate biplane flying boat designed by R J Mitchell, father of the legendary Spitfire. Its original design was to a 1931 Air Ministry Specification, amended by a 1935 specification for production Stranraers. The prototype first flew in 1935. It went into RAF squadron service in December 1936 and continued in first-line use in the RAF until 1940–41, after which it continued in service with the RCAF, until replaced by 'Canso' Catalinas in 1943. Of all-metal construction, a total of 58 Stranraers was built, 40 by Canadian-Vickers.

Left: **Supermarine Scapa S1648.**
Below: **Supermarine Southampton K2965 served with No. 201 Sqn at Calshot.**

Above: the Supermarine Stranraer
prototype later served with No. 210 Sqn.

Vickers Vimy

Type: heavy bomber.
Crew: three or four.
Power plants: two 360 hp Rolls-Royce Eagle
VIII.
Dimensions: span 68 ft; length 43 ft 6½ in;
height 15 ft 7½ in.
Weights: empty 7101 lb; loaded 12,500 lb.
Performance: maximum speed 103 mph at
ground level; climb to 5000 ft, 22 mins; service
ceiling 7000 ft; endurance 11 hrs.
Armament: one 0.303 in Lewis machine gun in
nose cockpit; one 0.303 in Lewis machine gun in
rear cockpit; up to 2476 lb of bombs.

Conceived, designed and built initially in 1917–
18, the Vimy was produced too late to undertake
operations in World War I, but finally entered
full squadron service with No.58 Squadron in
July 1919 as replacement for HP 0/400s. Other
squadrons, both in Britain and the Middle East,
became Vimy units shortly thereafter. The Vimy
stayed in first-line RAF use until 1925, and with
the AAF until 1929. Even after withdrawal from
RAF squadrons, Vimys continued as training
vehicles, and individual aircraft remained in
RAF livery until at least 1938. Civil Vimys
established several historic records; the best-
known of which include Alcock and Brown's
first ever direct trans-Atlantic flight of 1919, and
the Australian Smith brothers' England-Australia
flight of the same year.

Below: a Vickers Vimy of No. 4 FTS, Egypt.

Vickers Vernon II

Type: troop or cargo transport; air ambulance.
Crew: three or four.
Power plants: two 450 hp Napier Lion II.
Dimensions: span 68 ft; length 43 ft 8 in;
height 15 ft 3 in.
Weights: empty 7890 lb; loaded 12,500 lb.
Performance: maximum speed 118 mph at
ground level; climb to 6000 ft, 13½ mins;
service ceiling 7500 ft; range 320 miles at 80 mph.
Armament: nil.

Below: a Vickers Vernon transport.

The Vernon evolved via the Vimy Commercial
design, and was the first RAF transport designed
as such, though it eventually undertook various
different roles in actual service. It played a large
part in pioneering air mail routes in the Middle
East; acted as emergency ambulance for the
garrison army formations; lifted infantry to
trouble-spots quickly; and was even locally
modified on some squadrons as a makeshift
bomber. Successive attempts to improve the
Vernon's plodding performance by fitting up-
rated engines and other modifications made
little difference, and the type served from 1921–
27 before being superseded by the Vickers
Victoria and other designs.

Vickers Virginia X

Type: heavy bomber.
Crew: three or four.
Power plants: two 580 hp Napier Lion VB.
Dimensions: span 87 ft 8 in; length 62 ft 3 in;
height 18 ft 2 in.
Weights: empty 9650 lb; loaded 17,600 lb.
Performance: maximum speed 108 mph at
5000 ft; climb to 5000 ft, 10 mins; service ceiling
15,530 ft; range 985 miles.
Armament: one 0.303 in Lewis machine gun in
nose cockpit; one or two 0.303 in Lewis machine
gun in tail cockpit; up to 3000 lb of bombs.

Envisaged in 1920 as a 'stretched-Vimy', the
Virginia – 'Ginnie' to all its crews – was eventually produced in more variants and modified
versions over a longer period than virtually any
other RAF aircraft of the 1918–39 era. The prototype Virginia I first flew in November 1922, and

Above: a Vickers Virginia of No. 7 Sqn.

progressive development eventually produced the metal-winged Mark X. This was the most numerous variant used by the RAF, equipping nine RAF and AAF squadrons and remaining in first-line use until at least 1937, amounting to 50 of the 124 Virginias of all types delivered to the RAF. The figure of 50 does not include aircraft from several earlier Marks modified to Mark X standards retrospectively. On withdrawal from squadron use, several Virginias were used at Henlow for parachute training until 1940–41. The bomber version's rock-like stability can be judged by the record of No. 7 Squadron which won the Minot bombing trophy eight times.

Vickers Victoria

Type: troop transport.
Crew: three or four.
Power plants: two 570 hp Napier Lion XIB (Mk V); two 660 hp Bristol Pegasus IIL.3 (Mk VI).
Dimensions: span 87 ft 4 in; length 59 ft 6 in; height 17 ft 9 in.
Weights: empty 10,030 lb (Mk V), 9806 lb (Mk VI); loaded 17,760 lb (Mk V), 17,600 lb (Mk VI).
Performance: maximum speed 110 mph at sea level (Mk V), 130 mph at 5000 ft (Mk VI); climb to 5000 ft, 11 mins (Mk V), 8.5 mins (Mk VI); service ceiling 16,200 ft (both Mks); range 770 miles (Mk V), 800 miles (Mk VI).
Armament: nil.

As with the Vimy/Vernon relationship, so the Victoria was an 'extended Virginia', in that many Virginia bomber design components were interchangeable with those of the Victoria. The prototype Victoria I, J6860, was first flown in August 1922, and the first production Victorias – designated Mark III – totalled 15 aircraft in the initial May 1925 contract. Further Mark III contracts saw a number of this version accepted for squadron use in the Middle East. In the winter of 1928–29 several Victoria IIIs and IVs participated in the evacuation of civilians from Kabul. The Mark IV was basically a metal-structure wing variant; though the main production type of metal Victoria was the Mark V. Despite the great improvement of metal-constructed Victorias over the early wood-built variants, the Lion engines, though dependable, needed up-rating or replacement by a more powerful power plant by 1934. As a result Pegasus engines were installed, while all-round loadings were increased, resulting in the Victoria Mark VI. At this stage the Air Ministry insisted upon a fresh name for the latest types of Victoria, ostensibly to avoid confusion at maintenance level, and the structurally improved Victoria with Pegasus engines and increased weight limits was accordingly titled Valentia Mark I. New Valentia production from the Vickers factory amounted to 28 aircraft, but additional Valentias were provided by the conversion of 15 Victorias. Eventually a total of 54 conversions was made. Victorias and Valentias were aircraft which pioneered the roles of a future RAF Transport Command, and Valentias were still in individual service during the first two years of World War II, in the Middle East and northern India.

Below: a Vickers Victoria V serving with No. 216 Squadron is pictured here during a visit to Aden.

Below: **Vickers Valentias of No. 31 Squadron pictured at Dum Dum airfield in India in 1936.**

Above: **Vickers Vildebeests of No. 42 Squadron, 1938.**

Vickers Vildebeest

Type: torpedo bomber.
Crew: two or three.
Power plant: 600 hp Bristol Pegasus IM3 (Mk I); 635 hp Bristol Pegasus IIM3 (Mk III); 825 hp Perseus VIII (Mk IV).
Dimensions: span 49 ft; length 36 ft 8 in (Mks I and III), 37 ft 8 in (Mk IV); height 14 ft 8 in.
Weights: empty 4229 lb (Mk I), 4773 lb (Mk III), 4724 lb (Mk IV); loaded 8100 lb (Mk I), 8500 lb (Mks III and IV).
Performance: maximum speed 143 mph at 5000 ft (Mk III), 156 mph at 5000 ft (Mk IV); climb to 5000 ft, 7½ mins (Mk III), 6 mins (Mk IV); service ceiling 17,000 ft; range 1250 miles (Mk III), 1625 miles (Mk IV).
Armament: one fixed 0.303 in Vickers machine gun forward; one 0.303 in Lewis machine gun in rear cockpit; one 18-inch torpedo, or up to 1200 lb of bombs.

The Vildebeest I first entered service with No.100 Squadron at Donibristle in 1932, and was intended to replace the Hawker Horsley as the RAF's principal coastal defence aircraft. A re-engined version, the Mark II, was ordered in 1933. The Air Ministry then requested a re-

Below: **Vickers Vincents of No. 45 Sqn.**

designed rear cockpit to accommodate a third crew member, resulting in the Mark III version, which entered service with No.36 Squadron in 1934 and No.22 Squadron the following year. The final version, the Mark IV, was fitted with the sleeve-valve radial Perseus engine (progenitor of the Hercules and Centaurus engines later used widely in RAF aircraft), and this variant began RAF use with No.42 Squadron in 1937. In all, 194 Vildebeests were produced. At the outbreak of World War II Coastal Command possessed 30 Vildebeests in Britain – the RAF's sole torpedo-bomber force at that time in the UK – while Nos.36 and 100 Squadrons were based in Malaya until the Japanese invasion in late 1941, and were both decimated in subsequent operations.

Vickers Vincent

Type: army co-operation, general purpose.
Crew: two or three.
Power plant: 635 hp Bristol Pegasus IIM3.
Dimensions: span 49 ft; length 36 ft 8 in; height 17 ft 9 in.
Weights: empty 4229 lb; loaded 8100 lb.
Performance: maximum speed 142 mph at 5000 ft; initial rate of climb 765 ft per min; service ceiling 17,000 ft; range 1250 miles at 133 mph.
Armament: one fixed 0.303 in Vickers machine gun forward; one 0.303 in Lewis machine gun in rear cockpit; up to 1000 lb of bombs.

The first Vincent was Vildebeest Mark II, K4105, converted to become a general purpose aircraft to replace the Westland Wapiti and Fairey IIIF. Vincents entered squadron service with No.8 Squadron at Aden in late 1934 and eventually equipped 11 squadrons, all overseas. With an auxiliary fuel tank in place of a torpedo, the Vincent was dependable for long-range flights, while its ability to carry a wide range of army co-operation equipment gave the design wide versatility in its operational roles. In September 1939 a total of 84 Vincents was still on RAF charge, and a few continued in first-line operational use in Iraq until early 1942.

Vickers Wellesley

Type: long-range medium bomber.
Crew: two or three.
Power plant: 950 hp Bristol Pegasus XX.
Dimensions: span 74 ft 7 in; length 39 ft 3 in; height 12 ft 4 in.
Weights: empty 6235 lb; loaded (normal) 11,100 lb.
Performance: maximum speed 228 mph at 19,680 ft; climb to 10,000 ft, 10 mins 45 secs; service ceiling 32,500 ft; range 2270 miles.
Armament: one fixed 0.303 in Browning machine gun in starboard wing; one 0.303 in VGO K machine gun in rear cockpit; up to 2000 lb of bombs carried in underwing containers.

The elegant Wellesley first entered service with No.76 Squadron in March-April 1937 and was thus the first RAF squadron aircraft of geodetic construction to be taken into use. For its day the design was near-revolutionary in concept. Fully-cantilevered wings, enclosed cockpits, fully retractable landing gear, plus the greatly reduced structural weight which enabled heavy load-carrying over vastly increased range; all added up to a fresh concept in bomber design and operational capability. A total of 177 Wellesleys was eventually delivered to the RAF, equipping 10 squadrons and as many other types of RAF unit. The design achieved international fame in 1938 when three aircraft of the RAF Long Range Development Unit flew from Ismailia, Egypt to Australia; two of these establishing a world distance record which was to be unbeaten for seven years. When war with Germany erupted in 1939, UK-based Wellesleys had already been replaced in bomber squadrons, but the aircraft saw extensive operations against Italian forces in the Middle East until early 1943.

Below: **Vickers Wellesleys of No. 14 Squadron were based in Transjordan and later the Sudan.**

Westland Wapiti IIA

Type: general purpose bomber; army co-operation.
Crew: two.
Power plant: 480 hp Bristol Jupiter VIII or VIIIF; 500 hp Jupiter XFA.
Dimensions: span 46 ft 5 in; length 34 ft 2 in; height 11 ft 10 in.
Weights: empty 3810 lb (Jupiter VIIIF), 3320 lb (Jupiter XFA); loaded 5400 lb (Jupiter VIIIF), 5400 lb (Jupiter XFA).
Performance: maximum speed 140 mph at 5000 ft (Jupiter VIIIF), 160 mph at 12,000 ft (Jupiter XFA); climb to 10,000 ft, 9½ mins (VIIIF), 8 mins 12 secs (XFA); service ceiling 20,600 ft (VIIIF), 27,000 ft (XFA); range 530 miles normal (VIIIF), 310 miles (XFA).
Armament: one fixed 0.303 in Vickers machine gun forward; one 0.303 in Lewis machine gun in rear cockpit; up to 500 lb of bombs.

From 1928 to 1942 the rugged Wapiti saw highly active service with the RAF in Britain, the

Above: **Westland Wapiti IIa K1309 served with No. 5 Squadron. The unit was based in India.**

Middle East and, especially, India; being the main general purpose workhorse of its period. Conceived as a replacement for the equally long-serving DH9A and Bristol F2b, the first Mark I wood-constructed Wapitis entered RAF service with No.84 Squadron at Shaibah, Iraq in 1928. The Mark IIA was an all-metal version and was the type most widely employed by the RAF; 430 of the overall total of 517 Wapitis (all Marks). The Wapiti was widely used by the AAF until 1937, by which time several RAF squadrons overseas had relinquished their Wapitis for Hawker Harts and other types. At the outbreak of war, however, three squadrons in India, Nos.5, 27 and 60, were still equipped wholly or partly with the type which was used for initial coastal patrols and other tasks. One squadron of the Indian Air Force – a force created in 1933 with four Wapitis – continued operating the type until 1942.

Part Three
1939

Below: a De Havilland Tiger Moth training aircraft.

1945

Airspeed Oxford

Type: trainer.
Crew: three.
Power plants: two 375 hp Armstrong Siddeley Cheetah X; two 450 hp Pratt & Whitney Wasp Junior R-985-AN-6 (Mk V).
Dimensions: span 53 ft 4 in; length 34 ft 6 in; height 11 ft 1 in.
Weights: empty 5380 lb (Mk I and II), 5670 lb (Mk V); loaded 7600 lb (Mk I and II), 8000 lb (Mk V).
Performance (Mks I and II): maximum speed 188 mph at 8300 ft; climb to 10,000 ft, 12 mins; service ceiling 19,500 ft; range 925 miles.
Armament: one 0.303 in Vickers K machine gun in Armstrong Whitworth dorsal turret (Mk I only); up to 12 25 lb practice bombs in bomb bay if required.

Just as the DH Tiger Moth was responsible for virtually all *ab initio* flying instruction for RAF air crews, so the Oxford provided advanced training for embryo bomber crews. The prototype, L4534, first flew in June 1937, and first RAF deliveries went to the Central Flying School (CFS) in November 1937. Thereafter Oxfords were used in Britain and the Empire for pilot and

Above: an Airspeed Oxford of the Central Flying School, Upavon, late 1937.

navigational training throughout World War II, and continued in such use with the RAF until 1955. A total of 8558 Oxfords (all types) was produced.

Armstrong Whitworth Whitley

Type: night bomber.
Crew: five (normal).
Power plants: two 795 hp Tiger IX (Mk I); two 845 hp Tiger VIII (Mks II and III); two 1030 hp Rolls-Royce Merlin IV (Mk IV); two 1145 hp RR Merlin X (Mks V and VII).
Dimensions: span 84 ft; length 70 ft 6 in (Mk V); height 15 ft.
Weights (Mk V): empty 19,350 lb; loaded 33,500 lb.
Performance (Mk V): maximum speed 230 mph at 16,400 ft; climb to 15,000 ft, 16 mins; service ceiling 26,000 ft; range (normal) 1500 miles.
Armament: one or two 0.303 in machine guns in nose turret; four 0.303 in Browning machine guns in tail turret; up to 7000 lb of bombs.

First ordered into production in June 1935, straight from the drawing board, the prototype Whitley first flew in March 1936, the first production example was delivered in early 1937 and the first example to reach a squadron, K7184, was sent to No. 10 Squadron, Dishforth on 9 March 1937. Continued development eventually resulted in the Mark V, the most widely-built version, emerging initially in August 1939. At the outbreak of war the RAF had 196 Whitleys (various Marks) on charge, serving with four bomber squadrons. First operations were flown by 10 Whitleys on night of 3/4 September 1939 – a leaflet raid on the Ruhr area. The Whitley continued on bombing operations until officially withdrawn in mid-1942, though individual Whitleys from OTUs occasionally flew bombing and other sorties until at least mid-1944. From 1941–42 Mark VII Whitleys – longer-range versions fitted with Air-to-Surface Vessel Radar (ASV) – served with Coastal Command as anti-submarine bombers; while in 1940–41 other modified Whitleys were widely employed as glider-tugs and for training of paratroopers. A small number were used in 1942 for Special Duties, usually dropping agents in enemy-occupied territories in Europe. A total of 1814 Whitleys (all types) was built.

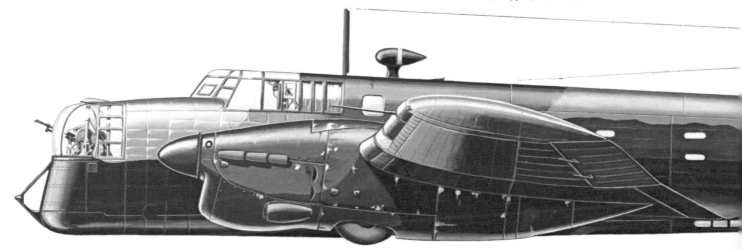

Armstrong Whitworth Albemarle

Type: glider-tug.
Crew: four.
Power plants: two 1590 hp Bristol Hercules XI.
Dimensions: span 77 ft; length 59 ft 11 in; height 15 ft 7 in.
Weights: loaded 36,500 lb (maximum, special transport), 22,600 lb (glider tug).
Performance: maximum speed 265 mph at 10,500 ft; service ceiling 18,000 ft; range (normal) 1300 miles.
Armament: four 0.303 in Browning machine guns in dorsal turret (bomber), or two 0.303 in Vickers K machine guns in dorsal cockpit.

Left: an Armstrong Whitworth Albemarle pictured at Grotaglie, Italy in 1943.
Below: an Armstrong Whitworth Whitley V.

Above: an Armstrong Whitworth Whitley V of No. 102 Sqn, Linton-on-Ouse, Yorks.

Intended initially as a medium bomber, the bulk of the eventual total of 602 Albemarles built was converted to special transport or glider-tug duties. First to be equipped with the type was No.295 Squadron in mid-1942 in the troop transporting role, and the first tug-variants joined the unit in January 1943. Albemarles were first used on operations in July 1943 during the invasion of Sicily; while the type played its part in Operation Overlord – the Normandy invasion – in June 1944, the Arnhem action in September 1944 and in other minor sorties.

Avro Manchester I & Ia

Type: heavy night bomber.
Crew: seven.
Power plants: two 1760 hp Rolls-Royce Vulture I.
Dimensions: span 90 ft 1 in; length 69 ft 4¼ in; height 19 ft 6 in.
Weights: empty 29,432 lb; loaded 56,000 lb.
Performance: maximum speed 265 mph at 17,000 ft; service ceiling 19,200 ft; range 1630 miles.
Armament: two 0.303 in Browning machine guns in FN5 turret in nose; two 0.303 in Browning machine guns in FN7 dorsal turret; four 0.303 in Browning machine guns in FN20 tail turret; maximum bomb load 10,350 lb.

Built to a 1936 Air Ministry Specification, the Manchester was powered by twin Vulture engines by official decree, despite the designers' misgivings about these unproven power plants. The first production contract, dated July 1937,

Right: **an Avro Manchester of No. 83 Squadron photographed in 1942.**
Below: **Avro Manchester L7320.**

specified 200 aircraft, built to an amended specification of 1937. First flight came in July 1939 and gave proof of the designers' doubts about Vulture engines, but production continued. In November 1940, No.207 Squadron was reformed at Waddington to introduce the design to operations; the first sorties being flown in February 1941. From then until the ultimate operational sorties of the type in June 1942, Manchesters were used by 13 squadrons. Of the 202 Manchesters delivered, some 40 per cent were lost on operations, and a further 25 per cent written off in crashes due to technical defects. In September 1939, seeking alternatives to the mistrusted Vulture engine, Avro designers proposed a four Rolls-Royce Merlin – engine version known as the Manchester III. This proposed variant later became the Avro Lancaster.

Below: an Avro Lancaster Mk II in service with No. 426 Squadron RCAF.
Bottom: a Lancaster Mk I pictured in service with No. 15 Squadron.

Avro Lancaster

Type: heavy bomber.
Crew: seven or eight.
Power plants: four 1280 hp Rolls-Royce Merlin XX (Mk I); four 1650 hp Bristol Hercules VI or XVI (Mk II); four 1300 hp Packard Merlin 28 (Mks III and X); four 1750 hp Rolls-Royce Merlin 85/102 (Mk VI).
Dimensions: span 102 ft; length 69 ft 4 in; height 20 ft 6 in.
Weights: empty 36,457 lb (Mks I, II and X); loaded 72,000 lb (with 22,000 lb bomb), 68,000 lb (Mk VII).
Performance: maximum speed 287 mph (Mks I, III and X); service ceiling 22,000 ft; range (maximum) 2500 miles.
Armament: two 0.303 in Browning machine guns in nose turret; two 0.303 in Browning machine guns in dorsal turret; four 0.303 in Browning machine guns in tail turret, or two 0.50 in Browning machine guns in tail Rose turret; up to 18,000 lb of bombs; one 12,000 lb or one 22,000 lb bomb if modified.

The Lancaster was first conceived as a Mark III variant of the Avro Manchester in late 1939. The prototype Lancaster, BT308, was a four-engined, modified Manchester, first flown in January 1941. The first Lancaster squadron was No.44 at Waddington from December 1941. The first Lancaster operations were in March 1942. The Hercules-engined Mark II version was first delivered in October 1942. The Mark X, the Canadian-built version with the Packard Merlin Mark III, first arrived in the UK in August 1943. By March 1945 RAF Bomber Command had 56 squadrons of Lancasters. Lancasters participated in such epic operations as the breaching of the Möhne and Eder dams in the Dambusters Raid, the famous daylight attack on Augsburg in April 1942, the sinking of the *Tirpitz* and the destruction of the German rocket research station at Peenemünde and many others. The Lancaster was the only Allied bomber able to carry the 12,000 pound *Tallboy* and 22,000 pound *Grand Slam* bombs. A total of 7378 Lancasters of all types was built. From 1946 Lancaster IIIs served with Coastal Command in Air-Sea Rescue and maritime training roles. The Lancaster also saw much post-1945 service with the RCAF, French and Argentinian air services. Nine of the 32 Victoria Crosses awarded to airmen in World War II went to Lancaster crew members.

Above: a cutaway view of the Lancaster.
Right: an Avro Lancaster Mk I of No. 106 Squadron based at Syerston, Notts.

Blackburn Skua/Roc

Type: naval dive bomber (Skua); naval fighter (Roc).
Crew: two.
Power plants: 840 hp Bristol Mercury IX (Mk I Skua); 890 hp Bristol Perseus XII (Skua Mk II and Roc).
Dimensions: span 46 ft 2 in; length 35 ft 7 in, 39 ft 4 in (seaplane); height 12 ft 6 in, 12 ft 1 in (Roc seaplane).
Weights: empty 5496 lb (Skua), 6124 lb (Roc landplane); loaded 8228 lb (Skua), 7950 lb (Roc).
Performance (Skua): maximum speed 225 mph at 6500 ft; service ceiling 19,100 ft; maximum range 435 miles (Skua II).
Armament (Skua): four fixed 0.303 in Browning machine guns in wings; one 0.303 in machine gun in rear of cockpit; one 500 lb bomb or eight 30 lb bombs.

The Skua was the first British dive bomber to enter FAA squadron service. The prototype Skua first flew in February 1937, after production had been contracted in July 1936. The first FAA deliveries arrived in late 1938, and by the outbreak of war 33 Skuas were in first-line use. A Skua of No.803 Squadron FAA from the carrier *Ark Royal* claimed the first British aerial victory of World War II on 25 September 1939. On 10 April 1940 seven Skuas of No.800 Squadron FAA dive-bombed and sank the German cruiser *Königsberg* in Bergen harbour, Norway, the first time a major warship had been sunk by dive bombers. The Skua subsequently saw operations during the Narvik campaign. By August 1941 the Skua had been withdrawn from first-line use and many were used thereafter as target-tugs. The Roc development incorporated a four-gun turret, the first such in FAA service, and was based on the same mistaken idea as the Boulton Paul Defiant. Though tested by FAA units from April 1939, Rocs did not see extensive service, being replaced by mid-1941. Totals of 192 Skuas and 136 Rocs were eventually built.

Blackburn Botha

Type: coastal reconnaissance; bomber.
Crew: four.
Power plants: two 880 hp Bristol Perseus X; two 930 hp Bristol Perseus XA.
Dimensions: span 59 ft; length 51 ft 0½ in; height 14 ft 7½ in.
Weights (Perseus XA): empty 12,036 lb; loaded 18,450 lb.
Performance: maximum speed 220 mph at 15,000 ft (Perseus XA); initial rate of climb 985 ft per min; service ceiling 18,400 ft (Perseus XA), 23,600 ft (Perseus X); range 1270 miles.
Armament: one fixed 0.303 in Vickers machine gun forward; two 0.303 in machine guns in dorsal turret; one Mk XII or XIV torpedo, or one 2000 lb bomb, or two 500 lb bombs, or four 250 lb bombs.

Above: a Boeing B-17 Fortress II of No. 206 Squadron, Benbecula in late 1943.

Though basically a good design, the Botha (pronounced 'Boater') suffered from under-powered engine installation for its intended operational role. Production commenced in 1937, and the production aircraft first flew in December 1938. A total of 580 Bothas was built in all. Service testing began in March 1939, and the first RAF delivery took place in December 1939. Only No.608 Squadron AAF flew Bothas on operations, until November 1940, after which all Bothas were relegated to training or other secondary duties; the last examples in service being with No.11 Radio School as late as April 1944.

Boeing Fortress I & II/III

Type: high altitude bomber; maritime patrol bomber.
Crew: seven or eight.
Power plants: four 1200 hp Wright Cyclone R-1820.
Dimensions: span 103 ft 9½ in; length 67 ft 10½ in; height 15 ft 4½ in.
Weights: empty 31,150 lb; loaded 45,470 lb.
Performance: maximum speed 320 mph at 20,000 ft (Mk I), 280 mph (Mk II); initial rate of climb 1300 ft per min (Mk I), 1400 ft per min (Mk II); maximum range 3160 miles (Mk I), 2740 miles (Mk II).
Armament: one 0.303 in machine gun in nose (Mk I), two 0.50 in machine guns (Mk II); four 0.50 in machine guns in dorsal, ventral and beam locations; up to 2500 lb of bombs (Mk I), 12,800 lb (Mk II).

Remembered chiefly as one of the mainstays of the USAAF's bombing campaigns of 1942–45, the Fortress first saw active operations in Europe with the RAF. A batch of 20 B-17Cs was modified as Fortress Mark Is, then issued to No.90 Squadron RAF in May 1941 for high level bombing sorties against German targets by day. Lack of adequate facilities to combat freezing conditions at altitude, poor defensive firepower and incorrect tactics led to high casualties, and operations ceased by 1942. The aircraft were transferred in small numbers to the North African Theatre. From mid-1942, however, improved B-17 variants were supplied to the RAF and were used mainly by Coastal Command as submarine hunters; commencing their maritime role in August 1942, and equipping four squadrons. Later in the war four more Coastal Command squadrons flew Fortresses on meteorological duties. For the last year of the war a number of Fortresses were used by No.100 Group as radio counter-measures vehicles in support of Bomber Command. In Coastal Command, Fortresses claimed at least 17 German U-Boats sunk or seriously damaged.

Boulton Paul Defiant

Type: fighter.
Crew: two.
Power plant: 1030 hp Rolls-Royce Merlin III (Mk I); 1260 hp Rolls-Royce Merlin XX (Mk II).
Dimensions: span 39 ft 4 in; length 35 ft 4 in; height 12 ft 2 in.
Weights: empty 6078 lb; loaded 8600 lb (maximum Mk I).
Performance: maximum speed 304 mph at 17,000 ft (Mk I); initial rate of climb 1900 ft per min; service ceiling 30,350 ft.
Armament: four 0.303 in Browning machine guns in rear Boulton Paul turret.

Conceived as a bomber interception fighter, using beam attack tactics, the Defiant first flew in prototype form in August 1937. Entry to RAF service began in late 1939 with No.264 Squadron, which unit first flew on operations in May 1940. Despite optimistic claims for enemy aircraft destroyed in the initial combats, the Defiant was no match for contemporary German fighters – it had no forward armament – and in the

Above left: a Blackburn Roc fighter.
Left: a formation of Blackburn Skuas.
Below: a Boulton Paul Defiant Mk I in night fighter finish. This aircraft served with No. 264 Squadron, based at Colerne, Wilts, in September 1941.
Bottom: a pair of Blackburn Bothas.

Above: **Boulton Paul Defiants of No. 264 Sqn at Kirton-in-Lindsey, Lincs, 1941.**

following months Defiant crews suffered high casualties. By the autumn of 1940 Defiants were redeployed to night-fighting duties, fitted with Airborne Interception (AI) radar sets. Replaced by Bristol Beaufighters in this latter role by mid-1941, Defiants then spent the rest of the war as target-tugs, air-sea rescue aircraft, gunnery trainers, or in other duties. Total production of Defiants comprised 1075 aircraft.

Bristol Blenheim I

Type: day bomber; fighter.
Crew: three.
Power plants: two 840 hp Bristol Mercury VIII.
Dimensions: span 56 ft 4 in; length 39 ft 9 in; height 12 ft 10 in.
Weights: empty 8100 lb; loaded 12,250 lb.
Performance: maximum speed 285 mph at 15,000 ft; climb to 15,000 ft, 11½ mins; service ceiling 32,000 ft; range 1125 miles.
Armament: one fixed 0.303 in Browning machine gun forward; one 0.303 in Lewis or Vickers K machine gun in dorsal turret; later, two Vickers K or two 0.303 in Browning machine guns in dorsal turret; four 0.303 in Browning machine guns in belly pack (Mk IF); maximum bomb load 1000 lb.

A military development of the civil Bristol Type 142, the Blenheim I entered RAF service as a medium bomber with No.114 Squadron RAF in March 1937. In December 1938 a fighter variant, Mark IF, entered squadron service, being

Below: **a Bristol Blenheim I of No. 211 Squadron in Greece, 1940.**

Below: a Bristol Blenheim IV of No. 40
Squadron based at Wyton, Hunts, 1940.

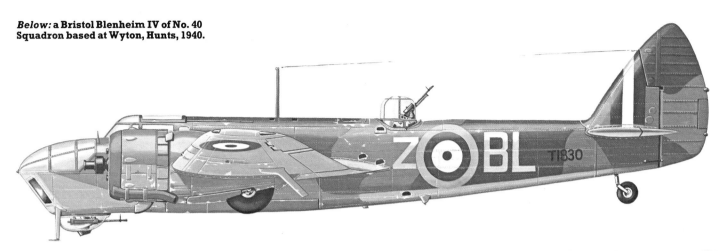

simply a re-armed standard Mark I, and was
later fitted with AI radar as a night-fighter. By
September 1939, the Blenheim Mark I bomber
was being superseded in that role, but had in the
interim equipped 26 squadrons in Britain and
overseas. In Malaya Squadron Leader A S K
Scarf of No.62 Squadron was awarded a
posthumous VC for his action during December
1941. Total production amounted to 1427 Mark
Is and variants.

Bristol Blenheim IV & V

Type: medium bomber.
Crew: two or three.
Power plants: two 920 hp Bristol Mercury XV
(Mk IV); two 950 hp Bristol Mercury 25/30 (Mk V).
Dimensions: span 56 ft 4 in (Mk IV), 56 ft 1 in
(Mk V); length 42 ft 9 in (Mk IV), 43 ft 11 in (Mk
V); height 12 ft 10 in (Mks IV and V).
Weights: empty 9800 lb (Mk IV), 11,000 lb (Mk
V); loaded 14,400 lb (Mk IV), 17,000 lb (Mk V).
Performance: maximum speed 295 mph (Mk
IV), 260 mph (Mk V); service ceiling 31,500 ft
(Mk IV), 31,000 ft (Mk V); range 1950 miles (Mk
IV), 1600 miles (Mk V).
Armament: one fixed 0.303 in Browning
machine gun forward; one or two 0.303 in VGO
or Browning machine guns in dorsal turret;
four 0.303 in Browning machine guns in belly
pack (IVF); maximum bomb load 1400 lb.

The 'long-nose' Blenheim IV bomber was first
ordered into production in 1938, and entered
RAF service with No.90 Squadron in March
1939; being at that time claimed to be the fastest

Left: a Blenheim V in North Africa, 1942.
Below: a Bristol Blenheim IV in service with
No. 13 Operational Training Unit.

Above: **Bristol Beauforts of No. 42 Sqn.**

bomber in the world. By August 1939 the RAF
possessed 18 Blenheim squadrons (mainly
equipped with Mark IVs) in Britain, and a
Blenheim IV of No.139 Squadron flew the RAF's
first wartime sortie on 3 September 1939. By
mid-1940 a total of 1375 four-gun conversion sets
had been produced, and Mark IVF variants
commenced service with Coastal Command.
Blenheim IVs continued on bombing operations
in Europe until August 1942, and remained in
first-line use in India, Burma and the Middle
East almost until the end of the war. The Mark
V, initially titled Bisley, had a new 'solid' nose
section with four Browning machine guns
installed originally, but evolved as a normal

bomber in operational use, and was employed
in the Middle and Far East theatres of war from
early 1942. In Canada Blenheims were produced in quantity and were named the Bolingbroke. Total production of Mark IVs and Vs
amounted to 4928 aircraft.

Bristol Beaufort

Type: torpedo bomber.
Crew: four.
Power plants: two 1130 hp Bristol Taurus VI,
XII or XVI (Mk I); two 1200 hp Pratt & Whitney
Twin-Wasp S3C4G (Mk II).
Dimensions: span 57 ft 10 in; length 44 ft 3 in;
height 14 ft 3 in.
Weights: empty 13,100 lb (Mk I), 14,070 lb (Mk
II); loaded 21,230 lb (Mk I), 22,500 lb (Mk II).
Performance: maximum speed 260 mph (Mk I),
265 mph (Mk II); service ceiling 16,500 ft (Mk I),
22,500 ft (Mk II); range 1600 miles (Mk I), 1450
miles (Mk II).
Armament: one or two 0.303 in Vickers K
machine guns in nose; one 0.303 in Vickers K
machine gun in Bristol dorsal turret; two 0.303 in
Vickers machine guns in beam locations; one
1605 lb torpedo, or up to 1000 lb of bombs.

Basically derived from the Blenheim design, the
Beaufort entered RAF use with No.22 Squadron
in November 1939, and by April 1940, alongside
No.42 Squadron, began maritime operations.
Seven other RAF squadrons eventually re-
equipped with Beauforts, flying many operations from 1940–43, in Europe and the Middle
East zones. A total of 1013 Mark Is were produced, while production of Mark IIs – introduced

Above: a Bristol Beaufort Mk II serving with No. 86 Squadron at Gosport, Hants, early in 1942.

from 1941 – amounted to 415 aircraft. The type was also built in Australia and used widely in the Burma campaigns and in the Pacific Theatre of war. One Beaufort pilot, Flying Officer K Campbell of No.22 Squadron was awarded a posthumous VC for a torpedo attack against the *Gneisenau* in Brest harbour on 6 April 1941.

Bristol Beaufighter

Type: fighter; torpedo-bomber.
Crew: two.
Power plants: two 1400 hp Bristol Hercules III, X or XI (Mk I); two 1250 hp Rolls-Royce Merlin XX (Mks II and V); two 1600 hp Bristol Hercules VI or XVI (Mk VI); two 1735 hp Bristol Hercules XVII (Mk X).
Dimensions: span 57 ft 10 in; length 41 ft 4 in (Mks I, VI, XI, 21), 42 ft 9 in (Mk II), 42 ft 6 in (Mk X). height 15 ft 10 in.
Weights: empty 13,800 lb (Mks I and II), 14,900 lb (Mk VI and XI), 15,600 lb (Mk X); loaded 21,000 lb (Mks I, II, V, VI, XI), 25,400 lb (Mk X).
Performance: maximum speed 330 mph; service ceiling 29,000 ft; range 1750 miles (maximum), 1500 miles (normal).
Armament: four 20mm cannon in belly; up to six 0.303 in Browning machine guns in wings; eight 3-inch rockets on wing rails; one 1605 lb torpedo, or up to 1000 lb of bombs.

Designed as a logical development of the Beaufort to meet an Air Ministry requirement for a fast, cannon-armed monoplane fighter, the prototype Beaufighter utilised the existing wings, tail unit and landing gear of the Beaufort married to a redesigned cockpit and nose area, and first flew in July 1939. With refinements and modifications, the Beaufighter I entered service with the RAF in July 1940; the first 50 machines being armed with four cannons only, but

Below: a Bristol Beaufighter Mk I of No. 604 Squadron based at Middle Wallop, 1941.

Above: a head-on view of a Bristol
Beaufighter TF X.
Left: a Beaufighter TF X carries rocket
projectiles underwing and a long-range fuel
tank beneath the fuselage.

subsequent production including wing machine guns. Initial operations were in the night-fighter role during the winter of 1940–41. The Merlin-engined Mark II became available from March 1941, while later that year long-range strike operations by Beaufighters for Coastal Command commenced. In North Africa the first Beaufighters arrived in May 1941. They played a large part in forward ground-strafing operations for the next two years and later operated in the Aegean zone as anti-shipping strike aircraft. In India and Burma the Beaufighter was flown on operations by No.27 Squadron from Christmas 1942, and by 1945 had been tasked with additional jungle rescue sorties. From 1942–45 complete strike wings of Beaufighters operated under the aegis of Coastal Command, striking as far afield as Norway and the Bay of Biscay. Some

Below: an Auster I air observation post.
Bottom: a Beaufighter VIF serving with No.
307 (Polish) Squadron at Exeter.

Beaufighters with these units were adapted as torpedo bombers. A total of 5564 Beaufighters was built before production ceased in Britain in 1945. A further 364 aircraft were built in Australia and equipped several RAAF squadrons during the closing months of the Pacific war. In late 1947 a target-tug (TT) variant was mooted, and produced from the following year. The ultimate Beaufighter in RAF use was a TT10, RD761, which made its final flight on 16 May 1960 from Seletar, Singapore.

British Taylorcraft(Auster)I-V

Type: air observation; artillery spotting;
communications.
Crew: two or three.
Power plant: 90 hp Cirrus Minor (Mk I); 130 hp
Lycoming (Mks II, IV, V).
Dimensions: span 36 ft; length 22 ft 5 in;
height 8 ft.
Weights: empty 1100 lb; loaded 1700 lb.
Performance: maximum speed 130 mph at
ground level; range 250 miles (normal).
Armament: nil.

Two thousand and forty-four Austers of all types were produced during World War II, and first

Left: **a formation of FAA Corsair IIs.**

examples to enter RAF service went to No.651 (AOP) Squadron in July 1941. The first 100 were Mark Is, but the main versions used throughout the war were the Mark III (470 built), Mark IV (254) and Mark V (804). Though administered and technically maintained by the RAF, Air Observation Post (AOP) squadrons were mainly manned by Army personnel 'attached RAF', and saw wide service in the Middle East, Burma and Northern Europe from 1941–45. Altogether 16 AOP squadrons were formed in World War II. Marks I and III were two-seaters, but subsequent marks included a third crew seat for an observer.

Chance-Vought Corsair

Type: naval fighter; fighter bomber.
Crew: one.
Power plant: 2000 hp Pratt & Whitney Double Wasp R-2800-8.
Dimensions: span 41 ft (Mk I), 39 ft 8 in (Mk IV); length 33 ft 4 in; height 15 ft 1 in.
Weights: empty 8800 lb (Mk I), 9100 lb (Mk IV); loaded (maximum) 11,800 lb (Mk I), 12,100 lb (Mk IV).
Performance: maximum speed 374 mph at 23,000 ft (Mk I), 415 mph at 19,500 ft (Mk IV); climb to 20,000 ft, $10\frac{3}{4}$ mins (Mk I), 10 mins (Mk IV); service ceiling 34,000 ft; maximum range 1125 miles (Mk I), 1560 miles (Mk IV).
Armament: four or six 0.50 in machine guns in wings; up to 2000 lb of bombs (Mk IV).

Renowned in USA aviation annals for its longevity of service (1942–54), the Corsair added to its laurels with excellent service with the FAA from June 1943 until 1945. At least 19 FAA squadrons eventually flew Corsairs. The Mark I Corsair was a pure fighter, but Mark IIs and subsequent variants accommodated bomb loads, or extra fuel tankage for long-range strikes. Used with some success in European operations, FAA Corsairs made their greatest contribution to the war in the Pacific Theatre as carrier-borne strike aircraft against Japanese targets. At the end of 1945 only four FAA squadrons still retained the type, and these were withdrawn by mid-1946.

Consolidated Catalina

Type: long-range ocean patrol flying boat.
Crew: seven to nine.
Power plants: two 1200 hp Pratt & Whitney Twin Wasp R-1830.
Dimensions: span 104 ft; length 65 ft $1\frac{3}{4}$ in; height 17 ft 11 in.
Weights: empty 14,240 lb; loaded 33,390 lb (maximum).
Performance: maximum speed 200 mph at 5700 ft; initial rate of climb 990 ft per min; service ceiling 24,000 ft; maximum range 4000 miles approximately.
Armament: one 0.303 in machine gun in nose; two 0.303 in VGO K or Browning machine guns in each side blister location; up to 4000 lb of bombs or depth charges.

In order to expand Coastal Command's strength for protection of merchant shipping, the RAF received a number of American-designed aircraft from 1939, including a modified version of the Consolidated PBY-5 flying boat from early 1941. From then until the end of the war, Catalinas served in European waters, in West Africa, and in the Far East. Their contribution to Coastal Command's anti-submarine campaign may be judged by the total of 45 U-Boats sunk or seriously damaged by Catalina crews; about one in every seven accounted for by the whole command throughout the war. Two of Coastal Command's four VC awards went to Catalina pilots. In some of the 22 Catalina-equipped squadrons an amphibious version, titled Canso, was used for a period. Nearly 700 Catalinas went into RAF service overall.

Below: **the Canso was the amphibious version of the Catalina.**
Bottom: **a Consolidated Catalina Mk VI.**

Consolidated Liberator

Type: heavy bomber; very long range (VLR) ocean patrol.
Crew: six to eight (normal).
Power plants: four 1200 hp Pratt & Whitney Twin Wasp R-1830.
Dimensions: span 110 ft; length 67 ft 1 in; height 17 ft 11 in.
Weights: empty 37,000 lb; loaded 62,000 lb.
Performance: maximum speed 270 mph at 20,000 ft; climb to 20,000 ft, 40 mins; service ceiling 32,000 ft; maximum range 2300 miles.
Armament: twin 0.30, 0.303 or 0.50 in machine guns in nose, dorsal and tail turrets; single 0.303 or 0.50 machine gun in waist positions; maximum bomb load 13,000 lb.

Alongside the Boeing B-17 Fortress, the Liberator made a huge contribution to the USAAF's daylight bombing offensive of 1942–45, but also saw considerable and successful service with the RAF. From early 1941 bomber-version Liberators saw service in the Middle East, while in the same year Very Long Range (VLR) Liberators joined Coastal Command's anti-submarine war. Early variants (bombers) relied on hand-operated defensive guns, but Mark II versions from late 1941 incorporated power-operated gun turrets. The Mark III VLR variant had increased fuel tankage; while later Marks had Leigh Lights and other specialised equipment installed. From early 1944 Liberators became the main heavy bomber in RAF use in Burma and a number were tasked with anti-submarine patrols over the Indian Ocean. In Coastal Command Liberators proved highly successful in attacking U-Boats, accounting for a total of 100 submarines destroyed or crippled; almost one third of the command's whole tally of U-Boats.

Curtiss Mohawk IV

Type: fighter.
Crew: one.
Power plant: 1200 hp Wright Cyclone GR-1820-G-205A.
Dimensions: span 37 ft 3½ in; length 28 ft 7¾ in; height 11 ft 8 in.
Weights: empty 4540 lb; loaded 6660 lb.
Performance: maximum speed 302 mph at 14,000 ft; climb to 10,000 ft, 4 mins; service ceiling 32,700 ft; range 620 miles.
Armament: two fixed 0.303 in machine guns in forward fuselage; two or four 0.303 in machine guns in wings; maximum bomb load 400 lb if required.

Left: a Consolidated Liberator GR VI on patrol over the Atlantic.
Below left: a Liberator II of No. 108 Squadron based at Fayid, Egypt, 1942.

The Mohawk was used operationally by the RAF in the Far East only, where it equipped three squadrons in 1942–44; though one squadron of the South African Air Force (SAAF) was also equipped in Middle East briefly. Ordered originally as an export version of the American P-36A by France, after May 1940 all were diverted to Britain and the RAF.

Curtiss Tomahawk

Type: fighter.
Crew: one.
Power plant: 1090 hp Allison V-1710-33.
Dimensions: span 37 ft 3½ in; length 31 ft 8¾ in; height 10 ft 8 in.
Performance: maximum speed 351 mph at 15,000 ft; climb to 15,000 ft, 5.65 mins; service ceiling 30,000 ft; range 606 miles (70% power).
Armament: two 0.303 in machine guns in nose four 0.303 in machine guns in wings.

Basically a re-engined and refined Curtiss Mohawk, the Tomahawk was initially diverted to RAF use from cancelled French orders in early 1940, and thereafter purchased by Britain in large quantity, an overall total of 1180 Model 81 Tomahawks being delivered ultimately, apart from 10 more Curtiss P-40C variants taken over from the US Army. The Tomahawk entered RAF service in Britain as a low-level reconnaissance aircraft and eventually equipped 17 RAF squadrons. In North Africa the type saw operational service as a fighter with five RAF,

Below left: a Curtiss Mohawk of No. 5 Squadron at Ramu, India in 1943.
Right: Tomahawks of No. 403 Sqn RCAF.
Below: Kittyhawks of No. 260 Squadron operated in North Africa in 1942.

two SAAF and one RAAF squadrons, the most famous of these units being No. 112 Squadron which introduced its legendary 'Sharkmouth' nose markings in September 1941. In the desert campaign Tomahawks were mainly used for low-level strafing sorties, being of inferior performance to their Messerschmitt Bf 109F opponents at altitude.

Curtiss Kittyhawk

Type: fighter.
Crew: one.
Power plant: 1600 hp Allison V-1710-81 (Mk III); 1470 hp Allison V-1710-99 (Mk IV).
Dimensions: span 37 ft 3½ in; length 31 ft 8½ in; height 10 ft 8 in.
Weights: empty 5922 lb; loaded 8515 lb.
Performance: maximum speed 362 mph at 5000 ft; climb to 15,000 ft, 9 mins; service ceiling 30,000 ft; range 1190 miles (maximum), 700 miles (normal).
Armament: four to six 0.50 in machine guns in wings and nose; up to 1000 lb of bombs if required.

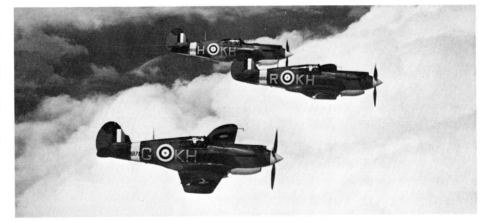

A more powerful, better-armed development of the Tomahawk, the Kittyhawk saw wide service with the American, Australian and New Zealand air services in the Pacific Theatre, but served only in the Mediterranean campaigns with the RAF, commencing in January 1942 and continuing in first-line squadrons until mid-1944. Its reputation as a tough, hard-hitting low-level ground support aircraft was high. More than 3000 Kittyhawks saw operational use with the RAF and its allied air forces, apart from wide use by the USAAF.

De Havilland Tiger Moth

Type: trainer.
Crew: two.
Power plant: 130 hp DH Gipsy Major IF.
Dimensions: span 29 ft 4 in; length 23 ft 11 in; height 8 ft 9½ in.
Weights: empty 1115 lb; loaded 1825 lb.
Performance: maximum speed 109 mph at 1000 ft; initial rate of climb 635 ft per min; service ceiling 14,000 ft; endurance 3 hrs.
Armament: nil.

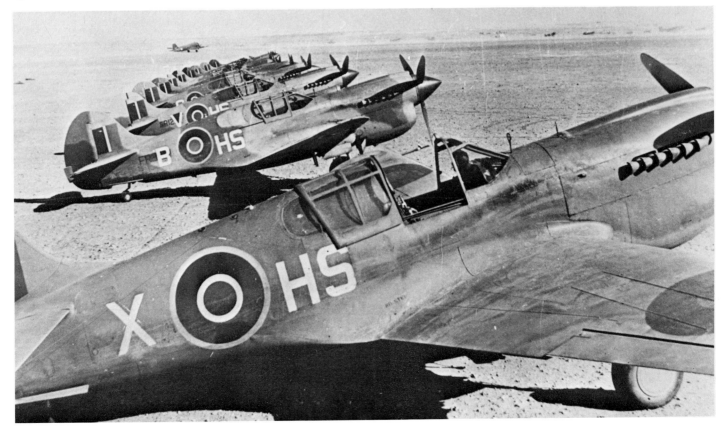

The DH Tiger Moth was the RAF's last biplane *ab initio* trainer, and served from 1932–47, during which period it was responsible for providing elementary flying instruction to virtually all RAF air crews. Fully aerobatic and of sturdy construction, its design remained almost unaltered throughout its service life. Slightly more than 8800 Tiger Moths were produced, including 420 Queen Bee pilotless, radio-controlled target versions for RAF and other services' gunnery practice. At the outbreak of war a few Tiger Moths were employed on anti-submarine coastal reconnaissance patrols, though without armament.

Left: a Canadian-built DH Tiger Moth fitted with an enclosed cockpit.
Below: a cutaway artwork illustrating the Mosquito FB VI variant.

Below: this DH Tiger Moth is preserved by the RN Historical Flight.

De Havilland Mosquito

Type: photo-reconnaissance; night fighter;
fighter bomber; bomber.
Crew: two.
Power plants: two 1280 hp Rolls-Royce Merlin
21 (prototype); two 1390 hp Rolls-Royce Merlin
23 (Mk II, night fighter); two 1480 hp Rolls-Royce
Merlin 21 or 23 (Mk IV, bomber); two 1635 hp
Rolls-Royce Merlin 25 (Mk VI, fighter bomber);
two 1650 hp Rolls-Royce Merlin 72 or 73 (Mk
XVI, bomber); two 1710 hp Rolls-Royce Merlin
76 (Mk XXX night fighter, PR34 reconnaissance).
Dimensions: span 54 ft 2 in; length 40 ft 6 in
(fighters), 40 ft $9\frac{1}{2}$ in (bombers), 41 ft 6 in
(PRU aircraft); height 15 ft 3 in.
Weights: empty 16,631 lb (PR34), 14,600 lb (Mk
XVI), 14,300 lb (Mk VI); loaded 25,500 lb (PR34),
23,000 lb (Mk XVI), 21,600 lb (Mk VI).
Performance: maximum speed 425 mph at
30,500 ft (PR34), 380 mph at 17,000 ft (Mk IV);
service ceiling 36,000 ft (PR34), 40,000 ft (Mk
XVI); range (maximum) 3500 miles (PR34),
1795 miles (Mk XVI).
Armament: four 20 mm Hispano cannon in
belly (fighters); four 0.303 in Browning machine
guns in nose (FB versions); maximum bomb load
4000 lb (bomber versions); eight 3-inch RP
under wings (Coastal strike aircraft); one 57 mm
shell gun in belly (Mk F.XVIII).

Like the Spitfire, Hurricane and Lancaster, the
all-wood Mosquito has achieved lasting international fame. Conceived as a private venture
project in 1938 as a wood-constructed, unarmed,
fast monoplane bomber, the 'Mozzie' found no
favour initially with officialdom due to its
unorthodoxy for a military machine. Reluctant

Above: **DH Mosquito Mk IV bombers of No. 105 Squadron at Marham, Norfolk, 1942.**
Below: **a Mosquito Mk VI of No. 21 Sqn pictured on a sortie against V1 sites.**
Right: **this Mosquito Mk IX served with No. 1409 BC Met Flight at Wyton, Hunts.**

acceptance of the concept by the Air Ministry in late 1939 led to a small production contract, from which emerged the first prototype (W4050) which made its first flight on 25 November 1940. By July 1941 large-scale production of the Mosquito had been begun, and the type first entered RAF service with the Photo-Reconnaissance Unit at Benson; making its first PRU sortie on 20 September 1941. Day bomber variants first entered operational use with No.105 Squadron in November 1941. Development of the basic design for fighter roles had been considered from the outset, and Mark II night-fighter versions entered first-line use with Nos.157 and 23 Squadrons in early 1942. Continuing development and improvement led to a wide variety of Mosquito versions, operating in many roles. In April 1943 the first Mosquitos to see service in the Far East were allotted to No.27 Squadron; while from early 1944 the Mosquito began to join Coastal Command's strike wings in Britain. The main Bomber Command offensive against Germany included a vast effort by Mosquito crews. They served as bombers, photo-reconnaissance aircraft, fighter escorts to the 'heavies', night intruders and path-finding marker aircraft as well as prodicing other examples of the design's ubiquity. From 1944–45 Mosquitos became particularly renowned for a series of precision bombing attacks on individual objectives. Mosquito production continued until late 1950, and the type remained in RAF service until December 1955. Overall production of Mosquitos amounted to 7781 aircraft.

Douglas Boston III-V

Type: light day bomber.
Crew: three.
Power plants: two 1600 hp Wright Cyclone GR-2600-A5B.
Dimensions: span 61 ft 4 in; length 47 ft 3 in; height 18 ft 1 in.
Weights: empty 15,051 lb; loaded 21,580 lb (maximum).
Performance: maximum speed 311 mph at sea level; initial rate of climb 2000 ft per min; service ceiling 25,170 ft; range 525 miles (normal), 1000 miles (maximum).
Armament: four fixed 0.303 in machine guns in nose section; two 0.303 in Browning machine guns in each of dorsal and ventral locations; maximum bomb load 2000 lb.

Initially ordered as slightly modified Douglas DB-7s from the USA, the first Boston Is were delivered to the RAF in mid-1940 and were used for crew conversion to tricycle-undercarriage bombers. The second variant, the Boston II, was converted by the RAF to the Havoc night fighter, and the third, the Boston III bomber, entered operational service in October 1941 with No.2 Group, Bomber Command, and with the Desert Air Force from late 1942. A further variant, the Boston IV, incorporated a power-operated dorsal turret. Bostons remained in service with the RAF until the end of the European war. Nearly 800 Boston IIIs, 200 Boston IIIAs, 170 Boston IVs, and 90 Boston Vs were delivered to the RAF and Commonwealth squadrons.

Above: a Douglas Havoc of No. 23 Sqn.

Douglas Havoc

Type: night fighter; intruder.
Crew: two or three.
Power plants: two 1200 hp Pratt & Whitney Twin Wasp S3C4-G.
Dimensions: span 61 ft 4 in; length 46 ft 11¾ in; height 15 ft 10 in.
Weights: empty 11,450 lb; loaded 19,050 lb.
Performance: maximum speed 295 mph at 13,000 ft; service ceiling 26,000 ft; range 1000 miles.
Armament: eight 0.303 in Browning machine guns in nose (night fighter); four 0.303 in Browning machine guns in nose, and one 0.303 in Vickers K machine gun in dorsal cockpit (intruder); up to 1000 lb of bombs if required (intruder).

Below: **Douglas Boston IIIs of No. 107 Sqn.**

Of the Douglas DB-7 bombers delivered (Boston IIs and a few IIIs), at least 185 are known to have been converted to the night fighter or intruder configuration, named Havoc by the RAF. Commencing in December 1940, Havocs continued night operations until mid-1942 before being withdrawn in favour of DH Mosquitos. Seventy Havocs were modified to incorporate a search-light in the nose, termed Turbinlite, for night interception in co-operation with single-seat fighters. Twenty others were used experimentally for carriage of aerial mines in night defence, though this form of operation, Pandora or LAM, was not a success.

Douglas Dakota

Type: transport.
Crew: three, 28 passengers.
Power plants: two 1200 hp Pratt & Whitney Twin Wasp R-1830-92.
Dimensions: span 95 ft; length 64 ft 5½ in; height 16 ft 11 in.
Weights: empty 16,970 lb; loaded 26,000 lb (normal).
Performance: maximum speed 230 mph at 8500 ft; initial rate of climb 1130 ft per min; service ceiling 23,200 ft; range 2100 miles (maximum).
Armament: nil.

The Dakota – or 'Dak' to all its crews – was the doyen of all RAF transport aircraft. Nearly 2000 Dakotas were supplied to the RAF and these served faithfully in every theatre of war, starting in April 1941 when 12 aircraft were received by No.31 Squadron RAF in India. These were Douglas DC2 transports, later supplemented by

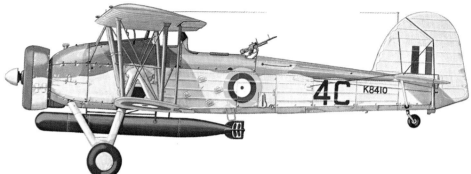

Above: **this Swordfish is preserved at Yeovilton, Somerset, by the RN Historical Flight.**
Left: **this Dakota is pictured in service with the Royal Aircraft Establishment.**

DC3s, and eventually C-47 Dakotas, military developments of the DC3 civil transport, first flown in 1935. In various guises Dakotas continued to serve the RAF until the ultimate Dakota flight in RAF markings in 1970. Apart from passenger and freight carriage, Dakotas figured largely in the role of glider tug, paratroop conveyance, ambulance, communications, propaganda 'sky-voices' fitted with loudspeakers, VIP vehicles, and general hacks.

Fairey Battle

Type: light bomber.
Crew: three.
Power plant: 1030 hp Rolls-Royce Merlin I, II, III or V.
Dimensions: span 54 ft; length 42 ft 4 in; height 15 ft 6 in.
Weights: empty 6647 lb; loaded 10,792 lb.
Performance: maximum speed 257 mph at 20,000 ft; climb to 10,000 ft, 8 mins 24 secs; service ceiling 25,000 ft; range 1000 miles (maximum).
Armament: one 0.303 in Vickers K machine gun in rear cockpit; one fixed 0.303 in Browning machine gun forward; maximum bomb load 1000 lb.

Above: **Fairey Swordfish Mk I K8410 served with No. 813 Squadron of the Fleet Air Arm, which operated from the aircraft carrier HMS Eagle in 1940.**

At its conception in 1932–34, the Battle was a reasonably advanced design of pleasing contours and performance, and the first prototype made its initial flight in March 1936. Ordered in large quantity, the Battle equipped a total of 15 squadrons in Bomber Command in September 1939. Ten of those squadrons moved to France that month, but in May–June 1940 were virtually wiped out during the German advance. Underarmed, with relatively inferior performance, the Battle was clearly obsolete for first-line operations by then. The first awards of VCs to RAF men went posthumously to two crew members of a No.12 Squadron Battle. After the Battle of France the Battle was quickly relegated to training or other roles. Total production of Battles was 2203 aircraft, more than half of which were despatched to Canada, Australia and elsewhere as trainers from 1939 onward.

Fairey Swordfish

Type: torpedo-bomber; maritime reconnaissance.
Crew: three.
Power plant: 690 hp Bristol Pegasus IIIM3 (Mks I and II); 750 hp Pegasus XXX (Mks II and III).
Dimensions: span 45 ft 6 in; length 35 ft 8 in (landplane), 40 ft 6 in (floatplane); height 12 ft 4 in (landplane), 14 ft 7 in (floatplane).
Weights: empty 4195 lb (landplane), 4997 lb (floatplane); loaded 7720 lb (landplane), 8900 lb (floatplane).
Performance: maximum speed 154 mph (landplane), 136 mph (floatplane); service ceiling 19,250 ft (landplane), 14,250 ft (floatplane); range 1000 miles (maximum).
Armament: one fixed 0.303 in Vickers machine gun forward; one 0.303 in Vickers K machine gun in rear cockpit; one 1610 lb torpedo, or up to 1500 lb of bombs; six–eight 3-inch rockets on underwing rails if required.

Below: **Fairey Battles of No. 226 Sqn were based at Harwell in early 1939.**

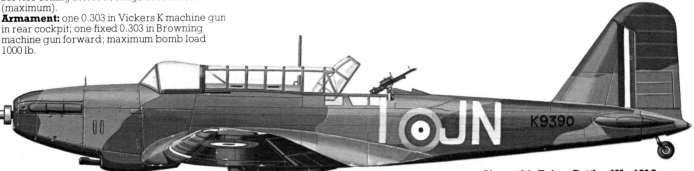

Above: **this Fairey Battle of No. 150 Sqn was shot down over Belgium in May 1940.**

Above: this Fairey Swordfish carries a
torpedo and underwing bomb racks.
Right: a Fairey Swordfish climbs away from
the deck of HMS *Furious.*

The 'Stringbag' – it's universal nickname –
achieved legendary fame in RAF and FAA
annals, serving throughout World War II on
first-line operational duties despite its apparent
obsolescence. Evolved from the Fairey S.9/30
and TSR private venture designs, the TSR II was
retitled Swordfish in early 1935, and first pre-
production examples were tested initially in
December 1935–February 1936, entering service use in the latter month. First production
Swordfish were titled the Mk I, and were followed by the Mk II having strengthened lower
wings and, latterly, being fitted with up-rated
engines. Mark IIIs were further modified for
carriage of a greater war load. FAA squadrons
began to re-equip with the Swordfish from July
1936 and by September 1939 the FAA had 13
first-line Swordfish squadrons, while a further
12 squadrons were formed during the war. The
Swordfish first came into the limelight during
operations in the 1940 Norwegian campaign,
and achieved international fame in November
1940 when 20 Swordfish crippled the Italian
Navy in an attack on Taranto harbour. Thereafter Swordfish crews were evident in most
operations in European and Mediterranean
waters. The sacrificial attack on German battle-
cruisers in the English Channel by six Swordfish
of No.825 Squadron FAA in February 1942
resulted in a posthumous award of a VC to their
leader, Lieutenant Commander E Esmonde,
DSO. From 1942–45 the Swordfish operated
mainly as an anti-submarine and anti-shipping
strike aircraft, and eventually accounted for
more tonnage of enemy ships sunk and seriously
damaged than any other British aircraft in the
same role. In January 1945 the FAA still possessed nine Swordfish squadrons, but the last of
these was disbanded in May that year. Total
production of the Swordfish amounted to 2399
aircraft.

Fairey Seafox

Type: maritime reconnaissance.
Crew: two.
Power plant: 395 hp Napier Rapier VI.
Dimensions: span 40 ft; length 33 ft 5 in; height 12 ft 2 in.
Weights: empty 3805 lb; loaded 5420 lb.
Performance: maximum speed 124 mph at 5860 ft; climb to 5000 ft, 15½ mins; service ceiling 9700 ft; range 440 miles.
Armament: one 0.303 in machine gun in rear cockpit.

Designed for catapult-launching from light cruisers, the Seafox was seriously under-powered with its Rapier engine – the only such aircraft fitted with this power plant in service use – and therefore was limited in performance. The first prototype first flew in May 1936, and a total of 66 aircraft was produced. In December 1939 a Seafox from HMS *Ajax* acted as gun-spotter for British cruisers attacking the German pocket battleship *Graf Spee*, and its pilot was awarded a Distinguished Service Cross (DSC); the first FAA officer to be decorated in World War II. Seafoxes served until mid-1943.

Fairey Albacore

Type: torpedo bomber.
Crew: three.
Power plant: 1130 hp Bristol Taurus XII.
Dimensions: span 50 ft; length 39 ft 10 in; height 14 ft 2 in.
Weights: empty 7250 lb; loaded 10,460 lb (normal).
Performance: maximum speed 161 mph at 4500 ft; climb to 6000 ft, 8 mins; service ceiling 20,700 ft; range 930 miles.
Armament: one fixed 0.303 in machine gun in wing; one or two 0.303 in Vickers K machine guns in rear cockpit; one 1610 lb 18-inch torpedo, or up to 2000 lb of bombs.

Intended as a replacement for the Swordfish, the Albacore first flew in December 1938, and entered FAA service in March 1940, with No.826 Squadron. A total of 800 Albacores was eventually built, production ceasing in 1943. Operations were flown until mid-1943 in European and Middle East Theatres, both from carriers and from land bases; while small numbers continued on anti-submarine duties until late 1944.

Below: Fairey Albacores of No. 827 Sqn from HMS *Indomitable.* over the Pacific.
Left: a Fairey Seafox under test in the Solent, July 1937.
Bottom: a Fairey Swordfish float version.

years after the prototype's first flight. From 1943–45 Barracudas gave important, if unspectacular service as dive bombers or torpedo bombers in each major war theatre, but are particularly remembered for their partially successful attacks on the German battleship *Tirpitz* in 1944. At least 21 FAA squadrons flew Barracudas, but most were quickly disbanded in late 1945. Total production of all Marks amounted to 2602 aircraft; 30 of these being post-war built Mark Vs which saw brief service in training roles in the late 1940s.

Fairey Firefly I

Type: naval fighter; reconnaissance.
Crew: two.
Power plant: 1730 hp Rolls-Royce Griffon IIB; 1990 hp Rolls-Royce Griffon XII.
Dimensions: span 44 ft 6 in; length 37 ft; height 12 ft 4 in.
Weights: empty 9750 lb; loaded 14,020 lb.
Performance: maximum speed 316 mph at 14,000 ft; climb to 5000 ft, $2\frac{1}{2}$ mins; service ceiling 28,000 ft; range 1300 miles (maximum).
Armament: four 20 mm cannon in wings; two 1000 lb bombs under wings, or eight 3-inch rockets.

The prototype Firefly first flew in December 1941, and entered FAA service in October 1943 with units of HMS *Indefatigable*. Operations were flown until the end of the war, the bulk of these being in the Pacific Theatre and Indian Ocean zone. Much of the 1944–45 operations involved concentrated attacks against enemy ground targets, and the Firefly's heavy firepower and bomb-carrying capacity were successful in such sorties.

Below: **Fairey Fireflies are shown aboard HMS *Indefatigable* on their return from a strike against a Sumatran oil refinery on 4 January 1945.**

Above: **a Fairey Fulmar drogue-towing aircraft pictured at El Arish, Egypt.**

Fairey Fulmar

Type: naval fighter.
Crew: two.
Power plant: 1080 hp Rolls-Royce Merlin VIII.
Dimensions: span 46 ft $4\frac{1}{2}$ in; length 40 ft 3 in; height 14 ft.
Weights: empty 6915 lb; loaded 9800 lb.
Performance: maximum speed 280 mph at 15,000 ft; service ceiling 26,000 ft; range (maximum) 800 miles.
Armament: eight fixed 0.303 in Browning machine guns in wings.

A naval fighter development of the Fairey P.4/34 light bomber, the Fulmar first flew in January 1940, and entered FAA squadron service with No.806 Squadron FAA in July 1940, aboard HMS *Illustrious*. This unit was quickly in action in the Mediterranean against Italian opponents and proved successful initially. From then until late 1942, Fulmars saw extensive service in European, Middle and Far East Theatres; accounting for some 80 claimed combat victories overall. Production of Fulmars, which ceased in early 1943, totalled 600 aircraft.

Fairey Barracuda

Type: torpedo bomber; dive bomber.
Crew: three.
Power plant: 1300 hp Rolls-Royce Merlin 30 (Mk I); 1640 hp Rolls-Royce Merlin 32 (Mks II and III); 2020 hp Rolls-Royce Griffon 37 (Mk V, postwar production).
Dimensions: span 49 ft 2 in (Mks I–III), 53 ft (Mk V); length 39 ft 9 in (Mks I–III), 41 ft 7 in (Mk V); height 15 ft 2 in (Mks I–III), 17 ft 3 in (Mk V).
Weights: empty 8700 lb (Mk I), 9350 lb (Mk II), 9407 lb (Mk III), 11,430 lb (Mk V); loaded 13,500 lb (Mk I), 14,100 lb (Mk II), 15,250 lb (Mk V).
Performance: maximum speed 235 mph at 11,000 ft (Mk I), 253 mph (Mk V); service ceiling 18,400 ft (Mk I), 20,000 ft (Mk III), 24,000 ft (Mk V); range (maximum) 1320 miles (Mk I), 1120 miles (Mk V).
Armament: two 0.303 in Vickers machine guns in rear cockpit; one 1620 lb torpedo, or up to 1800 lb of bombs.

Intended as replacement for the Albacore, the Barracuda was designed, built and flown in 20 months, yet was delayed by policy decisions in entering FAA service until January 1943; two

Below: **Barracudas from HMS *Indomitable*.**

Gloster Gladiator

Type: fighter.
Crew: one.
Power plant: 830 hp Bristol Mercury IX (Mk I);
840 hp Bristol Mercury VIIIA (Mk II); Mercury
VIIIAS (Sea Gladiator).
Dimensions: span 32 ft 3 in; length 27 ft 5 in;
height 11 ft 9 in.
Weights: empty 3217 lb; loaded 4592 lb
(normal).
Performance: maximum speed 250 mph at
17,500 ft (Mk I), 257 mph at 14,600 ft (Mk II); climb
to 10,000 ft, 4 mins 40 secs; service ceiling
32,800 ft (Mk I), 33,500 ft (Mk II); range 430–440
miles (normal).
Armament: two fixed 0.303 in Browning
machine guns in forward fuselage; two fixed
0.303 in Browning machine guns under lower
wings.

A development of the Gauntlet, the Gladiator
prototype – initially titled Gloster SS 37, then
Gloster F.7/30 – was named Gladiator on 1 July
1935; having made its first flight as the SS 37 in
September of the previous year. The first 70
production Gladiator Is had under-wing Lewis
or Vickers machine guns before Brownings
became standard equipment. The first RAF
squadron to receive Gladiators was No.72 at
Tangmere in February 1937, and by September
1939 the RAF's Fighter Command possessed a
total of 218 Gladiators; 76 of these in first-line
squadron use. By then Gladiators had re-
equipped units in the Middle East and in June
1940, when Italy declared war, were virtually
the only fighter defences throughout the Middle
East territories. From 1939–41 Gladiators flew in
combat over France, Norway, Greece, Crete,
Egypt, Aden, Malta and a dozen other war
zones; accumulating some 250 claimed combat
victories. From 1942 the Gladiator was relegated
to second-line duties, becoming meteorological
aircraft, fighter trainers, radar calibration

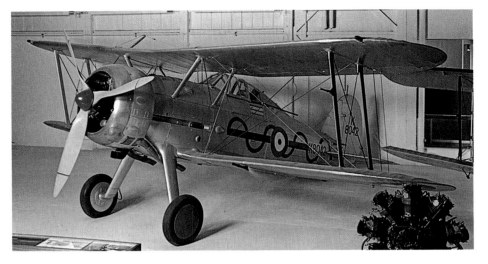

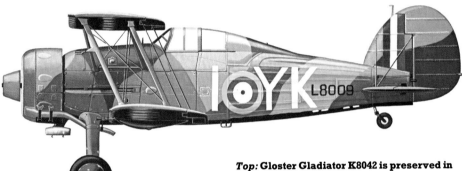

Top: **Gloster Gladiator K8042 is preserved in
No. 87 Sqn markings at the RAF Museum.**
Above: **Gloster Gladiator L8009 flew with No.
80 Squadron from Sidi Barrani in 1940.**

vehicles, and serving in sundry other minor
roles. In these guises Gladiators continued in
service until early 1945. The naval equivalent,
the Sea Gladiator, saw brief operational use in
European and Middle East waters from 1939–41,
though in small numbers. Total production of
Gladiators amounted to 378 Mark Is, 270 Mark
IIs, and 98 Sea Gladiators; an overall figure of
746 aircraft.

Gloster Meteor I-3

Type: fighter.
Crew: one.
Power plants (Mk I): two 1700 lb thrust Rolls-
Royce W.2B/23C Welland Series 1 turbo-jets.
Dimensions (Mk I): span 43 ft; length 41 ft 3 in;
height 13 ft.
Weights (Mk I): empty 8140 lb; loaded 13,795 lb.
Performance: maximum speed 415 mph at
10,000 ft; climb to 30,000 ft, 15 mins; service
ceiling 40,000 ft.
Armament: four fixed 20 mm British Hispano
cannon in front fuselage.

Britain's first operational jet aircraft of any type,
the prototype Meteor I first flew on 12 January
1944; while the first-ever RAF jet fighter unit was
No.616 Squadron at Culmhead, which received
its first Meteor I on 12 July 1944, and had completely equipped with the type by the end of
August 1944, being then based at Manston. The
unit's first aerial victory, a V1 unmanned flying
bomb, was achieved on 4 August; the first of 13
such bombs to be brought down by 616 Squadron's pilots. In January 1945, 616 Squadron
started a move to the Continent, being re-
equipped with F.3 Meteors, and flying ground
support sorties for the rest of the European
campaign. In March 1945 a second F.3-equipped
unit, No.504 Squadron AAF, also became based

Above: a Gloster Meteor F3 at Farnborough.
Left: Gloster Gladiators of No. 72 Sqn fly in
formation, 1937.

in Europe. The F.3 Meteor was intended to have
the more powerful W.2B/37, Derwent I engine,
but initial deliveries in 1945 had to be fitted with
W2B/23C Wellands.

Grumman Avenger (Tarpon) I-III

Type: torpedo bomber.
Crew: two or three.
Power plant: 1850 hp Wright Cyclone GR-
2600-8 (Mk I); 1750 hp Wright Cyclone R-2600-20
(Mk III).
Dimensions: span 54 ft 2 in; length 40 ft; height
15 ft 8 in.
Weights: empty 10,600 lb (Mk I), 10,700 lb (Mk
III); loaded 16,300 lb (Mk I), 16,400 lb (Mk III).
Performance: maximum speed 259 mph at
11,200 ft (Mk I), 262 mph at 16,600 ft (Mk III);
service ceiling 23,000 ft (Mk I), 25,000 ft (Mk III);
range (maximum) 1910 miles (Mk I), 2230 miles
(Mk III).
Armament: two fixed 0.50 in machine guns in
wings; one 0.50 in machine gun in dorsal turret;
one 0.30 in machine gun in ventral location; one
1921 lb 22-inch torpedo, or up to 1000 lb of
bombs; eight 3-inch rockets below wings if
required.

Below: a Grumman Avenger torpedo
bomber.

Regarded as one of the outstanding naval strike
aircraft of the war, and used widely by both
British and American naval air forces, the
Avenger entered FAA service under the title
Tarpon I initially, but reverted to its US designation from January 1944. First to equip with the
type was No.832 Squadron FAA in early 1943,
and 14 other FAA squadrons eventually flew
Avengers operationally. Though conceived as a
torpedo bomber, the Avenger was mainly used
as a naval bomber and general strike aircraft.
It operated with the FAA chiefly in northern
European waters and in the Far East until the end
of 1945. The Avenger finally left FAA service in
June 1946, though later versions were re-
introduced in the 1950s.

Above: a Grumman Martlet naval fighter.

Grumman Wildcat (Martlet) I-VI

Type: naval fighter.
Crew: one.
Power plant: 1200 hp Wright Cyclone G-205A
(Mk I); 1200 hp Pratt & Whitney Twin Wasp
S3C4-G (Mk II and III); 1200 hp Pratt & Whitney
Twin Wasp R-1830-86 (Mk V).
Dimensions: span 38 ft; length 28 ft 10/11 in;
height 9 ft 2½ in.
Weights: empty 4425 lb (Mk I), 4649 lb (Mks II–
V); loaded 5876 lb (Mk I), 6100 lb (Mks II–V).
Performance: maximum speed 310 mph (Mk I),
315 mph (Mks II and III), 330 mph (Mk V); service
ceiling 28,000 ft (Mks I–V); range 1100 miles
(Mk I), 1150 miles (Mks II–V).
Armament: four fixed 0.50 in machine guns in
wings (Mk I); six 0.50 in machine guns in wings
(Mks II–V).

Known to the USA's air services as the Grumman
F4F-3 Wildcat, the type was purchased by
Britain early in the war and retitled Martlet until
1944, then renamed Wildcat to conform with US
designation. The first six Martlets arrived in
Britain in August 1940, then entered FAA service
with No.804 Squadron FAA the following month.
The Martlet I had fixed wings and four wing
guns; Mark IIs had folding wings, a fresh engine,
and two extra guns in the wings. In operational
use Martlets proved tough, fast, hard-hitting,
highly manoeuvrable, and technically dependable. They continued in first-line use from 1940
until 1945. Mark III Martlets reverted to fixed
wings, and from January 1944 (when the name
was changed to Wildcat) Mark IV, V and VI
versions came into service. They were flown
from land bases and every form of sea-going
carrier, and operated in most war zones.

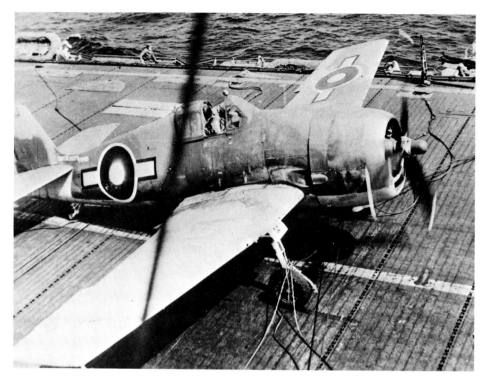

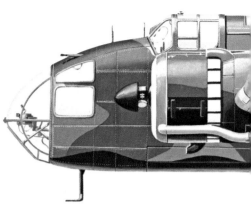

Below: a Handley Page Halifax B VI of No. 640 Squadron based at Leconfield, 1945.

Above: a Hellcat aboard HMS *Ruler.*

Grumman Hellcat

Type: naval fighter.
Crew: one.
Power plant: 2000 hp Pratt & Whitney Double Wasp R-2800-10W.
Dimensions: span 42 ft 10 in; length 33 ft 7 in; height 14 ft 5 in.
Weights: empty 9212 lb; loaded 13,753 lb (maximum).
Performance: maximum speed 371 mph at 17,200 ft; service ceiling 36,700 ft; maximum range 1530 miles.
Armament: six fixed 0.50 in machine guns in wings; up to 2000 lb of bombs, or six 3-inch rockets under wings.

Intended as a replacement for the Wildcat, a total of 1182 Hellcats was supplied to Britain under Lend-Lease arrangements before the end of the war. Until January 1944 the British versions were titled Gannet. Hellcats (Gannets) first entered FAA service in July 1943, and later equipped a total of 12 FAA squadrons on operations. With its better performance envelope than the Wildcat, the Hellcat was a match for virtually every opposing Japanese fighter in the Pacific zone.

Handley Page Hampden

Type: medium day bomber.
Crew: four.
Power plants: two 980 hp Bristol Pegasus XVIII.
Dimensions: span 69 ft 2 in; length 53 ft 7 in; height 14 ft 11 in.
Weights: empty 11,780 lb; loaded 18,756 lb (normal).
Performance: maximum speed 265 mph at 15,500 ft; climb to 15,000 ft, 18.9 mins; service ceiling 22,700 ft; range (with 4000 lb bomb load) 870 miles.
Armament: one fixed 0.303 in Vickers K machine gun in top forward fuselage; one 0.303 in Vickers K machine gun in nose; one or two 0.303 in Vickers K machine guns in dorsal cupola; one or two 0.303 in Vickers K machine guns in ventral cupola; maximum bomb load 4000 lb.

Essentially an interim design to bridge the gap between biplane and eventual heavy monoplane bombers, the Hampden emerged in prototype form in June 1936. The first Hampden delivered to the RAF (L4034) went initially to the Central Flying School, Upavon in August 1938, before joining the first Hampden squadron, No.49, at Scampton in September. By 3 September 1939, the RAF had a total of 212 Hampdens, mostly in first-line bomber squadrons, a figure representing some 10 per cent of the

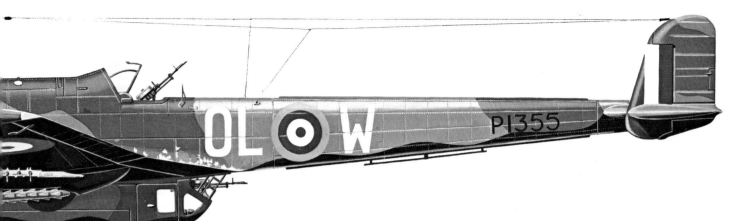

Above: **a Handley Page Hampden of No. 83 Squadron based at Scampton, Lincs, 1940.**

Left: **HP Hampden P5304 is pictured serving with No. 16 Operational Training Unit, based at Upper Heyford, Oxfordshire.**

RAF's overall aircraft strength then, and approximately 25 per cent of Bomber Command's offensive strength on that date. For almost exactly three years Hampdens operated by day and night, bombing and mining, before being withdrawn from first-line bomber squadrons; the ultimate Hampden bombing sorties being flown on 14/15 September 1942. For the next year several squadrons used modified Hampdens as torpedo-bombers under the aegis of Coastal Command, only ceasing this form of operation in December 1943. The main variant of the Hampden was the Napier Dagger-engined Hereford, used almost exclusively for training duties. Total production of Hampdens and Herefords amounted to 1584 aircraft; many Herefords being locally converted Hampdens.

Below: **a Handley Page Halifax B III.**

Handley Page Halifax

Type: heavy bomber.
Crew: six–eight.
Power plants: four 1280 hp Rolls-Royce Merlin X (Mk I); four 1390 hp Rolls-Royce Merlin XX/22 (Mks II and V); four 1615 hp Bristol Hercules XVI (Mk III); four 1800 hp Bristol Hercules 100 (Mk VI).
Dimensions: span 98 ft 10 in (Mks I, II, III, V), 104 ft 2 in (Mks IV and VI); length 70 ft 1 in (Mks I, II, III, V), 71 ft 7 in (Mks IV and VI); height 20 ft 9 in.
Weights: empty 36,000 lb (Mks I, II, V), 38,900 lb (Mks III and VI); loaded (maximum) 60,000 lb (Mk I), 63,000 lb (Mk V), 65,000 lb (Mk III), 68,000 lb (Mk VI).
Performance: maximum speed 280 mph (Mk I), 312 mph (Mk VI); service ceiling 22,800 ft (Mk I), 24,000 ft (Mk VI); maximum range 3000 miles (Mk I), 2350 miles (Mk III).
Armament: four 0.303 in Browning machine guns in tail turret (all Mks); two 0.303 in Brownin Browning machine guns in nose turret (Mk I); one hand-operated 0.303 in machine gun in nose, two in beam locations; four 0.303 in Browning machine guns in dorsal turret (III); maximum bomb load 13,000 lb.

The Halifax followed the Short Stirling into operational use with RAF Bomber Command; the first squadron, No.35, commencing bombing sorties in March 1941. It remained in service as a day or night bomber until 1945, serving in Europe and the Middle East in this role. Progressive modification and development produced a wide variety of other forms, including anti-submarine and meteorological patrol 'Hallies' for Coastal Command, special duties variants for spy and supply-dropping, radio counter-measures, glider-tugs, troop & VIP

transports and others. As a bomber the Halifax suffered relatively high casualty rates in the early stages of operations, due partly to its relatively low operating ceiling, but the rugged construction enabled it to absorb heavy damage to a great degree. Of the grand total of 6177 Halifaxes actually built, all but one were delivered for service; production finally ceasing in November 1946, and the last Halifax in first-line RAF use being withdrawn in March 1952.

Hawker Hurricane

Type: fighter.
Crew: one.
Power plant: 1030 hp Rolls-Royce Merlin II or III (Mk I); 1260 hp Rolls-Royce Merlin XX (Mk II); 1280 hp Rolls-Royce Merlin 24 or 27 (Mk IV).
Dimensions: span 40 ft; length 31 ft 4 in (Mk I), 32 ft 2¼ in (Mk II); height 13 ft 2 in.
Weights: empty 4743 lb (Mk I), 5467 lb (Mk II); loaded 6218 lb (Mk I), 7396 lb (Mk II).
Performance: maximum speed 320 mph at 18,200 ft (Mk I), 340 mph at 17,500 ft (Mk II); service ceiling 34,200 ft (Mk I), 36,300 ft (Mk IIA); range (maximum) 935 miles (Mk I, with extra tanks), 1090 miles (Mk IIA, with extra tanks).
Armament: eight fixed 0.303 in Browning machine guns in wings (Mk I); twelve fixed 0.303 in Browning machine guns in wings (Mk IIB); four 20 mm cannon in wings (Mk IIC); two Vickers 40 mm S guns & two 0.303 in Browning machine guns under/in wings (Mk IID); up to 1000 lb of bombs under wings.

Any short list of the world's classic fighter aircraft would have to include the doughty Hurricane. The RAF's (and the world's) first eight-gun, monoplane fighter capable of surpassing 300 mph in level flight with full war load, the Hurricane derived from a private project

Above: a Hawker Hurricane I completed to late production standard with metal wings and three-bladed propeller.
Below: Hawker Hurricane IIC fighters pictured in service with No. 94 Squadron based at El Gamil, Egypt, in 1942.

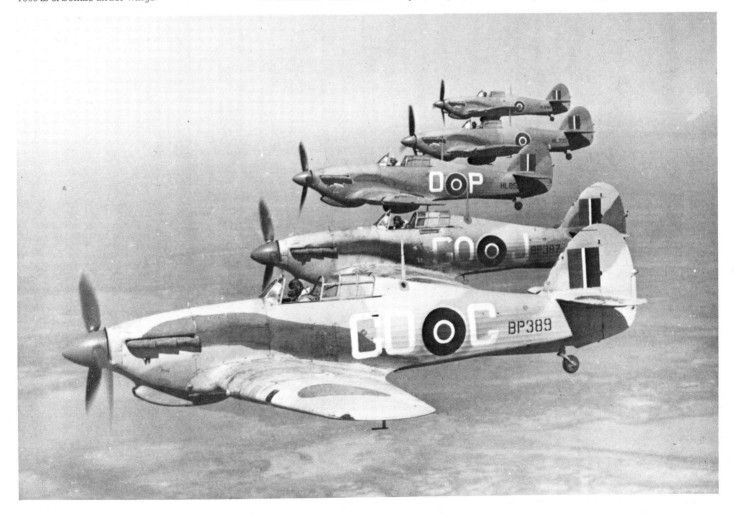

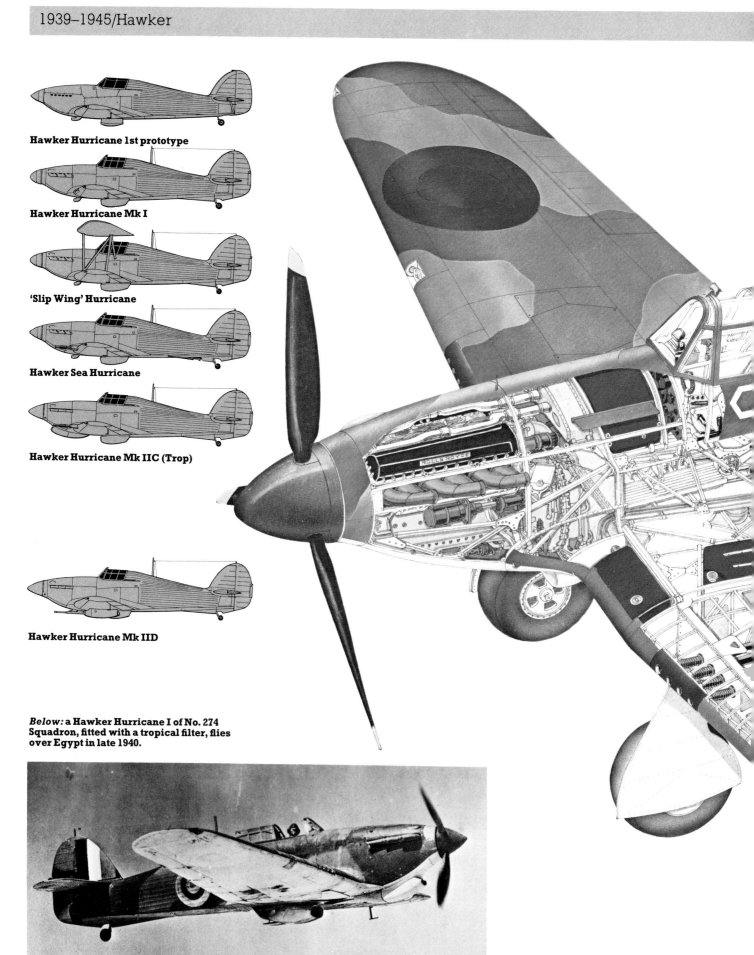

Hawker Hurricane 1st prototype

Hawker Hurricane Mk I

'Slip Wing' Hurricane

Hawker Sea Hurricane

Hawker Hurricane Mk IIC (Trop)

Hawker Hurricane Mk IID

Below: a Hawker Hurricane I of No. 274
Squadron, fitted with a tropical filter, flies
over Egypt in late 1940.

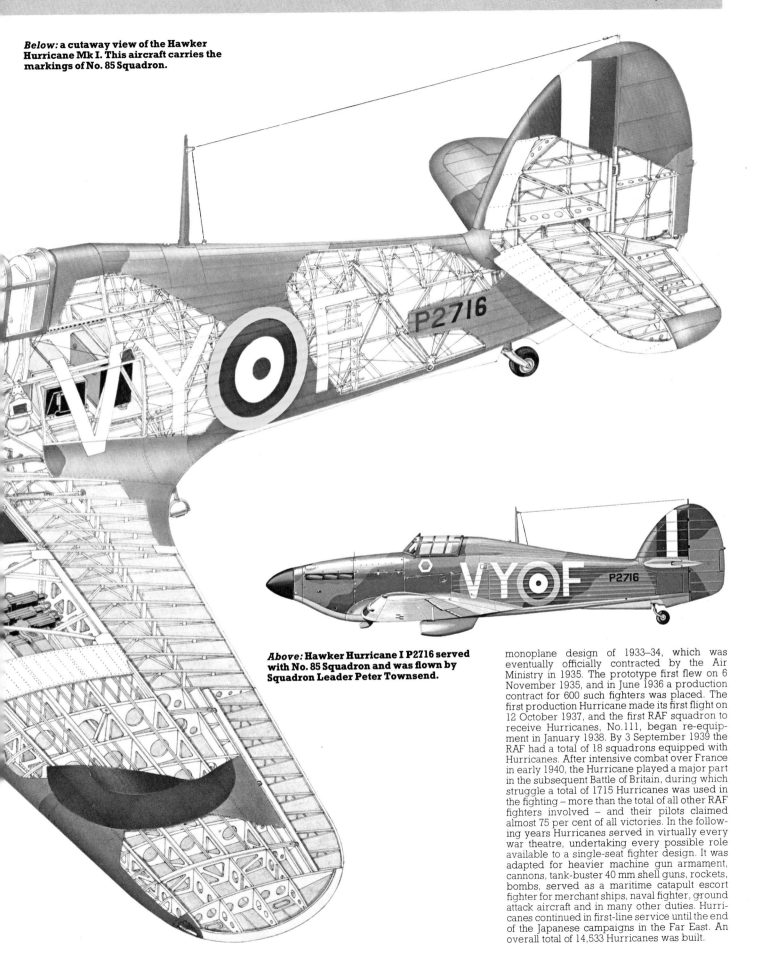

Below: a cutaway view of the Hawker Hurricane Mk I. This aircraft carries the markings of No. 85 Squadron.

Above: **Hawker Hurricane I P2716 served with No. 85 Squadron and was flown by Squadron Leader Peter Townsend.**

monoplane design of 1933–34, which was eventually officially contracted by the Air Ministry in 1935. The prototype first flew on 6 November 1935, and in June 1936 a production contract for 600 such fighters was placed. The first production Hurricane made its first flight on 12 October 1937, and the first RAF squadron to receive Hurricanes, No.111, began re-equipment in January 1938. By 3 September 1939 the RAF had a total of 18 squadrons equipped with Hurricanes. After intensive combat over France in early 1940, the Hurricane played a major part in the subsequent Battle of Britain, during which struggle a total of 1715 Hurricanes was used in the fighting – more than the total of all other RAF fighters involved – and their pilots claimed almost 75 per cent of all victories. In the following years Hurricanes served in virtually every war theatre, undertaking every possible role available to a single-seat fighter design. It was adapted for heavier machine gun armament, cannons, tank-buster 40 mm shell guns, rockets, bombs, served as a maritime catapult escort fighter for merchant ships, naval fighter, ground attack aircraft and in many other duties. Hurricanes continued in first-line service until the end of the Japanese campaigns in the Far East. An overall total of 14,533 Hurricanes was built.

Above: a Hawker Typhoon Mk IB fighter.

Hawker Typhoon

Type: fighter.
Crew: one.
Power plant: 2100 hp Napier Sabre I; 2180 hp
Napier Sabre IIA; 2200 hp Napier Sabre IIB;
2260 hp Napier Sabre IIC.
Dimensions: span 41 ft 7 in; length 31 ft 10 in
(early machines), 31 ft $11\frac{1}{2}$ in (later models);
height 14 ft 10 in (early machines, 15 ft 4 in
(later models).
Weights: empty 8840 lb; loaded 13,250 lb
(maximum).
Performance (Sabre IIB): maximum speed
412 mph at 19,000 ft; climb to 15,000 ft, 5 mins
50 secs; service ceiling 35,200 ft; range 510 miles
(normal).
Armament: twelve 0.303 in Browning machine
guns in wings (Mk IA); four 20 mm Hispano
cannon in wings (Mk IB); two 1000 lb bombs; or
eight 3-inch rockets under wings.

The Sabre-engined Typhoon prototype first flew
in February 1940, but delays and problems in
that year prevented the first production example
being flown initially until May 1941. Early

Above: a Hawker Tempest F6 of No. 249
Squadron based at Habbaniyah, Iraq, 1947.

deliveries to the RAF began in September 1941
but troubles with the early Sabre engines and
structural failures caused several accidents.
The Typhoon began its operational career in
December 1941 intercepting low-level 'sneak'
raiders along southern Britain, but found its true
métier as a ground attack strike aircraft from
1942 onwards, particularly when combining its
four 20 mm cannon with either a heavy bomb
load or lethal rocket projectile battery. This
latter role became highlighted from June 1944

Below: a Hawker Typhoon Mk IB in service
with No. 609 Squadron, Manston, Kent, 1943.

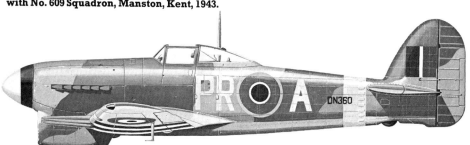

during the opening phases of the Allied invasion of Normandy. From then until the close of the European war Typhoons roamed far and wide, blasting paths forward for the ground forces, but were beginning to be replaced by Hawker Tempests in the final months of the fighting. Total production of Typhoons amounted to 3330 aircraft.

Hawker Tempest

Type: fighter.
Crew: one.
Power plant: 2520 hp Bristol Centaurus V or VI (Mk II); 2180 hp Napier Sabre IIA, B or C (Mk V); 2340 hp Napier Sabre V (Mk VI).
Dimensions: span 41 ft; length 34 ft 5 in (Mk II), 33 ft 8 in (Mk V); height 15 ft 10 in (Mk II), 16 ft 1 in (Mk V and VI).
Weights: empty 8900 lb (Mk II), 9000 lb (Mk V), 9150 lb (Mk VI); loaded 13,250 lb (Mk II), 13,450 lb (Mk V).
Performance: maximum speed 442 mph at 15,100 ft (Mk II), 426 mph at 18,500 ft (Mk V); climb to 15,000 ft, 4½ mins (Mk II), 5 mins (Mk V); service ceiling 37,500 ft (Mk II), 36,500 ft (Mk V); range (normal) 800 miles (Mk II), 740 miles (Mk V).
Armament: four 20 mm Hispano cannon in wings; up to 2000 lb of bombs.

The Tempest emerged as a highly refined development of the Typhoon, and the first production aircraft first flew in June 1943. Deliveries to the RAF began in April 1944, and the Tempest entered operations over Europe, attacking V1 flying bomb sites, ground installations, transport, and other ground targets. In aerial combat the Tempest proved highly manoeuvrable and destructive. Tempests remained in squadron use until 1949, before being replaced by jet fighters, while exported Tem-

pests served with the Indian and Pakistani air services until 1953. A total of 1395 Tempests (all Marks) was produced.

Lockheed Hudson

Type: maritime reconnaissance.
Crew: four.
Power plants: two 1100 hp Wright Cyclone GR-1820-G102A; two 1200 hp Pratt & Whitney Twin Wasp S3C4-G (Mk VI).
Dimensions: span 65 ft 6 in; length 44 ft 4 in; height 11 ft 10½ in.
Weights: empty 12,000 lb (Mk I), 12,929 lb (Mk VI); loaded 17,500 lb (Mk I), 18,500 lb (Mk VI).
Performance: maximum speed 246 mph at 6500 ft (Mk I), 284 mph at 15,000 ft (Mk VI); service ceiling 22,000 ft (Mk I), 24,500 ft (Mk VI); range 2160 miles.
Armament: two fixed 0.303 in machine guns forward; two 0.303 in machine in dorsal turret; one 0.303 in machine gun in ventral location; maximum bomb load 1600 lb.

A militarised version of the Lockheed 14 airliner, the Hudson was first purchased by Britain as a navigational trainer. when an order for 200 Hudsons was placed with Lockheed in mid-1938. Initial RAF deliveries arrived in Britain in February 1939, and first entered squadron service with No.224 Squadron in mid-1939. At the outbreak of war Coastal Command had 53 on charge. The Hudson served throughout the war in Europe and the Mediterranean theatres; mainly as a maritime patrol and anti-submarine aircraft, though in the later years many Hudsons undertook transport, communications, spy-dropping, and other roles. One Hudson of No.269 Squadron achieved unique fame in August 1941 by capturing a U-Boat, *U-570*, while other Hudsons (RAF and USN) sank at least four more submarines.

Above: a Lockheed Ventura of No. 21 Sqn awaits its bomb load.

Lockheed Ventura

Type: day bomber.
Crew: four–five.
Power plants: two 2000 hp Pratt & Whitney Double Wasp GR.2800-S1A4-G.
Dimensions: span 65 ft 6 in; length 51 ft 2½ in; height 11 ft 10½ in.
Weights: empty 20,100 lb; loaded 31,100 lb (maximum).
Performance: maximum speed 296 mph at sea level; service ceiling 26,300 ft; range 1660 miles (normal).
Armament: two fixed 0.50 in machine guns in nose; two or four 0.303 in machine guns in dorsal turret; two 0.303 in machine guns in ventral location; maximum bomb load 2500 lb.

The Ventura was introduced to operational service with No.21 Squadron RAF in October 1942, and began bombing sorties in the following month. In May 1943, when leading a daylight

Below: **Lockheed Hudson Mk III T9465 served with No. 269 Squadron in 1941–42.**

raid on Eindhoven, Squadron Leader L H Trent was shot down and later awarded a Victoria Cross. Despite the Ventura's relatively heavy defensive armament, its indifferent performance made it vulnerable to fighter attack and the type was withdrawn from bombing operations by the close of 1943; reverting thereafter to second-line duties with Coastal Command. A total of 394 Venturas was delivered to the RAF.

Martin Maryland

Type: day bomber; photo-reconnaissance.
Crew: three.
Power plants: two 1200 hp Pratt & Whitney Twin Wasp S3C4-G.
Dimensions: span 61 ft 4 in; length 46 ft 8 in; height 15 ft.
Weights: empty 11,213 lb; loaded 16,809 lb.
Performance: maximum speed 278 mph at 11,800 ft; service ceiling 29,500 ft (Mk I), 31,000 ft (Mk II); range (maximum) 1800 miles (Mk II).
Armament: four fixed 0.303 in Browning machine guns in wings; one 0.303 in machine gun in dorsal and ventral locations; maximum bomb load 2000 lb.

Though originally intended as an export ground attack bomber for the French air services, the Maryland was mainly delivered to Britain from 1940. The RAF used the aircraft chiefly in the Middle East as a light day bomber and general reconnaissance machine. In these roles the Maryland continued on operations until early 1943, by which time most had been replaced by Baltimores or other more powerful aircraft.

Below: **a Martin Maryland of No. 60 Sqn SAAF.**

Left: Martin Baltimores fly over Italy, 1944.

Martin Baltimore

Type: medium day bomber.
Crew: four.
Power plants: two 1660 hp Wright GR-2600-19 (Mks I–IV); two 1700 hp Wright GR-2600-19 (Mk (Mk V).
Dimensions: span 61 ft 4 in; length 48 ft 5¾ in; height 17 ft 9 in.
Weights: empty 15,200 lb (Mks I and II), 15,900 lb (Mk V); loaded 23,000 lb (maximum).
Performance: maximum speed 320 mph at 15,000 ft (Mk V); service ceiling 22,300 ft (Mk I), 25,000 ft (Mk V); maximum range 2800 miles.
Armament: four fixed 0.303 in Browning machine guns in wings; two or four 0.303 in Browning machine guns in dorsal turret; two machine guns in ventral location; maximum bomb load 2000 lb.

Used solely in the Mediterranean Theatre, the Baltimore was produced to British orders for the RAF, and entered operational use with No.223 Squadron in January 1942, and No.55 Squadron, in May 1942. Early examples were fitted with American dorsal turrets, but these were quickly replaced by British equivalents, and the Mark III, introduced in July 1942, had Boulton Paul turrets already installed. By mid-1943 some units were tasked with anti-submarine duties, but the Baltimore continued its main bombing and reconnaissance role until the end of the Italian campaign, though in reduced numbers. Baltimores equipped at least 10 desert squadrons of the RAF, SAAF and RAAF, apart from other units.

Martin Marauder

Type: medium bomber.
Crew: six or seven.
Power plants: two 2000 hp Pratt & Whitney Double Wasp R-2800-43.
Dimensions: span 71 ft; length 57 ft 6 in; height 20 ft.
Weights: empty 17,000 lb; loaded 37,000 lb.
Performance: maximum speed 317 mph at 14,500 ft; service ceiling 28,000 ft; range 1150 miles.
Armament: two 0.50 in machine guns in nose; two 0.50 in machine guns in dorsal turret; two 0.50 in machine guns in tail turret; single 0.50 in machine gun in each beam location; maximum bomb load 5200 lb.

One of the USAAF's standard bombers from 1942–45, the Marauder first entered RAF service with No.14 Squadron in the Mediterranean zone in mid-1942, and commenced operations with that unit in October 1942. Though known to its American crews as the 'Widow-maker', the

Below: Martin Marauder I 'Dominion Revenge' with No. 14 Squadron in 1942.

Marauder proved tough in action and incurred low casualty rates overall in both British and American service. The RAF operated the type solely in the Middle East campaigns from 1942 until the end of the European war. One modified variant had four fixed 0.50 in machine guns in the nose; while for a brief period some Marauders were utilised as torpedo bombers.

Miles Magister

Type: elementary trainer.
Crew: two.
Power plant: 130 hp DH Gipsy Major I.
Dimensions: span 33 ft 10 in; length 24 ft 7½ in; height 6 ft 8 in.
Weights: empty 1286 lb; loaded 1900 lb.
Performance: maximum speed 132 mph at 1000 ft; climb to 10,000 ft, 9 mins 15 secs; service ceiling 18,000 ft.
Armament: nil.

A contemporary of the biplane ab initio trainer the DH Tiger Moth, the all-wood constructed Magister, 'Maggie' to its crews, was introduced to RAF service in late 1937, but continued in wide use throughout World War II as an elementary trainer and light communications hack. It was

Above: a Miles Magister elementary trainer.

mainly used in Britain though several examples saw service in the Middle East as liaison aircraft. Total production amounted to 1293 aircraft.

Miles Master

Type: advanced trainer.
Crew: two.
Power plant: 715 hp Rolls-Royce Kestrel XXX (Mk I); 870 hp Bristol Mercury XX (Mk II); 825 hp Pratt & Whitney Wasp Junior (Mk III).
Dimensions: span 39 ft (Mk I), 35 ft 7 in (Mk III); length 30 ft 5 in (Mk I), 30 ft 2 in (Mk III); height 10 ft.
Weights: empty 4370 lb (Mk I), 4204 lb (Mk III); loaded 5573 lb (Mk I), 5570 lb (Mk III).
Performance: maximum speed 226 mph (Mk I), 232 mph (Mk III); service ceiling 27,000 ft (Mk I); range 490 miles (Mk I), 320 miles (Mk III).
Armament: one fixed 0.303 in Vickers machine gun forward if required; provision for light practice bombs if required.

Below: Miles Master Mk III advanced trainers were fitted with the Pratt & Whitney Wasp Junior engine.

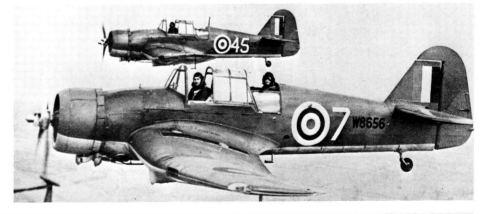

Above: a Miles Martinet target tug.

Developed from the Miles Kestrel projected trainer, the Master offered an excellent vehicle for interim-stage conversion of elementary-trained air crews to the fast monoplanes in squadron use by 1939. Production of Master Is began in 1938, and seven machines were on RAF strength by September 1939; a total of 900 Master Is being eventually produced for the RAF. By 1942 an overall total of 3450 Masters of all Marks had been built.

Miles Martinet

Type: target tug; trainer.
Crew: two.
Power plant: 870 hp Bristol Mercury XX or XXX.
Dimensions: span 39 ft; length 30 ft 11 in; height 11 ft 7 in.
Weights: empty 4640 lb; loaded 6750 lb (maximum).
Performance: maximum speed 240 mph at 5800 ft; service ceiling 24,000 ft; range 690 miles.
Armament: nil.

The Martinet is significant as the first RAF aircraft designed from the outset as a target tug. The prototype first flew in April 1942, and the type entered service in same year. Total production of Martinets amounted to 1793 aircraft, and the type remained in wide RAF use for several years after the war.

North American Harvard

Type: trainer.
Crew: two.
Power plant: 550 hp Pratt & Whitney Wasp R-1340-49.
Dimensions: span 42 ft 0¼ in; length 28 ft 11⅞ in; height 11 ft 8½ in.
Weights: empty 4158 lb; loaded 5250 lb.
Performance: maximum speed 205 mph at 5000 ft; service ceiling 21,500 ft; range 750 miles.
Armament: provision for light practice bomb load if required.

The Harvard, or 'Yellow Peril' as it was dubbed, was one of the first American designs ordered for RAF use prior to the war, in mid-1938. First deliveries to RAF training units commenced by January 1939, and the type remained in service use until the late 1950s. Along with the DH Tiger Moth, the Harvard trained many thousands of

Left: **HRH The Duke of Edinburgh flies over Windsor Castle in a North American Harvard II during his flying training after World War II. He received his wings in 1953.**

RAF and Commonwealth air crews during and after the war, in Britain, Canada, the USA, Rhodesia, Australia and elsewhere.

North American Mustang

Type: fighter; photo-reconnaissance.
Crew: one.
Power plant: 1150 hp Allison V-1710-39 (Mk I); 1120 hp Allison V-1710-81 (Mk II); 1680 hp Packard-Merlin V-1650-7 (Mk III and IV).
Dimensions: span 37 ft 0¼ in; length 32 ft 3 in; height 8 ft 8 in.
Weights: empty 6300 lb (Mks I and II), 7000 lb (Mk III); loaded 8600 lb (Mks I and II), 9200 lb (Mk III).
Performance: maximum speed 390 mph at 8000 ft (Mks I and II), 442 mph at 24,500 ft (Mk III); service ceiling 32,000 ft (Mks I and II), 42,500 ft (Mk III); range 1050 miles (Mk I and II), 1710 miles maximum (Mk III).
Armament: four fixed 0.50 in machine guns in wings (Mks I, II, III); four fixed 0.30 in machine guns fixed in wings (Mks I and II); maximum bomb load 1000 lb (Mk III); provision for rockets under wings if required.

Claimed by most sources as the outstanding fighter of World War 2, the Mustang was

Below: a North American Mustang I army-co-operation aircraft pictured serving with No. 2 Squadron.

originally designed specifically for RAF requirements. Mustang Is first reached Britain in October 1941, and entered first-line RAF use in April 1942 with No. 2 Squadron. Due to the original engine's poor high altitude performance, the design was allocated to low level army co-operation roles. By September 1944, modified Mustangs (Mark III and IVs), fitted with American-produced Merlin engines, extra fuel tankage, and other refinements, entered RAF fighter squadrons. These later versions provided excellent long range, high altitude performance, and equipped 28 squadrons in Europe and the Middle East during 1944–45.

North American Mitchell

Type: light day bomber.
Crew: four or five.
Power plants: two 1350 hp Wright Cyclone GR-2600 A-5B.
Dimensions: span 67 ft 6¾ in; length 54 ft 1 in; height 15 ft 9¾ in.
Weights: empty 16,000 lb; loaded 24,500 lb.
Performance: maximum speed 292 mph at 15,000 ft; service ceiling 20,000 ft; maximum range 1635 miles.
Armament: one 0.50 in machine gun in nose; two 0.50 in machine guns in dorsal turret; two 0.50 in machine guns in tail turret; one 0.50 in machine guns in ventral location or two machine guns in ventral turret; maximum bomb load 6000 lb.

Above: the North American Mitchell III was the RAF equivalent of the USAAF's B-25J, the major production variant.

Used principally in No. 2 Group, Bomber Command and, from mid-1944, by the 2nd Tactical Air Force (2nd TAF), the Mitchell supplemented the RAF's daylight bombing offensives from 1942–44. More than 800 Mitchells saw RAF service, the first entering operational use with Nos. 98 and 180 Squadrons in late 1942. Mitchells eventually equipped eight squadrons in the RAF and were superseded by Mosquito bombers by mid-1945.

Republic Thunderbolt I & II

Type: fighter bomber.
Crew: one.
Power plant: 2300 hp Pratt & Whitney Double Wasp R-2800-59.
Dimensions: span 40 ft 9$\frac{1}{4}$ in; length 36 ft 1$\frac{3}{4}$ in; height 12 ft 7$\frac{3}{4}$ in.
Weights: empty 10,000 lb; loaded 14,600 lb.
Performance: maximum speed 427 mph at 28,500 ft; service ceiling 37,000 ft; maximum range 1970 miles.
Armament: eight fixed 0.50 in machine guns in wings; maximum bomb load 2000 lb; six or eight 3-inch rockets under wings if required.

Below: a Republic Thunderbolt II of No. 30 Squadron in Burma, 1944.

Above: a Saro Lerwick of No. 209 Squadron photographed early in 1941.

Although the P-47 Thunderbolt entered USAAF operational use from 1942, the RAF's first Thunderbolts were not taken into service until May 1944, and were first flown operationally by RAF pilots in September that year. The RAF Thunderbolt II, the most-used variant, corresponded to the USAAF's P-47D with bubble canopy. All RAF Thunderbolts were used in the Burma theatre; No. 135 Squadron being the first to start re-equipment, and No. 261 Squadron the first to operate. Seven more RAF squadrons in Burma eventually flew the type, primarily as a dive-bomber and general ground attack aircraft. After the war Nos. 60 and 81 Squadrons retained their Thunderbolts to participate in the Dutch East Indies nationalist troubles, but both had been disbanded by late 1946. Of the 919 Thunderbolts allocated for RAF use, 89 were never delivered.

Saro Lerwick

Type: martime reconnaissance flying boat.
Crew: six or eight.
Power plants: two 1375 hp Bristol Hercules
II or IV.
Dimensions: span 80 ft 10 in; length 63 ft 7½ in;
height 20 ft.
Weights: loaded (normal) 28,500 lb, (maximum)
33,200 lb.
Performance: maximum speed 216 mph;
service ceiling 25,600 ft; range 1540 miles.
Armament: one 0.303 in Vickers K machine
gun in nose; two 0.303 in Browning machine
guns in dorsal turret; four 0.303 in Browning
machine guns in tail turret; maximum bomb load
2000 lb.

Entering service with No. 240 Squadron, Coastal
Command in June 1939, the ill-starred Lerwick
began its brief operational career with No. 209
Squadron in December 1939. Its general flying
and control characteristics were considered
poor, even difficult, and after an undistinguish-
ed operational effort throughout 1940, the type
was withdrawn from first-line use by early
1941, though it served again briefly with No.
422 Squadron RCAF in late 1942. Aerodynami-
cally unstable, too heavy, and with low engine
reliability for lengthy over-sea patrol work,
the Lerwick achieved little.

Short Sunderland

Type: maritime reconnaissance and patrol
flying boat.
Crew: ten (normal).
Power plants: four 1010 hp Bristol Pegasus
XXII (Mk I); four 1065 hp Bristol Pegasus XVIII
(Mks II and III); four 1200 hp Pratt & Whitney
Twin Wasp R-1830 (Mk V).
Dimensions: span 112 ft 9½ in; length 85 ft 4 in;
height 32 ft 10½ in.
Weights: empty 28,290 lb (Mk I), 33,000 lb
(Mks II and III), 37,000 lb (Mk V); loaded 50,100 lb
(Mk I), 58,000 lb (Mks II and III), 65,000 lb (Mk V).
Performance: speed 210 mph (Mk I), 205 mph
(Mks II and III), 213 mph (Mk V); service ceiling
17,900 ft (Mk V); maximum range 2110 miles
(Mk I), 2880 miles (Mk V); normal endurance
13½ hrs.
Armament: one 0.303 in Browning machine
gun in nose (Mk I); four 0.303 in Browning
machine guns in tail turret (most Mks); two
0.303 in Vickers K machine guns in beam
locations (Mk II); four 0.303 in Browning
machine guns in nose and tail turrets (Mk V);
four fixed 0.303 in Browning machine guns in
nose flanks (Mk III); maximum bomb load
4960 lb.

Top right: **a Short Sunderland GR5 pictured
in postwar service with No. 201 Squadron.**
Above right: **a Short Sunderland of No. 210
Squadron undergoes maintenance.**
Below: **a Short Sunderland Mk II of No. 10
Squadron RAAF, 1942.**

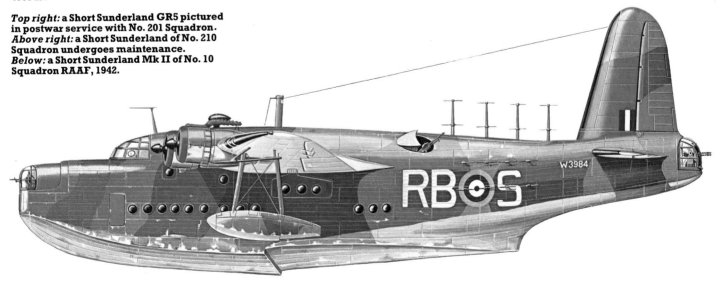

Produced in parallel to its contemporary civil Empire Class flying boat design, the Sunderland entered RAF service in June 1938 with No. 230 Squadron at Seletar, Singapore. By September 1939, 27 Sunderlands were on RAF charge, and by the end of the war at least 20 squadrons of the RAF, RCAF and RAAF had been equipped with the type. Production ceased in June 1946, by which time a total of 749 aircraft had been built. Sunderlands played a constant part in the main anti-submarine campaign in the Battle of the Atlantic and other waters, but were also employed as evacuation vehicles for Allied troops in Crete, Greece and Burma and in ambulance, supply, and general communications duties. Sunderlands accounted for at least 58 U-Boats sunk or severely damaged by 1945. After the war the Sunderland remained in RAF service until 1959, flying first-line operations during the Berlin Air Lift, the Malayan Emergency (Operation Firedog), and the Korean War, apart from seeing widespread use for specific expeditions and other service. When Sunderland GR5, ML797 of No. 205 Squadron made the type's ultimate flight in RAF livery on 20 May 1959, it also heralded the demise of the flying boat in RAF squadron use.

Short Stirling I-V

Type: heavy night bomber; transport.
Crew: seven or eight.
Power plants: four 1150 hp Bristol Hercules II (Mk I); four 1650 hp Bristol Hercules XVI (Mks III and V).
Dimensions: span 99 ft 1 in; length 87 ft 3 in; height 22 ft 9 in.
Weights: empty 44,000 lb (Mk I), 46,900 lb (Mk III), 43,500 lb (Mk V); loaded 59,400 lb (Mk I), 70,000 lb (Mk III), 71,000 lb (Mk V).
Performance: maximum speed 260 mph (Mk I), 275 mph (Mk III), 280 mph (Mk V); service ceiling 17,000 ft (Mks I and III), 18,000 ft (Mk V); range (maximum) 2330 miles (Mk I), 2010 miles (Mk III), 3000 miles (Mk V).
Armament (Mks I and III): two 0.303 in Browning machine guns in nose turret; two 0.303 in Browning machine guns in dorsal turret; four 0.303 in Browning machine guns in tail turret; maximum bomb load 14,000 lb.

The Stirling is historically significant as the RAF's first four engined monoplane bomber to see operational service. The first prototype flew in May 1939, and the type entered first-line service with No. 7 Squadron in August 1940.

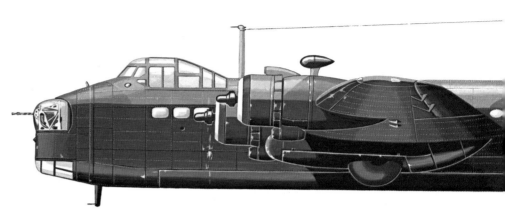

Below: a Short Stirling Mk I of No. 15 Squadron based at Wyton, late 1941.

Right: a Short Stirling Mk V of No. 196 Squadron pictured in 1945.
Bottom right: the second production Supermarine Walrus at Felixstowe.

Due to official restrictions in the original 1936 specification, the design of the Stirling limited its operational ceiling, leading to undue casualties in service. By mid-1942 Stirling Is were beginning to be replaced by Lancasters in many units, but an improved version, the Mark III, came into use by early 1943. In that year too production Stirlings for glider tug, paratroop carriage, and heavy transport of goods and personnel emerged, titled Mark Vs, having all gun turrets deleted, and internal redesign. Other variants were allotted to radio countermeasures squadrons, while from 1943 many Stirling bombers were employed extensively on mine-laying sorties. The ultimate Stirling sorties with Bomber Command were flown in September 1944, but Mark IV and V transport versions continued in use until the end of the war. Total production of Stirlings of all Marks was 2381 aircraft for the RAF. Of these, 160 were Mark Vs, while 641 Stirling bomber versions were lost to enemy action.

Below: a Short Stirling of No. 1651 Conversion Unit in 1942.

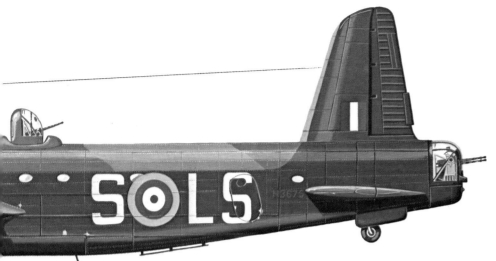

Supermarine Walrus

Type: amphibian, maritime reconnaissance; air-sea rescue.
Crew: three or four.
Power plant: 615-650 hp Bristol Pegasus II-VI.
Dimensions: span 45 ft 10 in; length 38 ft; height 16 ft 10½ in.
Weights: empty 4900 lb; loaded 7200 lb.
Performance: maximum speed 135 mph at 4750 ft; initial rate of climb, 1050 ft per min; service ceiling 18,500 ft; range 600 miles.
Armament: two 0.303 in Vickers K machine guns; maximum bomb load 760 lb.

Affectionately dubbed the 'Shagbat' (a legendary bird, whose reputed ever-decreasing, circular flightpath had an inevitable conclusion . . .), the Walrus was initially known as the Seagull V when, in prototype form, it first flew in June 1933. Initial production orders were placed in 1935, and the Walrus went into FAA service in March 1936. From then until 1945 the Walrus undertook a myriad of duties and roles, apart from its original fleet-spotter tasks. It

acted as a bomber in East Africa, anti-submarine patroller and photo-reconnaissance aircraft in European and Mediterranean waters, and, increasingly from 1941, as part of the growing Air-Sea Rescue Service. Walrus crews operated from such diverse zones as northern Norway and the Indian Ocean; serving faithfully for almost 10 years. Total production amounted to at least 26 Seagull Vs and 765 Walruses.

Supermarine Spitfire

Type: fighter, photo-reconnaissance.
Crew: one.
Power plant: 1030 hp Rolls-Royce Merlin II or III (Mk I); 1470 hp Rolls-Royce Merlin 45 (Mks V, PR.IV, PR.VII); 1710 hp Rolls-Royce Merlin 63a (Mk IX, F.VIII, PR.XI); 1580 hp Packard-Merlin (USA-built) (Mk XVI only); 1735 hp Rolls-Royce Griffon III or IV (Mk XII); 2035 hp Rolls-Royce Griffon 66 (PR.XIX); 2375 hp Rolls-Royce Griffon 64 (F.21 and 22); 2045 hp Rolls-Royce Griffon 85 (Seafire 45).
Dimensions: span 32 ft 10 in (Mk I), 36 ft 10 in (Mk VIII), 36 ft 11 in (F.21); length 29 ft 11 in (Mk I); 31 ft 3½ in (Mk VIII); 32 ft 8 in (F.21 and Seafire 45); height 12 ft 7¾ in (Mk I), 11 ft 8½ in (Mk VIII).
Weights: empty 5280 lb (Mk I), 7100 lb (Seafire 45); loaded 6200 lb (Mk I), 9500 lb (Seafire 45).
Performance: maximum speed 362 mph (Mk I), 452 mph (Seafire 47); maximum rate of climb 2500 ft per min (Mk I), 4800 ft per min (Seafire 47); service ceiling 34,000 ft (Mk I), 44,500 ft (Mk XIV); maximum range 575 miles (Mk I), 1475 miles (Seafire 47).
Armament: eight fixed 0.303 in Browning machine guns in wings (Mks I and IIa); two 20 mm Hispano cannon in wings, and four 0.303 in Browning machine guns in wings (Mks V–IX and XVI); two 20 mm Hispano cannon and two 0.50 in machine guns in wings (Mk XVIII); six or eight 3-in rockets under wings (later Marks); maximum bomb load 1000 lb (later Marks).

The Spitfire was unique in at least one respect, in being the only Allied fighter to begin full production prior to 1939 and continue to be produced until after 1945. In all more than 40 major variants were built, apart from numerous sub-variants. Designed by R J Mitchell, famed for his previous Schneider Trophy floatplane

Top left: **a Supermarine Spitfire Mk VC fitted with a tropical filter.**
Above left: **a Spitfire F24 of No. 80 Squadron flies over Hong Kong, 1950.**
Left: **a Spitfire Mk VB W3822 'Zanzibar IV' pictured in 1942.**
Right: **a Spitfire PR19 preserved in flying condition by the RAF.**
Above: **the prototype Seafire Mk III with wings folded for carrier stowage.**

designs, the prototype Spitfire first flew on 5 March 1936. The first production contract was issued in July 1936, and the Spitfire entered service with No. 19 Squadron at Duxford in August 1938. By 3 September 1939, 187 Spitfires were with 12 squadrons of RAF Fighter Command, with a further 83 machines in store. From then until after 1945 development of the Spitfire was unceasing. Mark IIs came into general use from late 1940, and in March 1941 Mark Vs came into service. In July 1942 Mark IX Spitfires entered operational use, ostensibly to counter the Luftwaffe's Focke Wulf Fw 190. The Mark XII introduced the Griffon engine to the Spitfire airframe and this powered most subsequent versions. By 1944 Marks XVIs, and by VE-Day, 1945, the F.21 had begun operations, albeit in small numbers. Adapations of the Mark I and other early versions for FAA use were dubbed Seafires. Spitfires served in every war theatre during World War 2, and with

Above: **Supermarine Spitfire Mk VB AB910
is preserved in flying condition.**
Right: **a cutaway view of a Supermarine
Spitfire Mk IX carrying the markings of
Wg Cdr JE 'Johnnie' Johnson.**

every Allied air force at some period. Actual
production of Spitfires ceased on 20 February
1948, by which date totals of 20,351 Spitfires and
2408 Seafires had been built. Of these myriad
variants, Mark Vs had been produced in
largest quantity (total 6479 machines), closely
followed by the second most-produced version,
the Mark IX (5665 aircraft). Spitfires remained
in first-line use with the RAF until April 1954.

Right: this Supermarine Spitfire Mk VA was flown by Wing Commander Douglas Bader, leader of the Tangmere Wing, when he was shot down over France on 9 August 1941.

Below: **Supermarine Spitfire Mk VB AB910 of the RAF Battle of Britain Memorial Flight formates on the Flight's Hawker Hurricane Mk II (foreground).**

Vickers Wellington

Type: night bomber; maritime reconnaissance; torpedo bomber.
Crew: six (normal); three (Mks V and VI).
Power plants: two 1050 hp Bristol Pegasus XVIII (Mks I, Ic, VIII); two 1145 hp Rolls-Royce Merlin X (Mk II); two 1425 hp Bristol Hercules III or XI (Mk III); two 1050 hp Pratt & Whitney Twin Wasp R-1830-S304-G (Mk IV); two 1675 hp Bristol Hercules VI or XVI (Mks X, XI, XII); two 1735 hp Bristol Hercules XVII (Mks XIII, XIV, XVIII).
Dimensions: span 86 ft 2 in; length 64 ft 7 in; height 17 ft 5 in.
Weights: empty 18,556 lb (Mk Ic); loaded 28,500 lb (Mk Ic), 34,500 lb (Mk III), 36,500 lb (Mk X).
Performance: maximum speed at operational height 235 mph (Mk Ic), 255 mph (Mk III), 299 mph (Mk IV), 255 mph (Mk X); service ceiling 18,000 ft (Mk Ic), 22,000 ft (Mks III, XI, XVIII); range (normal) 1805 miles (Mk Ic), 1470 miles (Mk III).
Armament: two 0.303 in machine guns in both nose and tail cupola turrets (Mk I); two 0.303 in Browning machine guns in nose turret, and four 0.303 in Browning machine guns in tail turret (Mk III and later versions); two single hand-operated 0.303 in machine guns in beam locations often installed in Mks I–III; up to 4500 lb of bombs, or mines, or two 18-inch torpedoes.

The 'Wimpy' – the universal nickname for the Wellington – was a real backbone for RAF Bomber Command from 1939–43, and played a not insignificant role with Coastal Command throughout the war. It was produced in greater quantity – 11,461 aircraft – than any other multi-engined aircraft built in Britain. It also served in every major war theatre, in a wide variety of roles, and did not retire from RAF service until early 1953; some 30 years after its original specification was produced. First production Wellingtons were delivered to No. 99 Squadron at Mildenhall in October 1938, and by September 1939 six bomber squadrons were fully equipped. During the first few months of war unescorted Wellingtons attempting daylight raids on Germany were heavily outfought by German defenders, and from 1940 Wellingtons became night bombers for such sorties. From late 1940, they became long-range bombers for the desert air forces in North Africa and from early 1942 commenced

Top right: **a Vickers Wellington Mk III pictured in service with No. 425 Sqn RCAF.**
Above right: **a Wellington XII of No. 407 Sqn RCAF flies off the Devon coast.**
Below: **a Wellington Mk IC of No. 214 Sqn based at Stradishall in 1940.**

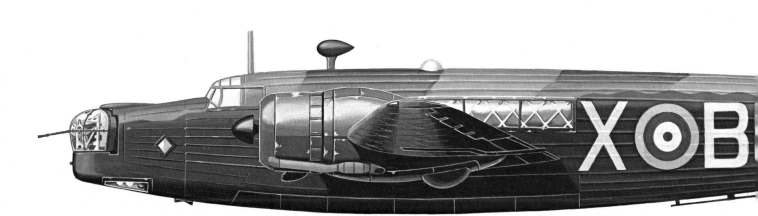

similar operations in India. Later in 1942 modified versions began long service with Coastal Command as submarine hunters, many equipped with Leigh Lights for night illumination of U-Boats. Mark X versions, basically improved variants of the Mark III, came into service from 1943, and were used after 1945 as navigational and general bomber trainers until retirement in 1953. Much experimental work on standard Wellingtons was accomplished during the type's long career. Marks V and VI were specifically built as pressure-cabin models for projected very high altitude work. The Wellington proved astonishingly versatile in the many diverse roles imposed upon it, while its ability to absorb heavy damage and still fly was due in no small measure to its geodetic structure; a practical application of geodesic lines instigated by Sir Barnes Wallis, who designed the Wimpy's basic configuration and construction style.

Vickers Warwick I-V

Type: heavy bomber (initially); maritime reconnaissance; air-sea rescue; transport.
Crew: two to six (according to role).
Power plants: two 1850 hp Pratt & Whitney Double Wasp R-2800-S1A4-G (Mk I); two 2520 hp Bristol Centaurus VII (Mk V).
Dimensions: span 96 ft 8½ in; length 72 ft 3 in (Mk I); 70 ft 6 in (Mks III and V); height 18ft 6 in.
Weights (ASR, Mk 1): empty 28,154 lb; loaded 45,000 lb.
Performance (ASR, Mk 1): maximum speed 224 mph at 3600 ft; climb to 10,000 ft, 16 mins 6 secs; service ceiling 21,500 ft; range (normal) 2300 miles.
Armament (Mk II): two 0.303 in Browning machine guns in nose turret; two 0.303 in Browning machine guns in dorsal turret; four 0.303 in Browning machine guns in tail turret; maximum bomb load 8000 lb.

Produced to a different specification and purpose than its stablemate the Wellington, the Warwick nevertheless closely resembled the Wellington in general configuration – almost a stretched Wimpy. Its genesis was as a heavy bomber design, but by the time production examples entered RAF service, in mid-1943, the Warwick was outdated for such a role and was instead used for maritime reconnaissance and air-sea rescue duties. Later, with added radar equipment and appropriate armament, it extended its role to include anti-submarine

Above: a Vickers Warwick Mk V serving with No. 179 Squadron, 1945.

sorties. From 1943 Mark I and III versions were produced as unarmed transport aircraft, with ample freight and/or passenger accommodation. Other roles allotted to Warwicks included meteorological sorties, Leigh Light anti-submarine work, and lifeboat carrying (in its ASR role). Often (mistakenly) referred to as a replacement for the Wellington, the Warwick was built specifically to be complementary to its illustrious brother.

Vultee Vengeance

Type: dive bomber.
Crew: two.
Power plant: 1700 hp Wright Cyclone GR-2600-A5B-5.
Dimensions: span 48 ft; length 40 ft; height 12 ft 10 in.
Weights: empty 10,300 lb; loaded 16,400 lb (maximum).
Performance: maximum speed 279 mph at 13,500 ft; climb to 15,000 ft, 11 mins 18 secs; service ceiling 22,300 ft; range 2300 miles (normal).
Armament: four or six fixed 0.50 machine guns in wings; two 0.303 in Browning machine guns in rear cockpit; maximum bomb load 2000 lb.

Built initially to a 1940 British order for an army-support dive bomber, the first RAF Vengeance made its first flight in July 1941. Further modification slightly delayed its introduction to RAF

operations – the first production model only made its initial test flight in June 1942 – and it was not until mid-1943 that Vengeances began to reach RAF units. By then the early myths about dive bombers had been rationalised, and the Vengeance was therefore used exclusively in Burma by the RAF, where aerial combat was less frequent than in other theatres. Four RAF squadrons, Nos. 45, 82, 84 and 110, flew Vengeances in Burma, providing effective strikes against Japanese ground targets until the end of the war. By late 1944 other Vengeances had been converted to target tugs in the UK.

Westland Lysander

Type: army co-operation; special duties; air-sea rescue.
Crew: two.
Power plants: 890 hp Bristol Mercury XII (Mk I); 905 hp Bristol Perseus XII (Mk II); 870 hp Bristol Mercury XX or XXX (Mk III).
Dimensions: span 50 ft; length 30 ft 6 in; height 14 ft 6 in.
Weights: empty 4065 lb (Mk I), 4160 lb (Mk II), 4365 lb (Mk III); loaded 5920 lb (Mk I), 6015 lb (Mk II), 6318 lb (Mk III).
Performance: maximum speed 219 mph at 10,000 ft (Mk I), 230 mph at 10,000 ft (Mk II), 212 mph at 5000 ft (Mk III); climb to 10,000 ft, 6.9 mins (Mks I and II), 8 mins (Mk III); service ceiling 26,000 ft (Mks I and II), 21,500 ft (Mk III).
Armament: one fixed 0.303 in Browning machine gun in each wheel spat; one 0.303 in Lewis machine gun, or two 0.303 in Browning machine guns in rear cockpit; maximum bomb load 500 lb.

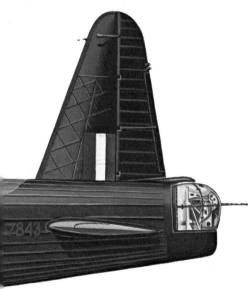

Right: a Vultee Vengeance Mk III in service with No. 84 Sqn in Burma, 1944.

The 'Lizzie' prototype first flew on 15 June 1936, and entered full RAF service with No. 16 (AC) Squadron at Old Sarum in June 1938. By September 1939, seven squadrons had been re-equipped with Lysander Is (including two AAF units) which in turn were in the process of being replaced by Lysander IIs. Six of these units went to France in support of the BEF, but by the end of May 1940, only some 50 (of more than 170 Lysanders despatched to France until then) had survived the fierce aerial combat. From 1939–41 Lysanders served with Nos. 6 and 208 Squadrons in the Middle East; while in India from late 1941 Nos. 5 and 28 Squadrons RAF received Lysanders, and later No. 20 Squadron RAF and units of the Indian Air Force were equipped with the type. These Far East examples were eventually withdrawn in 1943. In Britain Lysander III variants were employed from August 1941 by two squadrons to ferry Allied agents and supplies into German-occu-

Above: a Westland Lysander III which served with No. 276 Squadron on Air-Sea Rescue duties in late 1941.

pied territories in Europe, flying some 400 such sorties between 1941 and 1944. Total Lysander production amounted to 1652 (including two prototypes and 225 built in Canada under licence, and a number exported to Egypt and Finland). By 1945, however, few remained in RAF service.

Westland Whirlwind

Type: fighter; ground attack.
Crew: one.
Power plants: two 885 hp Rolls-Royce Peregrine I.
Dimensions: span 45 ft; length 32 ft 3 in; height 10 ft 6 in.
Weights: empty 8310 lb; loaded 10,356 lb (fighter).
Performance: maximum speed 360 mph at 15,000 ft; climb to 15,000 ft, 5.8 mins; service ceiling 30,000 ft.
Armament: four fixed 20 mm Hispano cannon in nose; maximum bomb load 1000 lb.

As the RAF's first twin-engined, single-seat fighter, the sleek Whirlwind was, at its conception, the fastest, most heavily-armed fighter interceptor in the world. Designed in 1936–37, the prototype first flew in October 1938, and incorporated several features well ahead of contemporary design philosophy. Its performance, especially at low altitudes, was considered magnificent, and in January 1939 production contracts were awarded. Nevertheless, first deliveries to the RAF for operational use were delayed until July 1940 when No. 263 Squadron received its first examples. Lack of engines from production lines further delayed progress – by October 1940, No. 263 Squadron possessed only eight Whirlwinds – and operations did not begin until December 1940. The disappointing high altitude performance – due to underpowered Peregrine engines – soon led to Whirlwinds being used primarily as ground-attack machines. In September 1941, No. 137 Squadron was re-equipped with Whirlwinds – the only other first-line unit to operate the type. In July 1942 Whirlwinds were modified to act as bomb carriers for their low-level role. By mid-1943 Whirlwinds had been replaced by Hawker Typhoons. Of the two prototypes and 400 aircraft initially contracted, only the prototypes and 114 Whirlwinds were actually built and delivered.

Left: a Westland Lysander of No. 28 Squadron flies on a supply-dropping sortie in the Burma theatre, 1942.
Below: a Westland Whirlwind I fighter pictured in flight. The Whirlwind was an imaginative concept, which failed to live up to expectations largely because of the disappointing performance of its Rolls-Royce Peregrine engines.

Part Four
POST

Below: **Hawker Hunter F6 fighters of No. 208 Squadron fly in echelon formation.**

Above: an AW Argosy of No. 114 Sqn.
Right: an Auster AOP9.

Armstrong Whitworth (HS) Argosy

Type: medium range tactical transport.
Crew: four (five if required).
Power plants: four 2470 ehp Rolls-Royce Dart RDa8.
Dimensions: span 115 ft; length 86 ft 9 in; height 29 ft 3 in.
Weights: empty 56,000 lb; loaded 97,000 lb (maximum).
Performance: cruising speed 253 mph; service ceiling 23,000 ft; maximum range 3450 miles.

The Argosy was Armstrong Whitworth's final venture in the civil aircraft field, and the last design to carry the makers' name before being brought under the aegis of Hawker Siddeley. The civil Argosy first flew in January 1959, and in the same month an order for 20 aircraft for the RAF was placed, later increased to 56 aircraft. Considerable modification was necessary to meet RAF needs, and the Argosy C1 military version first flew in March 1961. The type entered first-line service with No. 114 Squadron in March 1962, and by April 1964 all 56 Argosies ordered had been delivered to the RAF. These, incidentally, had been purchased on a fixed-price basis, and caused a £5-million loss to the Armstrong Whitworth firm. Argosies served in Britain, the Middle and Far East until 1974 and the type was withdrawn shortly after, having equipped a total of six squadrons.

Armstrong Whitworth Meteor NF.11-14

Type: night fighter.
Crew: two.
Power plants: two 3600 lb thrust Rolls-Royce Derwent 8 turbojets.
Dimensions: span 43 ft; length 48 ft 6 in; height 13 ft 11 in (NF.11).
Weights: loaded 22,000 lb (NF.11).
Performance: maximum speed 579 mph at 9842 ft (NF.11); initial rate of climb 5797 ft per min; service ceiling 43,000 ft; range 920 miles.
Armament: four fixed 20 mm Hispano cannon.

Though ostensibly a development of the Gloster-designed Meteor 8, the NF11-14 versions were entirely designed and built by the Armstrong Whitworth firm, hence their designation.

Right: an AW Meteor NF 14 of No. 46 Sqn.

The NF11 prototype first flew in May 1950, and production aircraft entered RAF operational use with No. 29 Squadron in January 1951; the first jet night fighter taken into squadron service. The NF12 variant had a lengthened nose section to house more modern radar equipment; while the NF13 version was tropicalised for Middle East operational employment. The final production version, the NF14, incorporated a one-piece, perspex, sliding canopy for the cockpits. Total production of Meteor night fighters was 592 aircraft. The last first-line aircraft were withdrawn from squadrons by August 1961, though a number of NF11s continued in use until 1968 as target tugs. In all, 19 squadrons had been equipped with NF Meteors at some period.

Auster AOP.6-9

Type: artillery spotter; communications aircraft.
Crew: one or two.
Power plant: 145 hp DH Gipsy Major VII (AOP 6); 180 hp Blackburn Cirrus Bombardier 203 (AOP 9).
Dimensions: span 36 ft (AOP6), 36 ft 5 in (AOP9); length 23 ft 9 in; height 8 ft 5 in.
Weights: empty 1413 lb (AOP6), 1461 lb (AOP9); loaded 2160 lb (AOP6), 2130 lb (AOP9).
Performance: maximum speed 127 mph (AOP9); service ceiling 14,000 ft (AOP6), 18,500 ft (AOP9); range 250 miles.
Armament: nil.

The excellent operational record of the early Auster light aircraft from 1941–45 led to its adoption in improved forms by the post-war RAF. The first post-1945 variant, the AOP6, entered service in 1947 and soon became the standard Air Observation Post (AOP) machine. Though serviced by RAF technical personnel, Auster pilots and observers were almost exclusively from the army. In early 1955 the AOP9 version began to replace AOP6s in service and continued in their ubiquitous duties with the RAF until September 1957, in which month the army took over all responsibilities for AOP duties from the RAF. Austers gave prodigious operational service in the

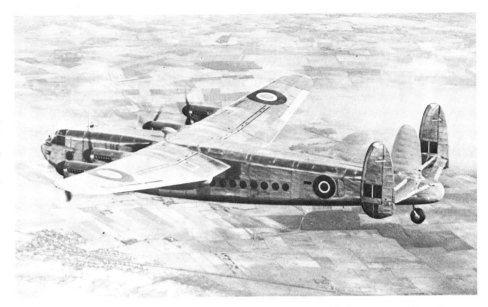

Korean War and, particularly, in Operation Firedog in Malaya. In the latter extended campaign Austers flew an accumulated total well in excess of 143,000 sorties, including leaflet-dropping, gun-spotting, and other duties. Seventy-seven two-seat dual training versions, titled T7, were supplied to the RAF. These were mainly converted AOP6s.

Avro York C.1

Type: transport.
Crew: five (and up to 24 passengers).
Power plants: four 1620 hp Rolls-Royce Merlin T.24; four 1620 hp Rolls-Royce Merlin 502.
Dimensions: span 102 ft; length 78 ft 6 in; height.16 ft 6 in.
Weights: empty 42,040 lb; loaded 68,000 lb.
Performance: maximum speed 298 mph at 21,000 ft; cruising speed 233 mph; initial rate of climb 1500 ft per min; service ceiling 26,000 ft; range 2700 miles.

Above: an Avro York transport aircraft.

Though conceived and flown by the RAF during World War 2, the York saw its main operational use after the war. Using the Lancaster's wings, engines, undercarriage and tail assembly, Avro added an all-metal, square-section, deeper fuselage with twice the cubic capacity of the Lancaster, and the prototype York first flew on 5 July 1942. Due to a contemporary agreement that all transport aircraft during the war would be American-designed, the York was not mass-produced immediately, and only three were built in 1943. Slightly increased production, three per month in 1944, allowed several to be used as VIP transports by the RAF, and some were loaned to BOAC for civil transport and freight duties. The first unit wholly-equipped with the type was No. 551 Squadron at Lyneham in 1945, and eventually eight other squadrons used the York. Total production for the RAF amounted to 208 Yorks.

In 1948 Yorks made a huge contribution to the RAF's efforts during the Berlin Air Lift; almost half the gross tonnage carried by the RAF.

Avro Lincoln

Type: heavy bomber.
Crew: six to eight.
Power plants: four 1750 hp Rolls-Royce Merlin 85 (Mk I); four 1750 hp Packard-Merlin 68/300 (Mk II); four 1750 hp Rolls-Royce Merlin 85a (Mk IV); four 1750 hp Rolls-Royce Merlin 102 (Mk 30B).
Dimensions: span 120 ft; length 78 ft 3½ in; height 17 ft 3½ in.
Weights: empty 43,778 lb (Mk I), 44,148 lb (Mk II); loaded 82,000 lb (Mk I and Mk II).
Performance: maximum speed 295 mph at 15,000 ft; initial rate of climb 820 ft per min; service ceiling 22,000 ft; maximum range 3570 miles.
Armament: twin 0.50 in machine guns in each of nose, dorsal, tail turrets (Mk I); two 0.50 in machine guns in nose turret, two 0.50 in machine guns in tail turret, one 0.50 in machine gun in ventral position, two 20 mm Hispano cannon in dorsal turret (Mk II); maximum bomb load 14,000 lb.

Intended initially as the Lancaster IV or V – a longer-range, heavier-armed variant of the Lancaster for Far East operations – the prototype Lincoln first flew on 9 June 1944. Too late to see operations in World War 2, Lincolns entered service with No. 57 Squadron in September 1945, and later equipped a total of 20 squadrons of the RAF. From March 1950, UK-based Lincoln squadrons were detached on rotation basis to Tengah, Singapore for participation in Operation Firedog – bombing Chinese terrorists in the Malayan Emergency campaign; alongside No. 1 Squadron RAAF, also Lincoln-equipped and based at Tengah. Many individual Lincolns came to be used for a variety of experimental installations of engines and other equipment. Lincolns were withdrawn from first-line use in the RAF by mid-1955.

Below: **an Avro Lincoln heavy bomber.**

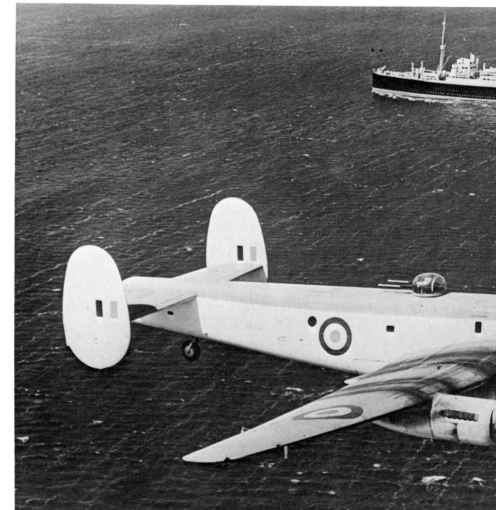

Avro Shackleton

Type: long range maritime reconnaissance, anti-submarine aircraft.
Crew: six to ten.
Power plants: four 2450 hp Rolls-Royce Griffon 57 or 57a.
Dimensions: span 120 ft (MR1 and 2), 119 ft 10 in (MR3); length 77 ft 6 in (MR1), 87 ft 3 in (MR2), 92 ft 6 in (MR3); height 17ft 6 in (MR1), 16 ft 9 in (MR2), 23 ft 4 in (MR3).
Weights (MR3): empty 57,800 lb; loaded 100,000 lb.
Performance (MR3): maximum speed 302 mph; initial rate of climb 850 ft per min; service ceiling 19,200 ft; range 4215 miles at 200 mph at 1500 ft.
Armament: two 20 mm Hispano cannon in nose; two 20 mm Hispano cannon in B.17 dorsal turret; two 0.50 in machine guns in tail (MR1); two 20 mm cannon in nose only (MR2 and 3); bomb bay adaptable for various maritime loads.

Left: **an Avro Shackleton MR1.**
Below: **the Shackleton MR3 variant first flew in September 1955.**

Above: **a Shackleton AEW2 of No. 8 Sqn.**

The prototype Shackleton first flew on 9 March 1949, as an obvious development of the Lancaster/Lincoln stablemates, specifically for Coastal Command. First RAF squadron to receive the type was No. 120 at Kinloss in early 1951. By 1953 seven squadrons were equipped with Shackletons (MR1s and MR1as), but refined variants (MR2s) then began reaching squadrons as replacements. In 1954 there was further redesign, culminating in the tricycle-undercarriage MR3 version, which entered squadron service eventually from 1957. The last MR3 based in Britain was ultimately retired in late 1971; but an Airborne Early Warning variant (AEW Mark 2) began service with No. 8 Squadron in January 1972.

Avro Andover

Type: transport.
Crew: three.
Power plants: two 3245 hp Rolls-Royce Dart RDa12 Mk 201C turboprops.
Dimensions: span 98 ft 3 in; length 78 ft; height 30 ft 1 in.
Weights: empty 27,709 lb; loaded 44,500 lb.
Performance: maximum speed 302 mph at 15,000 ft; service ceiling 23,800 ft; range (normal) 380 miles, (maximum) 2700 miles.

A military development of the civil Avro 748 airliner, the Andover was the last design to bear the Avro prefix; later designs having Hawker-Siddeley designations from 1 July 1963, when the Avro firm was absorbed in the new company. In its RAF version, the Andover offered short take-off and landing (STOL) capabilities, combined with a multi-role employment as transport, ambulance, freighter, or troop conveyance; while its novel 'kneeling' undercarriage gave easy access for awkward freight loads. The prototype first flew in July 1965, and Anovers entered RAF service with No. 46 Squadron. Only 31 aircraft were ordered

Below: **an Avro Andover C1 of No. 46 Sqn.**

for RAF use; while six luxury CC2 versions were equipped solely for VIP passenger transportation. Though mainly withdrawn from RAF use in 1975, a few examples were still in use in the early 1980s. A maritime patrol variant, titled Coastguarder, was used by several other countries from 1977.

Avro Vulcan

Type: high altitude bomber; low-level strategic reconnaissance.

Crew: five.

Power plants: four 11,000 lb thrust Bristol Olympus 101 (B.1); four 12 or 13,000 lb thrust Olympus 102 or 103 (B.1); four 17,000 lb thrust Bristol-Siddeley Olympus 201 (B.2); four 20,000 lb Olympus 301 (B.2).

Dimensions: span 99 ft (B.1), 111 ft (B.2); length 97 ft 1 in (B.1), 99 ft 11 in (B.2); height 26 ft 6 in (B.1), 27 ft 1 in (B.2).

Weights: loaded (approx) 180,000 lb (B.2).

Performance (B.2): maximum speed approximately Mach 0.98 (approximately 650 mph); service ceiling (approximately) 60,000 ft; maximum range 5750 miles (with in-flight refuelling).

Armament 21 1000 lb HE bombs (conventional); or various missile loads.

Designed for Air Ministry Specification B.35/46 (issued early in 1947), the Vulcan was a radical departure from conventional heavy bomber concepts of its era, and emerged as the world's first delta-winged truly heavy bomber. The first prototype made its initial flight on 30 August 1952, and the production Vulcan B.1 first flew in February 1955. After acceptance trials at Boscombe Down, the Vulcan B.1 entered

RAF service with No. 230 Operational Conversion Unit (OCU) at Finningley in mid-1956; while the first squadron to be equipped was No. 83 at Waddington in July 1957. Vulcan B.1 production totalled 45 aircraft. Later a slightly larger version with uprated powerplants, the B.2, went into production and No. 83 Squadron was again first to receive this type; the initial example arriving with the unit in December 1960. In 1962, No. 617 Squadron became the first V-bomber unit to become operational with the Blue Steel stand-off missile. From 1964 Vulcans (and the other V-bombers) were expected to undertake low-level contour-hugging tactics, and were accordingly fitted with

Above: **an Avro Vulcan B1 of No. 230 OCU visits Pinecastle Air Force Base, Florida.**

appropriate radar equipment; becoming operational in this role from 1966. In April 1968, when Bomber Command was merged into the newly-created Strike Command, Vulcans equipped eight squadrons of the RAF. From 1973, No. 27 ('Flying Elephants') Squadron pioneered the Vulcan SR2, a terrain-hugging strategic reconnaissance version converted from the B.2.

Right: **the third production Vulcan B1.**
Below: **an Avro Vulcan B2 in service with No. 617 Squadron, 'The Dambusters'.**

BAC Lightning F.1-6

Type: fighter interceptor.
Crew: one.
Power plants: two 15,680 lb thrust Rolls-Royce Avon 302 turbojets.
Dimensions: span 34 ft 10 in (F.6); length 53 ft 3 in (F.6); height 19 ft 7 in (F.6).
Weights: empty approximately 28,000 lb (F.6); loaded approximately 50,000 lb (F.6).
Performance: maximum speed 1500 mph at 40,000 ft (F.6); initial rate of climb 50,000 ft per min (F.6); service ceiling over 60,000 ft; range 800 miles.
Armament: packs for two Red Top or Firestreak missiles, or 22 spin-stabilised rockets; two 30 mm Aden cannon in pack.

Britain's first true supersonic fighter, the Lightning was designed by W E W Petter and his English Electric Company team, and was a bold concept for producing a transonic interceptor in one scratch-to-squadron stage. The first prototype (WG760, titled P.1) made its initial flight on 4 August 1954, and the production Lightning 1 first flew on 30 October 1959. In July 1960 No. 74 ('Tiger') Squadron at Coltishall, Norfolk became the first squadron to begin requipment with the type. The early Service Mark 1a was warmly received by RAF crews, and had twice the performance of the Hawker Hunter. The Lightning was produced and designed from the outset as an integrated weapons system. Mark 2 aircraft incorporated fully variable reheat capability and other progressive refinements. The Mark 2 was followed by the much-improved standard F3 version in 1964. In 1965 the F6 development entered RAF service, incorporating greater range and endurance by virtue of increased tankage and inflight refuelling equipment, and advanced radar and armament. Two-seat trainer versions of the Lightning were designated T4 or T5. Total production of Lightnings (all types) was 338 aircraft, including 57 exported to foreign air services in the Middle East.

Left: **a BAC Lightning F6 interceptor.**
Below: **a Lightning F3 of No. 29 Sqn is armed with Red Top air-to-air missiles.**
Right: **a Lightning F1A of No. 56 Sqn.**

Above: a BAC VC10 C1 of No. 10 Squadron.

BAC VC10 C.1

Type: long-range transport.
Crew: four (plus 5 to 7 stewards).
Power plants: four 21,000 lb thrust Rolls-Royce Conway RCO42; four 22,500 lb thrust Rolls-Royce Conway RCO43 (C1).
Dimensions: span 146 ft 2 in; length 158 ft 8 in; height 39 ft 6 in.
Weights: empty 142,220 lb; loaded 322,000 lb.
Performance: maximum speed 580 mph; service ceiling 38,000 ft; range 6300 miles.

Designed originally for the British Overseas Airways Corporation (BOAC), the first VC10 flight was made on 29 June 1962, received its certificate of airworthiness in April 1964, and commenced BOAC use in the same month. RAF orders for VC10s were placed in September 1961 and August 1962; a total of 14 aircraft being converted to military requirements. In its RAF role the VC10 carried up to 150 troops and their equipment for approximately 4000 miles non-stop; while as a pure freighter the VC10 could lift a service load of 59,000 lb. Accommodation for up to 78 stretcher cases could be provided in the casualty-evacuation role. First deliveries to the RAF were made to No. 10 Squadron in July 1966.

BAC Jet Provost T.1-5

Type: jet trainer.
Crew: one or two.
Power plant: 1750 lb thrust Armstrong Siddeley Viper ASV5 (T1); 1750 lb thrust Bristol Siddeley Viper 102 (T3); 2500 lb thrust Bristol Siddeley Viper 201 (T5).
Dimensions: span 35 ft 2 in (T1), 36 ft 11 in (T2 and 5 with tip tanks); length 31 ft 11 in (T1), 32 ft 5 in (T3), 33 ft 7½ in (T5); height 12 ft 8 in (T1), 10ft 2 in (T3 and 5).
Weights: empty 4347 lb (T3); loaded 7200 lb (T3), 9200 lb (T5).
Performance: maximum speed 330 mph (T1), 409 mph (T5); service ceiling 36,700 ft (T5); range 900 miles (T5).

A development, in essence, of the piston-engined Hunting Percival Provost trainer, the Jet Provost prototype first flew in June 1954, and commenced RAF use in 1955. By 1957 the T3 version was adopted as the RAF's standard jet

Left: the first Jet Provost T3 XM346.

trainer, and began service use in June 1959. This variant was followed in 1961 by the T4, an up-rated version. The need for a high altitude trainer, fitted with pressurised cabin, produced the T5 version, which commenced RAF service in September 1969. Jet Provosts (T3 and 5s) formed the equipment of various noted RAF aerobatic teams.

Blackburn Firebrand 1-5

Type: naval fighter; torpedo bomber.
Crew: one.
Power plant: 2305 hp Napier Sabre III (Mks I and II); 2400 hp Bristol Centaurus VII (Mk III); 2520 hp Bristol Centaurus IX (Mk III); 2520 hp Bristol Centaurus IX/57 (Mks 4, 5, 5a).
Dimensions: span 50 ft (Mk I), 51 ft 3½ in (Mks II–5a); length 38 ft 2 in (Mk I), 38 ft 9 in (Mks 4, 5, 5a); height 13 ft 4 in (Mk I), 13 ft 3 in (Mks 4, 5, 5a).
Weights: empty 11,100 lb (Mk I), 11,835 lb (Mk 5); loaded 13,643 lb (Mk I), 17,500 lb (Mk 5).
Performance: maximum speed 353 mph (Mk I), 342 mph (Mks 4 and 5); service ceiling 32,500 ft (Mk I), 34,000 ft (Mk 4), 28,500 ft (Mk 5); range 805 miles (Mk I), 745 miles (Mks 4 and 5).
Armament: four fixed 20 mm Hispano cannon in wings; one 1850 lb torpedo, or up to 2000 lb of bombs, or six or eight rockets.

Though first flown as a prototype Mark I as early as July 1942, the Firebrand only entered FAA service trials in 1944, and FAA squadron service (with No. 813 Squadron FAA) in September 1945. These latter versions were Mark 4s and were deployed as torpedo bombers primarily. Total Firebrand production was 220 aircraft, the final Mark 5 and 5a versions entering squadron service in April 1947. By 1953 Firebrands were being replaced in first-line use by Westland Wyverns, and remaining machines were allocated to training establishments, mainly as non-flying airframes.

Left: a pair of BAC Jet Provost T4s.
Below: a Blackburn Firebrand Mk 4.
Bottom: a Blackburn Beverley C1 transport.

Blackburn Beverley

Type: transport and freight supply.
Crew: six.
Power plants: four 2850 hp Bristol Centaurus 173.
Dimensions: span 162 ft; length 99 ft 5 in; height 38 ft 9 in.
Weights: empty 79,230 lb; loaded 135,000 lb (maximum).
Performance: maximum speed 238 mph; service ceiling 16,000 ft; range 1300 miles (29,000 lb load).

A development of the civil Universal Freighter, the Beverley entered RAF service with No. 47 Squadron in March 1956; the largest aircraft in RAF service at that date, and the first specially designed for dropping heavy army equipment in a supply role. Between then and October 1960, four more squadrons received Beverleys, Nos. 53, 30, 84 and 34 respectively in order of equipment. These served faithfully in Britain, the Middle and Far East zones until 1967. The type officially retired from the RAF in December 1968. A total of 47 aircraft were built for the RAF.

Blackburn Buccaneer

Type: low-level strike.
Crew: two.
Power plants: two 7100 lb thrust DH Gyron Junior DGJ.1 (Mk 1); two 11,100 lb thrust Rolls-Royce RB168-1A Spey (Mk 2); two 11,100 lb thrust Rolls-Royce RB168 Spey and two Bristol Siddeley BS605 rocket engines (Mk 50).
Dimensions: span 44 ft; length 63 ft 5 in; height 16 ft 3 in.
Weights: loaded (maximum) approximately 56,000 lb.
Performance: maximum speed approximately 720 mph at sea level; tactical radius 600 miles maximum.
Armament: variety of conventional and/or missile loads up to 4000 lb (internal) plus 4000 lb (wing pylons).

Originally designed to Admiralty requirements, the Buccaneer prototype first flew in April 1958, and was known at that time as the N.A.39. On 26 August 1960 the name Buccaneer was officially adopted, and FAA service trials commenced in March 1961. The first operational Buccaneer squadron was No. 801, FAA, from July 1962. In March 1965 the improved Mark 2 version entered FAA service. In 1968 Buccaneers were selected for re-equipment of RAF units as a low-level, long-range strike or reconnaissance aircraft, and began their RAF service with No. 12 Squadron in October 1969 in a dual RAF/maritime strike role. A total of 42 Buccaneers

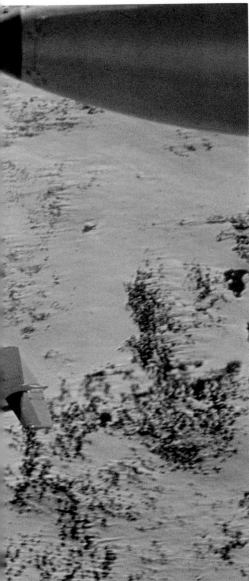

Left: Buccaneer S2s of No. 809 Squadron FAA.
Above: a Buccaneer of No. 809 Sqn FAA about
to be catapulted from HMS *Ark Royal*.

was specifically ordered for the RAF, and a
further 60 approximately were inherited from
the FAA. Highly manoeuvrable at near-ground
level, and structurally tough, the Buccaneer,
with its complex terrain-hugging and armament
radar equipment is well suited to its role.

Boeing Washington

Type: long-range heavy bomber.
Crew: ten.
Power plants: four 2200 hp Wright Cyclone
Eighteen R-3350.
Dimensions: span 141 ft 3 in; length 99 ft;
height 27 ft 9 in.
Weights: empty 74,500 lb; loaded 140,000 lb
(maximum).
Performance: maximum speed 350 mph at
25,000 ft; service ceiling 38,000 ft; maximum
range 4100 miles.
Armament: two 0.50 in machine guns in each of
four turrets; bomb load 17,500 lb (1000 miles
range).

Taken into service essentially as a stop-gap
machine, to maintain the RAF's bomber strength
between the ageing Avro Lincoln and the
advent of Britain's V-bomber force, the Wash-

Below: a Boeing Washington of No. XV
Squadron in a night bombing colour scheme.

ington was the RAF title for the ex-USAAF
Boeing B-29 Superfortress. First examples were
flown to Britain in March 1950, and these
entered first-line RAF use with No. 149 Squadron at Coningsby in November that year.
Seven other RAF squadrons eventually received Washingtons, and they remained in RAF use
until 1955. All aircraft incorporated pressurised
cockpit cabins; something of a novelty to most
RAF air crews of the period. A total of 88 aircraft
was delivered for RAF use.

Bristol Brigand

Type: torpedo bomber; strike bomber.
Crew: three.
Power plants: two 2500 hp Bristol Centaurus 57.
Dimensions: span 72 ft 4 in; length 46 ft 5 in;
height 17 ft 6 in.
Weights: empty 25,600 lb; loaded 39,000 lb.
Performance: maximum speed 360 mph;
service ceiling 26,000 ft; range 2800 miles (with
drop tanks), 2000 miles (normal).
Armament: four 20 mm Hispano cannon in
forward belly; eight 3-inch rockets on
underwing rails; maximum bomb load 2000 lb.

The ultimate piston-engined attack aircraft in
RAF service, the Brigand was originally design-
ed as a torpedo bomber, and the first prototype
flew in December 1944. The first 11 production
Brigands entered service with Nos. 36 and 42
Squadrons, Coastal Command in 1946, but were
soon withdrawn for factory conversion to light
bombers for tropical service in the Middle and
Far East zones. Entering RAF service in the
latter guise in early 1949, Brigands equipped
No. 84 Squadron in Iraq and No. 8 Squadron in
Aden. In 1950 they were also supplied to No. 45
Squadron in Malaya. From 1950–53 Brigands
flew a host of strike operations during Operation Firedog (Malayan Emergency); but ceased
these duties from mid-1953. In Britain the type
continued in RAF use until early 1958, mainly as
a radar training machine. Total Brigand production was 147 aircraft, all but four being delivered to the RAF.

Below: Bristol Brigands of No. 84 Sqn return
to their base at Tengah, Singapore, in 1951
after a jungle strike operation.

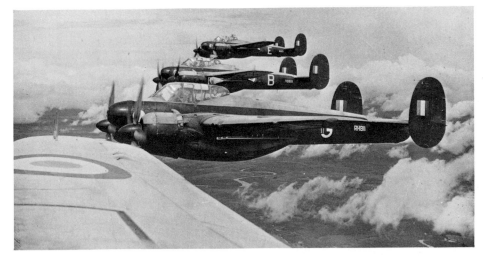

Above: **Bristol Britannia C1 XM520.**

Bristol Britannia C.1/2

Type: long-range transport.
Crew: four.
Power plants: four 4445 ehp Bristol Siddeley Proteus 255.
Dimensions: span 142 ft 3 in; length 124 ft 3 in; height 37 ft 6 in.
Weights: empty 90,600 lb; loaded 185,000 lb.
Performance: cruising speed 360 mph; range with maximum payload 4268 miles; maximum range 5334 miles.

Only 23 Britannias saw RAF service, but the type was the RAF's first turboprop transport aircraft. Developed from the successful civil Britannia airliner, the RAF version entered service with No. 99 Squadron in June 1959, followed by the only other Britannia unit, No. 511 Squadron from December 1959. Both squadrons continued flying the type until their disbandment in January 1976.

De Havilland Hornet F.1-3

Type: long-range fighter.
Crew: one.
Power plants: two 2070 hp Rolls-Royce Merlin 130/131; two 2030 hp Rolls-Royce Merlin 133/134.
Dimensions: span 45 ft; length 36 ft 8 in; height 14 ft 2 in.
Weights: empty 12,502 lb (Mk I), 12,880 lb (Mk 3); loaded 17,700 lb (Mk I), 20,900 lb (Mk 3).
Performance: speed 472 mph at 22,000 ft (Mks 1 and 3); initial rate of climb 4000 ft per min (Mks 1 and 3); service ceiling 37,500 ft (Mk I), 35,000 ft (Mk 3); range 2500 miles (Mk 1), 3000 miles (Mk 3).
Armament: four 20 mm Hispano cannon in belly; eight 3-inch rockets on underwing rails; maximum bomb load 2000 lb under wings.

Above: a DH Hornet of No. 45 Squadron.

Like its predecessor the DH Mosquito, of which design it was basically a slimmed-down version, the Hornet was originally a private venture project which was later officially approved for production. Its concept was as a long-range, ultra-fast fighter for opposing the Japanese air forces in the Pacific. The prototype first flew on 28 July 1944 – only 13 months after the start of detail designs. The first production Hornet reached the RAF for service trials on 28 February 1945, but actual squadron equipment began with No. 64 Squadron in May 1946. Hornets remained in first-line RAF service until 1951 in Britain, but were then used by Nos. 33, 45 and 80 Squadrons in the Far East. This trio of units flew strike operations in Malaya until mid-1955. With its exceptional speed, climb and manoeuvrability, the Hornet was the fastest piston-

Below: armourers load 3-inch rocket projectiles onto a DH Hornet of No. 33 Sqn at Butterworth, Malaya, in 1952.

engined fighter in RAF use and, indeed, the service's ultimate such fighter design prior to jet-engined successors. Late in 1944 prototypes of a naval version for aircraft carrier use were put in hand, resulting in the Sea Hornet; the prototype for which version first flew in April 1945. Designated Sea Hornet F.Mk 20 production aircraft entered full FAA service with No. 801 Squadron in mid-1947 and remained in service until 1951. Total production of Hornets was 203 (plus two prototypes), and 206 Sea Hornets (plus three prototypes).

De Havilland Chipmunk

Type: elementary trainer.
Crew: two.
Power plant: 145 hp DH Gipsy Major 8.
Dimensions: span 34 ft 4 in; length 25 ft 5 in; height 7 ft 1 in.
Weights: empty 1425 lb; loaded 2100 lb.
Performance: maximum speed 138 mph at ground level; service ceiling 16,000 ft; range 280 miles; endurance $2\frac{1}{4}$ hrs.

Successor to the DH Tiger Moth as the RAF's standard elementary trainer, the Chipmunk was designed by DH Canada of Toronto, and the prototype first flew in May 1946. Chipmunks entered RAF service in February 1950, providing *ab initio* instruction to thousands of regular and national service airmen, university graduates, and even royalty – HRH the Duke of Edinburgh receiving his elementary flying instruction in Chipmunk WP861 in November 1952.

Below: a DH Chipmunk T10 of the Empire Test Pilots School.

De Havilland Comet

Type: turbojet transport.
Crew: four–six.
Power plants: four 7300 lb thrust Rolls-Royce Avon 118 (Mk 2); four 10,500 lb thrust Rolls-Royce Avon 350 (Mk 4).
Dimensions: span 115 ft (Mk 2), 114 ft 10 in (Mk 4); length 96 ft (Mk 2), 118 ft (Mk 4); height 28 ft 4 in (Mk 2), 28 ft 6 in (Mk 4).
Weights: loaded 120,000 lb (Mk 2), 162,000 lb (Mk 4).
Performance: cruising speed 490 mph (Mk 2), 503 mph (Mk 4); crusing altitude 40,000 ft (Mk 2), 39,000 ft (Mk 4); maximum stage with full payload 2100 miles (Mk 2), 2650 miles (Mk 4).

Internationally famed as the world's first jet-engined commercial airliner, the prototype DH 106 Comet first flew on 27 July 1949. On 2 May 1952, BOAC flew the world's first pure jet flight with fare-paying passengers (from London to Johannesburg). The obvious potential for RAF long-haul transportation led to modified Comet Series 2 aircraft being introduced to RAF service in July 1956, and No. 216 Squadron became the first military jet transport unit in the world in 1956. In February 1962 the RAF began receiving Mark 4 variants, again via No. 216 Squadron, a version which increased passenger accommodation from 44 to 94, or could be simply converted to carry 12 stretchers, 47 'sitting patients', and six medical attendants with full medical facilities in a casualty-evacuation role. Comet Mark 2s were withdrawn from RAF service by May 1967, and Mark 4s were eventually withdrawn from squadron use in June 1975. Two units, Nos. 51 and 192 Squadrons, flew Comets on signal duties.

Below: the DH Comet C2 jet transport.

De Havilland Vampire/ Sea Vampire

Type: fighter; fighter bomber.
Crew: one.
Power plant: 3100 lb thrust DH Goblin 2 (Mks 1, 3, 5); 4400 lb thrust DH Ghost 2/2 (Mks 1, 3, 5); 3350 lb thrust DH Goblin 3 (Mk 9).
Dimensions: span 40 ft (Mk 1), 38 ft (Mks 5 and 9); length 30 ft 9 in; height 8 ft 10 in.
Weights: empty 6372 lb (Mk 1), 7134 lb (Mk 3), 7253 lb (Mk 5), 7283 lb (Mk 9); loaded 10,840 lb (Mk 1), 12,360 lb (Mk 5), 12,390 lb (Mk 9).
Performance: maximum speed 540 mph (Mk 1), 535 mph (Mk 5), 548 mph (Mk 9); initial rate of climb 4300 ft per min (Mk 1), 4800 ft per min (Mk 9); service ceiling 40,000 ft (Mk 5), 48,000 ft (Mk 9); range 730 miles (Mk 1), 1170 miles (Mk 5), 1220 miles (Mk 9).
Armament: four 20 mm Hispano cannon in belly; eight 3-inch rockets under wings, or 2000 lb of bombs.

Originally to be titled Spider-Crab, the diminutive Vampire was the RAF's second jet-engined fighter to enter service. The prototype first flew on 20 September 1943, and the first production

Above: **a DH Comet C4 transport of No. 216 Squadron based at Lyneham.**

aircraft on 20 April 1945. The Vampire entered first-line use with No. 247 Squadron in April 1946 (Mark 1s). In 1948 Vampires became the first jets to equip units of the Royal Auxiliary Air Force; while in the same year six Vampire F3s of No. 54 Squadron made the first RAF trans-Atlantic flight ever by jet fighters under their own power. In 1949 the Mark 5 started replacing former versions on squadrons, serving in Britain, Germany, the Middle and Far East areas. In the latter zone Vampires flew intensive operations over Malaya from late 1950 until 1953; being replaced in turn by Mark 9s from then until late 1954. A naval version, the Sea Vampire, was tested in December 1945, the first pure jet ever to operate from an aircraft carrier, and from 1948 production Sea Vampires helped train a generation of FAA jet pilots. A further version, the Sea Vampire T.22 two-seat trainer supplemented these duties.

Right: **DH Vampire F3s of No. 54 Squadron made the first trans-Atlantic flight by RAF jet aircraft in July 1948.**
Below: **a DH Vampire T11 jet trainer.**

Above: **DH Venom NF2s of No. 23 Sqn.**

De Havilland Venom/ Sea Venom

Type: fighter bomber; night fighter; naval fighter.
Crew: one; two (night fighter).
Power plant: 4850 lb thrust DH Ghost 103 (Mks I–4); 4950 lb thrust DH Ghost 104 (3/FAW Mk 21/53); 5300 lb thrust DH Ghost 105 (FAW Mk 22).
Dimensions: span 41 ft 8 in (Mk 1), 42 ft 11 in (Mk 22); length 31 ft 10 in (Mk 1), 33 ft 1 in (NF2), 36 ft 7 in (FAW Mk 22); height 6 ft 2 in (Mk 1), 7 ft 7 in (NF2), 8 ft 6$\frac{1}{4}$ in (FAW Mk 22).
Weights: loaded 15,400 lb (Mk 1), 15,800 lb (FAW Mk 22).
Performance: maximum speed 640 mph (Mk 1), 630 mph (NF3), 575 mph (FAW Mk 22); service ceiling 49,200 ft (NF3), 40,000 ft (Mk 22); range 1000 miles (NF3), 705 miles (FAW Mk 22).
Armament: four 20 mm Hispano cannon in belly; up to 2000 lb of bombs, or eight 3-inch rockets under wings.

Intended to replace the Vampire, the Venom was a completely fresh design despite its similar appearance. A new wing design, more powerful Ghost engine, and wing-tip jettison-able fuel tanks – the latter being the first tip tanks to be fitted to an RAF fighter design – led to far superior performance than the Vampire's. Venoms entered RAF service with No. 11 Squadron in Germany in August 1952 as day fighter bombers; joined Middle East operations in 1954, and Far East service in 1955. From 1953 Venoms modified to accommodate extra radar and a radar-navigator in the cockpit entered service as interim night-fighters. Navalised variants commenced with the Sea Venom NF Mark 20, which had carrier trials in July 1951, and FAA deliveries commenced in April 1954. Venoms saw active operations in the Suez Crisis of 1956, and in the 1957 Oman rebellion, apart from operational use in Malaya. Total Venom production was 1143 aircraft (including foreign contracts), of which 775 were RAF aircraft and 256 were Sea Venoms. Both versions were gradually superseded in RAF and FAA service in 1960.

Left: a DH Sea Vixen FAW2 with wings folded.

De Havilland Sea Vixen

Type: naval all-weather jet fighter.
Crew: two.
Power plants: two 11,230 lb thrust Rolls-Royce Avon 208.
Dimensions: span 51 ft; length 55 ft 7 in; height 11 ft.
Weight: loaded 35,000 lb.
Performance: maximum speed 645 mph at 10,000 ft; climb to 40,000 ft, $7\frac{1}{2}$ mins; service ceiling 48,000 ft (approximately).
Armament: four Firestreak homing missiles, or four Microcell rocket packs, plus 28 two-inch missiles; maximum bomb load 2000 lb.

The Sea Vixen, initially projected in 1946, was the final and biggest development of the Vampire-Venom theme. Originally considered for RAF use as a four 30 mm Aden gun-armed night fighter, the DH 110 (its makers' designation) was passed over in favour of the Gloster Javelin for such a role, and the design was re-worked to naval requirements. In early 1955 production contracts for Sea Vixens were placed, and the first squadron, No. 892, FAA, was formed in July 1959. The Sea Vixen at that date was the heaviest aircraft ever to enter British naval use, and also the first British interceptor to dispense with gun armament and carry missiles only. In FAA service Sea Vixens replaced Sea Venoms from 1960; while from 1963 improved versions, titled FAW2s, entered squadron service and were eventually withdrawn in 1972.

English Electric Canberra

Type: bomber; photo-reconnaissance; night intruder; electronic counter-measures aircraft.
Crew: two or three.
Power plants: two 6500 lb thrust Rolls-Royce Avon 101 (B2); two 7500 lb thrust Rolls-Royce Avon 109 (B(I)8)); two 11,250 lb thrust Rolls-Royce Avon 206 (PR.9).
Dimensions: span 63 ft $11\frac{1}{2}$ in (B2, PR7, B(I)8)), 67 ft 10 in (PR9); length 55 ft 6 in (B2, B(I)8)), 66 ft 8 in (PR7/9); height 15 ft 7 in (all types).
Weights: empty 22,200 lb (B2), 27,950 lb (B(I)8)); loaded (maximum) 46,000 lb (B2), 55,000 lb (PR), 54,950 lb (B(I)8)).
Performance: maximum speed 570 mph (B2), 580 mph (PR), 540 mph (B(I)8)); service ceiling 48,000 ft (B2, PR, B(I)8)); range (normal) 2660 miles (B2), 4340 miles (PR); 805 miles (maximum bomb load) (B(I)8)).
Armament: bomb load 6000 lb (B2), 5000 lb (B(I)8)); four 20 mm cannon in belly pack (B(I)8)).

The RAF's first jet bomber, the Canberra first flew on 13 May 1949, and entered RAF service as a bomber (B2) with No. 101 Squadron in May 1951. Total B2 production came to 430 aircraft, which eventually equipped 40 RAF squadrons

Below left: a Sea Vixen FAW2 (foreground) flies with a pair of Sea Vixen FAW1s.
Below: Canberra B6s of No. 12 Sqn at Hal Far, Malta, during the Suez Crisis.
Bottom: Canberra B2s of No. 27 Squadron based at Scampton, Lincs, in 1955.

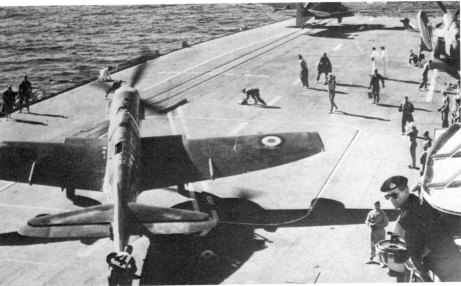

Above: **Canberra PR9s of No. 13 Sqn, 1970.**
Below left: **an English Electric Canberra B2 flies with a Gloster Javelin FAW9.**

Top: **HRH The Duke of Edinburgh watches Fireflies operating from HMS *Theseus*, 1952.**
Above: **a Fairey Firefly Mk 4.**

in Europe, Middle and Far East. A proliferation of variants soon followed the B2 light bomber version, and Canberras in some guise continue in RAF service in the early 1980s. Of these possibly the most significant operational variants were the range of photo-reconnaissance (PR) variants, designated PR3–PR9, and the B8 night intruder; the latter entering squadron service from mid-1956, and being withdrawn eventually in mid-1972. Other Canberras were used as target tugs, unmanned target drones, ECM aircraft; while many foreign air forces employed modified variants, notably the USAF, Martin-General Dynamics B-57 derivative. Total Canberra production in Britain was 925 aircraft but others were built abroad. RAF Canberras saw brief operational service in the Suez Crisis, and also served in the Malayan Emergency, while USAF versions saw active operations in the Vietnam War.

Fairey Firefly FR.4-AS.6/7

Type: fighter, reconnaissance.
Crew: two or three.
Power plant: 2100 hp Rolls-Royce Griffon 74 (FR4); 1965 hp Rolls-Royce Griffon 59 (AS7).
Dimensions: span 41 ft 2 in (FR4), 44 ft 6 in (AS7); length 38 ft (FR4), 38 ft 3 in (AS7); height 13 ft 11 in (FR4), 13 ft 3 in (AS7).
Weights: empty 9674 lb (FR4), 11,016 lb (AS7); loaded 13,479 lb (FR4), 13,970 lb (AS7).
Performance: maximum speed 367 mph (FR4), 300 mph (AS7); service ceiling 31,900 ft (FR4), 25,500 ft (AS7); range 760 miles (FR4), 860 miles (AS7).
Armament: four 20 mm cannon in wings (FR4–AS6), 16 3-inch rockets, or up to 2000 lb of bombs (FR4–AS6).

Developed from the wartime Firefly I, the Firefly Mark 4 first flew in 1944, but only

entered FAA operational service with Nos. 810 and 825 Squadrons FAA in late 1947. These were soon followed by Mark 5 variants – FR5s for fighter-recce roles, and AS5s for anti-submarine duties – the most prolific variants of the Firefly design, some 352 Mark 5s being eventually built. The Mark 5 variant introduced the power-operated folding wing for stowage and parking. Mark 5s began squadron service in 1948, and saw wide active operational use during the Korean War. From 1953 Mark 6 versions began to replace Mark 5 Fireflies in squadrons and remained in service until 1956. The AS7 unarmed anti-submarine search version was the final Firefly variant, which saw brief service until 1955. From 1941, an overall total of 1702 Fireflies of all types was produced.

Below: **a Fairey Firefly preserved by the RN Historical Flight.**

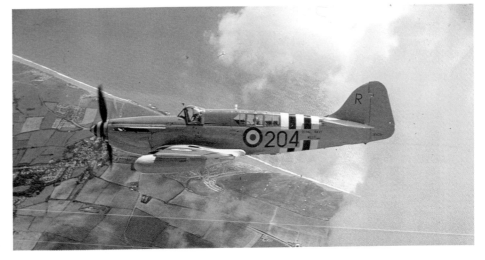

Fairey Gannet

Type: anti-submarine search, strike or torpedo bomber.
Crew: three.
Power plant: one 2950 hp Armstrong Siddeley Double Mamba 100 (AS1); one 3035 hp Armstrong Siddeley Double Mamba 101 (AS4); one 3875 hp Armstrong Siddeley Double Mamba 102 (AEW3).
Dimensions: span 54 ft 4 in; length 43 ft (AS1 and 4), 44 ft (AEW3); height 13 ft 8½ in (AS1 and 4), 16 ft 10 in (AEW3).
Weights: empty 15,069 lb (AS1), 14,069 lb (AS4); loaded 19,600 lb (AS1), 21,387 lb (AS4), approximately 25,000 lb (AEW3).
Performance: maximum speed 300 mph (AS4), 250 mph (AEW3); service ceiling 25,000 ft; range 660 miles (AS4), 700 miles (AEW3).
Armament: two homing torpedoes in bomb bay, or equivalent stores; 16 3-inch rockets under wings if required.

The Gannet was the first FAA aircraft capable of combining the full search and strike roles, and the first in the world to have a double airscrew/turbine power plant. It was also the first British-built maritime aircraft capable of stowing all weaponry internally. First flown in September 1949, the Gannet became the FAA's standard carrier-borne anti-submarine strike aircraft from its entry to squadron service with No. 826 Squadron FAA in January 1955, until early 1960. Progressive development improved the Gannet's strike capability, while in February 1960 the unarmed AEW3 variant came into use with No. 849 Squadron; a much redesigned version packed with sophisticated radar detection equipment.

Below: the third prototype of the Fairey Gannet anti-submarine aircraft.

Gloster Meteor F.4 – PR.10

Type: fighter; fighter reconnaissance; trainer; photo-reconnaissance.
Crew: one or two.
Power plants: two 3500 lb thrust Rolls-Royce Derwent 5 (F4); two 3600 lb thrust Rolls-Royce Derwent 8 (F8).
Dimensions: span 37 ft 2 in (short span), 43 ft (long span) (F4), 37 ft 2 in (F8), 43 ft (PR10); length 41 ft (F4), 44 ft 7 in (F8), 44 ft 3 in (PR10); height 13 ft.
Weights: empty 11,217 lb (F4), 10,684 lb (F8), 10,993 lb (PR10); loaded 14,545 lb (F4), 15,700 lb (F8), 15,400 lb (PR10).
Performance: maximum speed 580 mph at 10,000 ft (F4), 598 mph at 10,000 ft (F8), 576 mph at 10,000 ft (PR10); climb to 30,000 ft, 6 mins (F4), 6½ mins (F8), 6 mins 18 secs (PR10); service ceiling 44,500 ft (F4), 43,000 ft (F8), 44,000 ft (PR10).
Armament: four 20 mm Hispano cannon in nose (all fighters); eight 3-inch rockets under wings if required.

The postwar F4 development was faster and stronger than previous Marks, having up-rated Derwents, and it superseded the F3 from 1948. Five F4s, specially modified, achieved new world speed records in 1945–46. Total production of F4s amounted to 583 aircraft. In 1949, the T7 two-seat trainer version entered RAF service. The next significant Meteor was the F8 fighter which became the RAF's primary day interceptor from 1950–55, equipping 19 Fighter Command squadrons and 10 squadrons of the Royal Auxiliary Air Force. An off-shoot of the F8, adapted to carry cameras in the nose, the

Left: a Gloster Meteor PR10 photographic reconnaissance aircraft.
Below: Meteor T7s of the CFS.

FR9, was employed on low-level fighter-reconnaissance duties from 1950. It was succeeded by an unarmed reconnaissance variant, the PR10, from 1951. Meteors were ultimately withdrawn from squadron use in 1961. Though no RAF Meteors saw operational use in war after 1945, Meteor F8s of the Royal Australian Air Force were used in combat during the early stages of the Korean War; the only British-built jet fighters to see combat in that conflict. Total British production of Meteors, came to 3545 aircraft, of which the F8 was produced in greatest quantity – 1183 aircraft, while a further 658 were F4s.

Gloster Javelin 1-9

Type: all-weather day and night fighter.
Crew: two.
Power plants: two 8000 lb thrust Armstrong Siddeley Sapphire Sa6 (Mks 1, 4, 5); two 11,000 lb thrust AS Sapphire Sa7 (Mk 7), Sa7R (Mk 8).
Dimensions: span 52 ft; length 56 ft 3 in (Mks 1–8), 56 ft 9 in (Mk 9); height 16 ft.
Weights: take-off 31,580 lb (Mk I), 35,690 lb (Mk 7), 38,100 lb (Mk 9).
Performance: maximum speed 620 mph at sea level (Mk 9); climb to 45,000 ft, 9.8 mins (Mk 1), 6.6 mins (Mk 7); service ceiling 52,500 ft (Mk 1), 52,800 ft (Mk 7).
Armament: two 30 mm Aden guns in nose, and four DH Firestreak missiles; or four packs of 37 2-inch rockets (air-to-air).

Below: a Gloster Javelin FAW8 of No. 41 Sqn.

Above: armourers work on a Gloster Meteor F4 of No. 66 Squadron at Duxford in 1949. *Right:* Gloster Meteor F8 fighters of No. 245 Squadron are refuelled from a converted B-29 tanker of the USAF.

The first twin-jet delta-winged fighter in the world, the Javelin first flew in prototype form in November 1951, and entered RAF service with No. 46 Squadron in February 1956. Improved versions were successively produced and put into service until the final withdrawal of the type in April 1968. Total production of all types amounted to 435 aircraft, of which the most-produced variant was the Mark 7 (142 aircraft). The latter, designated officially as the FAW7, first introduced Firestreak missiles as standard armament for the type. Apart from eight Marks of Javelin fighter, a two-seat, dual control training version, the Javelin T3, was produced.

Handley Page Hastings

Type: transport.
Crew: five.
Power plants: four 1675 hp Bristol Hercules 106.
Dimensions: span 113 ft; length 82 ft 8 in; height 22 ft 6 in.
Weights: empty 37,750 lb (C1), 48,427 lb (C2), 48,600 lb (C3); loaded (maximum) 75,000 lb (C1), 80,000 lb (C2, 3, 4).
Performance: maximum speed 354 mph (C1); service ceiling 26,700 ft; range 3260 miles (C1), 4250 miles (C2), 3280 miles (C3), 4250 miles (C4).

Above: a HP Hastings C1 takes off.
Right: a HP Hastings C1A.

Successor to the Avro York as the RAF's main heavy, long-range transport, the Hastings proto-type first flew in May 1946, and equipped the first RAF unit, No. 47 Squadron, from October 1948. It almost immediately flew a year's intensive operations in the Berlin Airlift. In late 1950 the C2 version came into use, having greater fuel tankage with consequent greater range, carrying the same passenger or paratroop load as the C1. Further versions, mainly internally modified, undertook meteorological roles, freight carriage, VIP transport and other duties. Hastings provided stalwart service from 1948 until 1968, including participation in the Suez Crisis operations. Total production (including two prototypes) came to 151 aircraft.

Handley Page Victor

Type: bomber; tanker.
Crew: five; four (tankers).
Power plants: four 11,000 lb thrust Bristol Siddeley Sapphire 200 (B1); four 19,750 lb thrust Rolls-Royce Conway R.Co17, Mk 201 (B2).
Dimensions: span 110 ft (B1), 120 ft (B2); length 114 ft 11 in; height 28 ft 1½ in.
Weights: maximum 205,000 lb (B1), 216,000 lb (B2).
Performance: maximum speed Mach 0.95 at approximately 45,000 ft; range 6000 miles (maximum); service ceiling 56,000 ft (B1), approximately 60,000 ft (B2).
Armament: bomb load 35,000 lb (HE), or one Blue Steel missile.

The aesthetically graceful Victor was the third of Britain's V-bombers to enter RAF service; being delivered initially to No. 232 OCU, Gaydon in November 1957, and achieving operational status with No. 10 Squadron at Cottesmore in April 1958. The more powerful B2 bomber version began to supersed the B1 in squadrons in early 1962, and B1s were then converted to K1A refueller-tankers and began RAF use in this guise in 1965. From 1964 Victor B2 bombers came to be used in the low-level bomber role, but were withdrawn from bomber duties by 1969. Thereafter B2s were in turn converted to K2 tankers; the first example being delivered to the RAF in May 1974. In its strategic reconnaissance role the B/SR2 Victor continued in service until 1974.

Above right: a HP Victor B1 of No. XV Sqn.
Right: the Victor prototype WB771 in 1953.
Below: a HP Victor K1A of No. 57 Sqn.

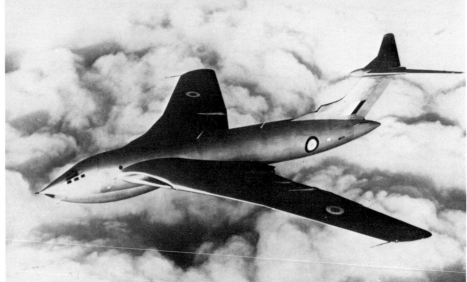

Below: a HP Victor K1A of No. 55 Sqn based
at Marham refuels a pair of No. 29 Sqn's BAC
Lightning F3s.

Hawker Sea Fury

Type: naval fighter.
Crew: one.
Power plant: 2480 hp Bristol Centaurus 18.
Dimensions: span 38 ft 4¾ in; length 34 ft 8 in
(Mk 20); height 15 ft 10½ in.
Weights: empty 9240 lb (Mk 11); loaded
12,500 lb (Mk 20).
Performance: speed 460 mph at 18,000 ft
(Mk 11); service ceiling 35,800 ft; range
(maximum) 1040 miles.
Armament: four 20 mm Hispano cannon in
wings; bomb load 2000 lb, or 12 3-inch rockets
under wings.

Developed from the Tempest, the Sea Fury
became the FAA's ultimate piston-engined
fighter in operational squadrons. The prototype
first flew in February 1945, and production
aircraft entered first-line FAA service with No.
807 Squadron in August 1947. From then until
the type was eventually superseded in 1953,
Sea Furies were the FAA's chief single-seat
fighters, and saw highly active operational use
during the Korean War from December 1950,
mainly as carrier-borne ground attack aircraft
but having a fair share of air-to-air combat with
opposing Soviet-built MiG-15 jet fighters. The
two-seat training version, the Mark 20, came
into naval use in 1950, production totalling 60
aircraft for RN service, though larger quantities
were built for export. Total Sea Fury production
was 860 machines.

Right: a Sea Fury X flies over Portsmouth.
Below: a Sea Fury of the RN Historical Flt.

Hawker Hunter F.1 – FR.10

Type: fighter; fighter reconnaissance.
Crew: one.
Power plant: 7500 lb thrust Rolls-Royce Avon 113/115 (Mk 1); 10,000 lb thrust Rolls-Royce Avon 203 (Mk 6); 10,150 lb thrust Rolls-Royce Avon 207 (FGA9 and FR10).
Dimensions: span 33 ft 8 in; length 45 ft 10½ in (all, except FR10); height 13 ft 2 in.
Weights: empty 12,128 lb (Mk 1), 12,760 lb (Mk 6), 13,010 lb (Mk 9); loaded 16,200 lb (Mk 1), 17,750 lb (Mk 6), 18,000 lb (Mk 9).
Performance: maximum speed 715 mph at sea level (Mach 0.95); service ceiling 51,500 ft; range (maximum fuel) 1840 miles.
Armament: four 30 mm Aden guns in interchangeable belly pack; up to 1000 lb war load under wings.

Tracing its ancestry from the Hawker P.1040, Hawker's first venture in jet propulsion, via the P.1081 and P.1067, the Hunter first flew in prototype form (WB188) on 20 July 1951 with Squadron Leader Neville Duke, DSO, DFC at its controls. The first production Hunter (WT555) made its first flight in May 1953, and the first Hunter to reach an RAF first-line unit was WW599 which arrived on No. 43 Squadron on 29 July 1954. Initial F.1 Hunters experienced problems with engine surge when firing their guns at high altitude, but F.2 versions, powered by AS Sapphire engines and issued to squadrons from late 1954, soon cured this defect. F.4 Hunters provided increased range and reached squadrons from 1955. The more powerful F.6 version, the most-produced Hunter variant, was introduced in 1956, and had become standard for most squadrons by 1958. The F.6's superiority over preceding versions led to its adoption for aerobatics teams within the RAF; the most famous being No. 111 Squadron's 'Black Arrows' and, later, No. 92 Squadron's 'Blue Diamonds'. F.6s were gradually phased out of first-line, UK-based squadrons

Right: **Hawker Hunter GA11s of the RN's 'Blue Herons' aerobatic team.**

Below: two Hawker Hunter FGA9s formate on a pair of HS Harrier GR1s.

from 1962, but FGA9s had already entered service by 1960 and continued in use overseas until late 1971. The FR10 version was a camera-equipped fighter-reconnaissance variant. Nearly 2000 Hunters of all types were built (including several hundreds built abroad), while at least 700 were refurbished after service and resold as export orders for foreign air forces.

Hawker Sea Hawk

Type: naval fighter.
Crew: one.
Power plant: 5000 lb thrust Rolls-Royce Nene RN4, Mk 101 (Mks 1/4); 5200 lb thrust Rolls-Royce Nene Mk 103 (Mks 5 and 6).
Dimensions: span 39 ft; length 39 ft $10\frac{1}{2}$ in (Mk 3), 39 ft 8 in (Mk 6); height 8 ft 9 in (Mk 3), 8 ft 8 in (Mk 6).
Weights: empty 9190 lb (Mk 3), 9560 lb (Mk 6); loaded (maximum) 16,200 lb (Mk 6).
Performance: maximum speed 524 mph at 10,000 ft (Mk 6); service ceiling 44,500 ft (Mk 6).
Armament: four 20 mm cannon under nose; 1000 lb bombs, and 10 rockets beneath wings.

The Sea Hawk served with first-line FAA units from 1953–60, superseding the Sea Fury and Supermarine Attacker in operational squadrons. The first prototype flew in September 1948, and production aircraft first equipped No. 806 Squadron FAA in March 1953. Sea Hawks saw brief active service in the support role in operations during the Suez Crisis. A total of 536 Sea Hawks was produced, excluding 25 supplied to India and other foreign orders.

Right: **this Sea Hawk FGA6 is preserved in the markings of No. 806 Sqn FAA.**
Below: **Hawker Sea Hawk F1 WF159.**

Hawker-Siddeley Gnat

Type: jet trainer.
Crew: two (in tandem seats).
Power plant: 4230 lb thrust Bristol Siddeley Orpheus 100.
Dimensions: span 24 ft; length 31 ft 9 in; height 9 ft 7½ in.
Weights: empty 5140 lb; loaded (maximum) 8630 lb.
Performance: maximum speed 714 mph (F1), 636 mph (T1); initial rate of climb 9850 ft per min (T1); service ceiling 48,000 ft (T1); range (maximum) 1180 miles.
Armament: two 30 mm Aden guns and up to 1100 lb load of bombs or rockets (export F1 versions only).

Originally ordered by the RAF (six aircraft only) as lightweight jet fighters, Gnats were used only as trainers in service. The Gnat first entered RAF service in February 1962 and superseded the Vampire T.11 trainer. Intended as an advanced trainer – following pupil instruction on Jet Provosts – the Gnat formed the equipment of the 'Red Arrows' aerobatics team until replaced by the Hawker Siddeley Hawk. Capable of supersonic speeds in a shallow dive, the Gnat offered all the qualities of a first-line jet fighter to its pupil pilots. Total deliveries to the RAF amounted to 105 aircraft.

Below: **a HS (Folland) Gnat trainer prototype.**

Hawker-Siddeley Dominie

Type: advanced navigation trainer.
Crew: four.
Power plants: two 3310 lb thrust Bristol Siddeley Viper 520 turbojets.
Dimensions: span 47 ft; length 47 ft 5 in; height 16 ft 6 in.
Performance: maximum speed approximately 570 mph (Mach 0.78); cruising speed 472 mph at 25,000 ft; maximum range 1340 miles; service ceiling 40,000 ft.

Above: **a Hawker-Siddeley Dominie T1.**

A militarised version of the HS 125 executive transport, the Dominie T1 was designed specifically as a jet-powered navigation trainer. It was the RAF's first such purpose-built aircraft in that category, entering service in December 1965. The Dominie CC1 was used for passenger and internal communications duties and was later supplemented by CC2 versions; the latter having lengthened belly fairing to house Decca doppler equipment.

Hawker-Siddeley Harrier GR.3/Sea Harrier FRS.1

Type: V/S TOL ground attack; fighter; naval strike.
Crew: one.
Power plants: one 21,500 lb thrust Bristol Siddeley Pegasus 103 two-shaft vectored-thrust turbofan.
Dimensions: span 25 ft 3 in; length 45 ft 6 in, 47 ft 2 in (laser nose), 55 ft 9½ in (two-seat trainer); height 11 ft 3 in, 13 ft 8 in (two-seat trainer).
Weights: empty 12,200 lb (FR1); loaded 23,000 lb (maximum).
Performance: maximum speed 737 mph at low level (Mach 0.972); initial rate of climb 50,000 ft per min, service ceiling over 50,000 ft; tactical radius (without drop tanks) 260 miles.
Armament: two 30 mm Aden guns in under-belly pods; up to 5000 lb of bombs and other stores under wings and fuselage.

The world's first Vertical/Short Take Off and Landing (VSTOL) combat aircraft to enter first-line service, the Harrier has its origins in the Hawker P.1127, via the Kestrel designs. The first true production Harrier flew on 28 December 1967, and entered RAF service with No. 1 Squadron in July 1969. Though fully capable of air-to-air combat, the Harrier's prime role is as a ground attack platform for a wide variety of sophisticated weaponry. A navalised version, the Sea Harrier, has a redesigned nose section, including raised cockpit, and improved all-round performance envelope. Trials of the Sea Harrier commenced in 1977, with a view to squadron use by 1981 at the latest, and by late 1978 orders for at least 34 aircraft for the FAA had been placed.

Left: **Hawker-Siddeley Gnats of the 'Red Arrows' aerobatic team.**
Right: **a HS Harrier GR3 of No. 233 OCU.**
Below: **a Sea Harrier FRS1 of 800 Sqn FAA lands aboard HMS *Invincible* in 1980.**

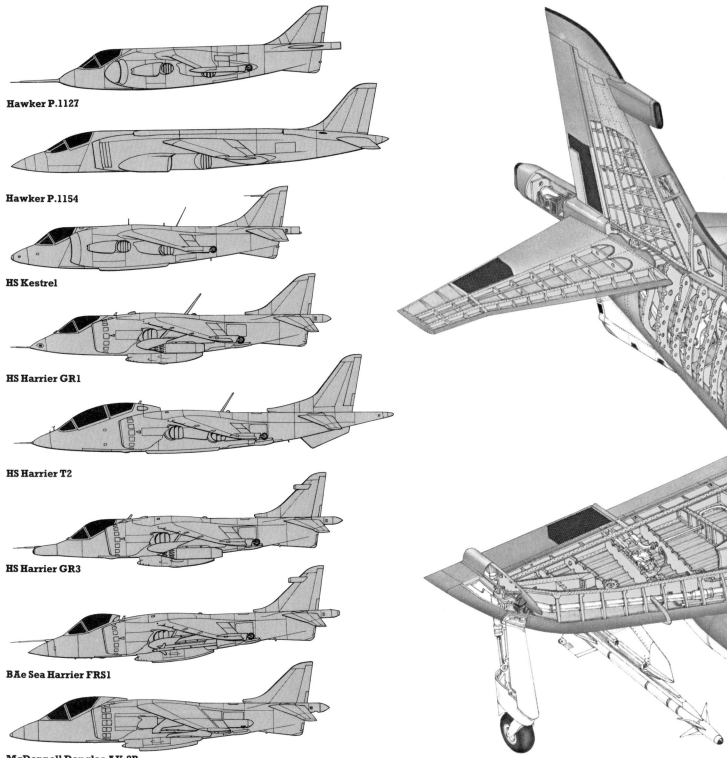

Hawker P.1127

Hawker P.1154

HS Kestrel

HS Harrier GR1

HS Harrier T2

HS Harrier GR3

BAe Sea Harrier FRS1

McDonnell Douglas AV-8B

Above: a Hawker-Siddeley Harrier T2
operational conversion trainer.
Left: a cutaway artwork shows the Fleet Air
Arm's Sea Harrier FRS1.

Left: Hawker-Siddeley Harrier GR1s of No. 20
Squadron based at Wildenrath, Germany, in
1971.

Hawker-Siddeley Hawk

Type: jet trainer.
Crew: two.
Power plant: 5340 lb thrust Rolls-Royce Turbomeca 151 Adour.
Dimensions: span 30 ft 10 in; length 39 ft 2½ in (over probe); height 13 ft 5 in.
Weights: empty 7450 lb; loaded 12,000 lb (trainer), 16,260 lb (attack version).
Performance: maximum speed 630 mph at low level (Mach 1.1 in shallow dive); initial rate of climb 6000 ft per min; service ceiling 50,000 ft; endurance 3 hrs (maximum).
Armament: provision for bomb/war load (external) of up to 5000 lb; two 30 mm cannon if required.

Designed to meet a rationalised multi-purpose jet trainer requirement, thereby replacing the Hunter T7, Gnat and Jet Provost in most roles, the Hawk production aircraft made its first test flight in August 1974. It entered RAF service in 1976. A total of 175 Hawks were initially ordered for the RAF, most of which had been delivered by late 1979. Provision for relatively heavy armament enables crews to undertake practical multi-role, tactical instruction, and in this guise the Hawk has already evoked strong interest from several foreign air forces who desire Hawks for operational equipment. Hawks now form the equipment of the RAF's premier aerobatics team, the famed 'Red Arrows'.

Left: a Hawker-Siddeley Hawk T1 of No. 1 Tactical Weapons Unit flies from Brawdy.
Above: a Hawker-Siddeley Nimrod MR1.
Below: a Nimrod MR1 of No. 203 Sqn flies over Grand Harbour, Valetta, Malta in 1977.

Hawker-Siddeley Nimrod

Type: maritime reconnaissance; anti-submarine warfare.
Crew: twelve.
Power plants: four 11,995 lb thrust Rolls-Royce Spey 250; four 12,160 lb thrust Rolls-Royce RB168 Spey 250.
Dimensions: span 114 ft 10 in; length 126 ft 9 in; height 29 ft 8½ in.
Weights: empty 92,000 lb; loaded 192,000 lb.
Performance: maximum speed 575 mph; range up to 5800 miles approximately; endurance approximately 12 hrs.
Armament: 50 ft bomb bay with provision for variety of anti-submarine stores, including homing torpedoes, AS bombs, nuclear weapons.

Evolved from the basic DH Comet, the Nimrod replaced the Shackleton as the RAF's prime maritime search and anti-submarine aircraft. The first prototype made its initial flight in May 1967, and the Nimrod began its RAF service in October 1969, a total of 46 MR1 versions being earmarked for RAF squadron use. Constant improvement in the Nimrod's already highly sophisticated electronic and radar equipment has followed the type's operational service; one result being the AEW3 variant due in service in 1982 to replace the aged Shackleton AEW aircraft in use as airborne early warning guardians of Western airspace. Originally dubbed 'The Pregnant Comet', the Nimrod is without doubt the fastest, quietest, most heavily-armed maritime hunter to serve with the RAF, with the bonus of superb flying qualities.

Above: a Pembroke of the Finnish AF.

Hunting Percival Pembroke

Type: communications; navigation or signals trainer; photo-reconnaissance.
Crew: two (plus eight passengers).
Power plants: two 560 hp Alvis Leonides 127.
Dimensions: span 64 ft 6 in; length 46 ft; height 16 ft.
Weights: empty 9589 lb; loaded 13,500 ft.
Performance: maximum speed 224 mph at 2000 ft; service ceiling 22,000 ft; range 1150 miles.

The Pembroke was accepted by the RAF as an urgent replacement for the ageing Avro Anson in the internal communications role, and it entered service in 1953. A total of 44 Pembroke C1s was delivered to the RAF. The Pembroke proved to be a huge improvement in passenger accommodation, performance, and adaptability over the Anson, and the type served overseas in Germany and the Middle East. In its trainer duties, the Pembroke could have dual pilot control easily installed and adequate instructional equipment fitted internally. In 1956, six Pembrokes fitted out for photo-reconnaissance duties were sent to No. 81 Squadron in Singapore. By 1975 No. 60 Squadron, based at Wildenrath, Germany, was the only squadron wholly equipped with Pembrokes.

Hunting Percival Provost

Type: elementary trainer.
Crew: two (side-by-side).
Power plant: 550 hp Alvis Leonides 126.
Dimensions: span 35 ft 2 in; length 28 ft 8 in; height 12 ft 2½ in.
Weights: empty 3350 lb; loaded 4400 lb.
Performance: maximum speed 200 mph at sea level; service ceiling 25,000 ft; endurance 4 hrs.

The Provost superseded the Percival Prentice as the RAF's basic trainer, entering RAF service at the Central Flying School in July 1953. It was then half the equipment for a planned piston and jet-engined training syllabus – the other half being the Vampire two-seat trainer – to enable qualified pupils to proceed to either type of

Right: **a Hunting Percival Provost T1 of the Central Flying School, September 1961.**

aircraft on squadrons. In the event the Jet Provost development meant that the Provost became the RAF's last piston-engined elementary trainer. A total of 387 Provosts was produced, and the type was retired in late 1969.

Lockheed Neptune

Type: maritime patrol; anti-submarine warfare.
Crew: seven.
Power plants: two 3250 hp Wright Turbo-Cyclone R-3350-30W.
Dimensions: span 104 ft; length 78 ft 3 in; height 28 ft 1 in.
Weights: empty 39,900 lb; loaded 72,000 lb.
Performance: maximum speed 353 mph at 9500 ft; service ceiling 26,000 ft; range 4200 miles.
Armament: two 0.50 in machine guns in nose turret (early versions); two 0.50 in machine guns in dorsal turret; two 20 mm cannon in tail turret; bomb load 8000 lb, or internal stowage for homing torpedo, sonic gear and other stores; provision for external rocket rails.

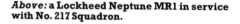

Above: **a Lockheed Neptune MR1 in service with No. 217 Squadron.**

The RAF equivalent of the USN's Lockheed P2V-5, the Neptune MR1 entered RAF service in January 1952 and remained in first-line use until 1957. It provided Coastal Command with a supplementary very long-range reconnaissance aircraft and submarine hunter until Shackletons became available in sufficient quantities to re-equip all such squadrons. Early deliveries to the RAF retained their nose turrets, but many of the later aircraft had this turret removed and replaced by a full Perspex cone-nose, and had a MAD (magnetic anomoly detector) tail 'sting' extension. Neptunes equipped just four squadrons of the RAF, Nos. 36, 203, 210 and 217 and 52 examples were delivered.

Lockheed Hercules

Type: medium-range tactical transport.
Crew: five.
Power plants: four 4910 hp Allison T56-A-15 turboprops.
Dimensions: span 132 ft 7¼ in; length 98 ft 9 in; height 38 ft 3½ in.
Weights: empty approximately 65,000 lb; loaded (maximum) 155,000 lb.
Performance: maximum speed 385 mph; maximum cruising speed 368 mph (normal, 340 mph); service ceiling 33,000 ft; maximum range 4780 miles.

The 'Herk' is the RAF's equivalent of the USAF's Lockheed C-130E, and the first example for the RAF arrived in Britain in December 1966. Intended as a replacement for the Argosy, the Hercules entered RAF squadron service in August 1967 with No. 36 Squadron. By mid-1968 five RAF squadrons were equipped with the type. Of the 61 aircraft in service by 1975, thirteen were withdrawn due to budget restrictions. In RAF use the Hercules can provide accommodation for 92 fully-kitted soldiers, or 64 paratroops, or in an ambulance role, 74 stretcher cases with attendant medical staff.

Below: a Lockheed Hercules C1 tactical transport aircraft serving with RAF Air Support Command. Thirty Hercules are to be modified by 'stretching' the fuselage by 13 ft 4 in, these aircraft being designated Hercules C3.

Above: a Phantom FG1 of No. 892 Sqn FAA
refuels from a Buccaneer of 809 Sqn.
Above right: a Phantom FG1 of 892 Sqn is
about to be catapulted from *Ark Royal.*
Right: a Phantom FGR2 of No. 17 Sqn, 1971.

McDonnell Douglas Phantom

Type: interceptor; ground attack.
Crew: two.
Power plants: two 12,250 lb thrust Rolls-Royce
Spey 202.
Dimensions: span 38 ft 4¾ in; length 58 ft 11 in;
height 16 ft 3 in.
Weights: empty 31,000 lb; loaded (maximum)
58,000 lb.
Performance: maximum speed 1386 mph at
40,000 ft (Mach 2.1); initial rate of climb
32,000 ft per min; service ceiling 60,000 ft;
maximum range 1750 miles.
Armament: one 20 mm Vulcan rotary cannon
below fuselage pod-mounted (FGR2); maximum
bomb load 11,000 lb (FGR2); 126 SNEB 68 mm
AP rockets (FGR2); four Sparrow air-to-air and
four Sidewinder air-to-air missiles.

Originally ordered for naval use, the Phantom
entered RAF operational use initially with No.
6 Squadron in May 1969. Two basic versions
are in RAF use; the FG1 air defence interceptor,
and the FGR2 originally used as a ground attack
and tactical reconnaissance variant, hence
different weaponry. The FG1 first entered
squadron use in September 1969 with No. 43
Squadron. By October 1969 a total of 168
Phantoms had been delivered to Britain. By
1974 Phantom FGR2s were being replaced in
their role by Sepecat Jaguars, reverting then
to pure air defence roles. In April 1968 the
Phantom also entered FAA service, as originally
envisaged, and, in small numbers, remained in
use for 10 years, these nval versions being
FG1s.

Below: a McDonnell Douglas Phantom FGR2 pictured during an armament training sortie.

Above: **NA Sabres of No. 112 Squadron.**

North American Sabre

Type: fighter.
Crew: one.
Power plant: 5200 lb thrust General Electric J-47GE-13.
Dimensions: span 37 ft 1 in; length 37 ft 6 in; height 14 ft 7 in.
Weights: empty 10,000 lb; loaded 16,500 lb.
Performance: maximum speed 670 mph; initial rate of climb 7500 ft per min; service ceiling 53,000 ft; maximum range 2350 miles.
Armament: six 0.50 in machine guns in forward fuselage.

The North American F-86 swept-wing Sabre jet was one of the most successful jet fighters of the post-1945 decade, becoming internationally publicised during the American part in the Korean War. The RAF ordered Sabres for its European responsibilities as an interim measure while awaiting new jet fighter designs from British manufacturers and the first batch was handed over to the RAF in January 1953. A total of 430 Sabres was eventually delivered to Britain, and the first in operational use were those of Nos. 3, 67 and 71 Squadrons from mid-1953. Eventually 12 squadrons, 10 of these in Germany, were equipped with Sabres, but by 1957 all had been replaced in Germany by Hawker Hunters.

Percival Prentice

Type: elementary trainer.
Crew: two.
Power plant: 251 hp DH Gipsy Queen 32.
Dimensions: span 46 ft; length 31 ft 3 in; height 12 ft 10½ in.
Weights: empty 3232 lb; loaded 4200 lb.
Performance: maximum speed 143 mph at 5000 ft; climb to 5000 ft, 6½ mins; service ceiling 18,000 ft; endurance 3 hrs 25 mins.

The Prentice superseded the DH Tiger Moth for basic flying training in the RAF, until it was in turn replaced by the piston-engined Provost. The prototype first flew in March 1946, and served at most RAF Flying Training Schools (FTS) from 1948 to 1953. Its side-by-side pilot seating was new to the RAF, and the roomy cabin offered good facilities for day or night

Right: **a Percival Prentice in service with No. 7 RFS at Desford, 1952.**

instruction, and for necessary equipment for training air signallers. After withdrawal from service, several were converted to represent Junkers Ju 87 Stuka divebombers for the epic film *Battle of Britain*.

Panavia Tornado

Type: multi-role combat.
Crew: two.
Power plants: two 15,000 lb thrust Turbo-Union RB199 Mk 101.
Dimensions: span 45 ft 7¼ in (full), 28 ft 2½ in (folded); length 54 ft 9½ in; height 18 ft 8½ in.
Weights: empty approximately 24,000 lb; loaded approximately 60,000 lb.
Performance: maximum speed at sea level approximately 910 mph (Mach 1.2); maximum speed at altitude at least 1320 mph (Mach 2); service ceiling 50,000 ft-plus; range (maximum) approximately 3000 miles, approximately 1000 miles (normal).
Armament: two 27 mm Mauser cannon in forward fuselage; external war load (variable) up to 18,000 lb.

Produced by a European consortium (British/German/Italian), the MRCA Tornado will be the key combat aircraft of the 1980s, with an order for 385 aircraft destined for RAF service. Its

Above: **Panavia Tornado prototype O6.**
Below right: **a Panavia Tornado prototype carries ECM jamming pods.**

purpose will be to replace Vulcans, Buccaneers and, to some extent, Jaguars in various roles; thereby near-rationalising much of the Western European air defence/offensive armoury. The Tornado F2 is a specialized air defence variant. It will, incidentally, be the first swing-wing design to enter RAF service. Training on the Tornado commenced at RAF Cottesmore in January 1981.

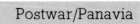

Above: Pioneer CC1s of No. 209 Sqn.
Left: Tornado prototype O3.

Scottish Aviation Pioneer CC.1

Type: communications; casualty evacuation.
Crew: two (five seats).
Power plant: 520 hp Alvis Leonides 502/4.
Dimensions: span 49 ft 9 in; length 34 ft 4 in; height 11 ft 4 in.
Weights: empty 3835 lb; loaded 5800 lb.
Performance: maximum speed 145 mph at 1500 ft; service ceiling 16,000 ft; range (maximum) 650 miles.

Designed specifically for RAF operations from small, unprepared airfields, the Pioneer entered service with the RAF in August 1953. Its short take-off run (75 yards) and landing run (66 yards) made it nearly ideal for operations in the Middle East and the Malayan jungle campaigns. First to be Pioneer-equipped was No. 267 Squadron at Kuala Lumpur, Malaya and Pioneers proved invaluable as 'jungle-hopper' communications, supply, and casualty evacuation vehicles. Only 40 aircraft were supplied to the RAF, but most remained on active service until 1968–69.

Below: **Twin Pioneers of No. 209 Sqn.**

Scottish Aviation Twin Pioneer

Type: communications; supply; casualty evacuation.
Crew: three (plus up to 16 passengers).
Power plants: two 550 hp Alvis Leonides 514; two 640 hp Alvis Leonides 531.
Dimensions: span 76 ft 6 in; length 45 ft 3 in; height 12 ft 3 in.
Weights: empty 10,200 lb; loaded 14,600 lb.
Performance: maximum speed 165 mph at 2000 ft; service ceiling 20,000 ft; range (16 passengers) 400 miles.

Known to its crews as the 'Two-Pin' or 'Twin-Pin', the Twin Pioneer exploited the outstanding STOL qualities of its single-engined stablemate. It entered RAF service with No. 78 Squadron at Khormaksar, Aden in 1958 and replaced the 'single' Pioneers used by that squadron since April 1956. Twin Pioneers saw active operations in Aden, Kuwait, Kenya and Borneo in subsequent years; while No. 78 Squadron at one period utilised their aircraft for 'sky-shout' propaganda sorties. The 'Twin-Pin' could operate effectively from a clear area only 900 feet by 100 feet and its slow-flying control characteristics proved a boon to its crews on operational sorties. The type was eventually retired from RAF first-line use by 1969.

Left: a Sepecat Jaguar GR1 of No. 226 OCU.

Sepecat Jaguar

Type: tactical strike fighter; advanced trainer.
Crew: one (GR1); two (T2).
Power plants: two 7305 lb thrust Rolls-Royce Turbomeca Adour 102; or two 8000 lb thrust RR Turbomeca Adour 804.
Dimensions: span 28 ft 6 in; length 50 ft 11 in, 53 ft 11 in (T2); height 16 ft 1½ in.
Weights: empty approximately 15,000 lb; loaded 34,000 lb (maximum).
Performance: maximum speed at high altitude 1055 mph (Mach 1.6); attack radius 500 miles approximately.
Armament: two 30 mm DEFA 553 guns forward; war load up to 10,000 lb.

Produced by an Anglo-French consortium, the Jaguar will serve alongside the Tornado for many years to come. Projected production for RAF use includes 165 single-seat attack versions (GR1) and 35 T2 two-seat advanced trainers. The first British-built Jaguar first flew in October 1969, and the RAF received its first examples in September 1973, at Lossiemouth. No. 54 Squadron became the first Jaguar squadron, receiving its first machine on 29 March 1974. Within two years eight RAF first-line squadrons were wholly equipped with the type. The Jaguar's prime combat role is ground attack, for which it is fitted with highly sophisticated navigation and strike equipment (NAVWASS) as well as a laser rangefinder. Supersonic at virtually all operational altitudes, the Jaguar can operate from relatively small, forward airfields with ease. Continuing development of more powerful power plants offers the possibility of even higher performance parameters in the future, while the existing optional multi-sensor pod fitment already achieves accurate reconnaissance capability.

Left: Short Belfast XR366 'Atlas' of No. 53 Squadron based at Brize Norton.
Right: a Supermarine Attacker serving with No. 800 Squadron FAA.
Below: an Attacker is catapulted from HMS *Eagle* past Skyraiders and Fireflies.

Short Belfast

Type: strategic freighter.
Crew: six.
Power plants: four 5730 hp Rolls-Royce Tyne RTy12 101 turboprops.
Dimensions: span 158 ft 10 in; length 136 ft 5 in; height 47 ft.
Weights: empty 125,000 lb; loaded 230,300 lb (maximum).
Performance: maximum crusing speed 358 mph; service ceiling 35,000 ft; maximum range 5200 miles.

Only 10 Belfasts were delivered to the RAF, all going to No. 53 Squadron which received its first example on 20 January 1966. On its introduction the Belfast was the largest aircraft ever to enter RAF service, and was then also the world's largest design to incorporate a fully operational automatic landing system. Its cargo hold could accommodate loads exceeding 11,000 cubic feet in bulk and up to 77,000 pounds in weight, or it could simply be converted to lift 150 troops and their immediate kit. The Belfast became yet another victim of defence budget cuts, and was phased out of RAF service by the close of 1976.

Supermarine Attacker

Type: naval fighter.
Crew: one.
Power plant: 5100 lb thrust Rolls-Royce Nene 3 (F1).
Dimensions: span 36 ft 11 in; length 37 ft 6 in; height 9 ft 11 in.
Weights: empty 8434 lb; loaded 11,500 lb.
Performance: maximum speed 590 mph at sea level (F1); climb to 30,000 ft, 6 mins 36 secs; service ceiling 45,000 ft; maximum range 1200 miles.
Armament: four 20 mm cannon in wings; maximum bomb load 2000 lb, or eight 3-inch rockets under wings.

Initially projected as an RAF fighter, the proto-type Attacker first flew in July 1946. In the event the RAF declined the type and the first navalised Attacker was air-tested in June 1947. The Attacker entered FAA service with No. 800 Squadron in August 1951, the first standard jet fighter in squadron service in FAA history. Attackers eventually equipped four FAA squadrons until being superseded by Sea Hawks and Sea Venoms by 1955, and continued in service with RNVR squadrons until 1957. The

FB2 development was powered by the slightly more powerful Nene 102 engine. Totals of 61 F1/FB1 versions and 84 FB2s were produced.

Supermarine Scimitar

Type: naval fighter.
Crew: one.
Power plants: two 11,250 lb thrust Rolls-Royce Avon 202 turbojets.
Dimensions: span 37 ft 2 in; length 55 ft 4 in; height 15 ft 3 in.
Weights: loaded 41,000 lb.
Performance: maximum speed 710 mph at 10,000 ft; maximum range approximately 1300 miles.
Armament: four 30 mm Aden guns in nose; or four Sidewinder homing missiles; or rocket pod for 2-inch rockets; or atomic bomb; or up to 2000 lb of bombs.

Superseding the Sea Hawk in FAA service, the Scimitar represented a huge advance in sophistication of design and potential strike capability; being the first swept-wing jet fighter in naval aviation use by the FAA, and that service's first design fitted for carriage of a nuclear weapon. Early examples entered FAA service trials in August 1957, and the initial first-line unit, No. 803 Squadron, was formed in June 1958. Three other first-line squadrons were equipped with Scimitars, and a total of 76 aircraft was built.

Right: a Supermarine Scimitar F1.
Below: the Supermarine Scimitar prototype during trials aboard HMS *Ark Royal*, 1956.

Above: **Vickers Valetta prototype VL249.**

Supermarine Swift

Type: jet fighter; fighter reconnaissance.
Crew: one.
Power plants: 7500 lb thrust Rolls-Royce Avon RA7 (F1); 7175 lb thrust Rolls-Royce Avon 114 turbojet (FR5).
Dimensions: span 32 ft 4 in; length 41 ft 5½ in (F1), 42 ft 3 in (FR5); height 12 ft 6 in (F1), 13 ft 6 in (FR5).
Performance: maximum speed 685 mph at sea level (FR5); initial rate of climb 12,000 ft per min; tactical radius (normal) 240 miles.
Armament: two 30 mm Aden guns (F1); four 30 mm Aden guns (F2).

Developed as an insurance against the possible failure of the Hawker Hunter, the Swift, in the event, proved to be a failure in its intended fighter role and, after disappointing service

Below: **a Swift F7 carries Fairey Fireflash air-to-air missiles.**

with No. 56 Squadron, the F1 version was withdrawn from first-line use by early 1955. With a lengthened nose section housing three cameras, the Swift was produced as a fighter-reconnaissance aircraft (FR5) and entered service with No. 2 Squadron in 1956, and later equipped No. 79 Squadron, both units being based in Germany then. These remained in service until mid-1961 before being replaced by Hunters. Twelve Swifts, modified further for development trials with guided missiles, titled F7, saw brief RAF service from 1957. A Swift F4, prototype of the final fighter version, established a world speed record of 737.7 mph on 25 September 1953.

Vickers Valetta

Type: medium-range transport; freighter; troop carrier.
Crew: four.
Power plants: two 2000 hp Bristol Hercules 230.
Dimensions: span 89 ft 3 in; length 62 ft 11 in; height 19 ft 7 in.
Weights: empty 24,980 lb; loaded 36,500 lb (maximum).
Performance: maximum speed 258 mph at 10,000 ft; initial rate of climb 1275 ft per min; service ceiling 21,500 ft; range 1460 miles.

In essence a militarised version of the Vickers Viking civil airliner, the Valetta pioneered the conception of the multi-role air transport. It could be converted simply to various major freight or passenger roles and was in effect a form of general workhorse of the type originally established by its forebears the Vernon, Victoria and Valentia overseas in the 1930s. The prototype Valetta first flew in June 1947, and the initial production aircraft in January 1948; in which latter year the type entered RAF first-line use. Valettas gave sterling service in Malaya and the Middle East, including the Suez Crisis operations, and in Britain was used equally as VIP transport, flying navigational classroom, radar instructional vehicle, mobile ambulance and in other maid-of-all-work tasks. Valettas remained in second-line use until 1967. Total production was 263 aircraft.

Vickers Valiant

Type: long-range bomber; air tanker.
Crew: five (seven in tanker role).
Power plants: four 10,000 lb thrust Rolls-Royce Avon RA28 (201).
Dimensions: span 114 ft 4 in; length 108 ft 3 in; height 32 ft 2 in.
Weights: empty 75,881 lb; loaded 140,000 lb (maximum).
Performance: maximum speed 567 mph at 30,000 ft; initial rate of climb 4000 ft per min; service ceiling 54,000 ft; maximum range 4500 miles (with underwing tanks).
Armament: one 10,000 lb bomb, or 21 1000 lb bombs.

The Valiant will always be remembered as being the first four-jet V-bomber to enter RAF squadron use. With the Vulcan and Victor it provided Britain with its nuclear deterrent V-bomber force of the 1950–60s. The prototype Valiant first flew on 18 May 1951, and the type entered first-line service with No. 138 Squadron in February 1955, the first of 10 squadrons eventually to fly Valiants. In 1956 Valiants participated in bombing operations during the Suez Crisis, and, on 11 October that year, Valiant WZ366 of No. 49 Squadron released an atomic bomb over Maralinga in South Australia, the first such trial. On 15 May 1957 another Valiant, XD818 of No. 49 Squadron, dropped the first British H-bomb, in the Pacific. Four types

Left: **Vickers Valiant B1 WZ365 was an early production aircraft.**
Right: **the Vickers Varsity prototype.**

of Valiant entered service: the B1 bomber, B(PR)1 bomber or PR, B(K)1 flight-refuelling receiver (bomber or tanker role), and the B.PR(K)1 flight-refuelling receiver (bomber, PR or tanker roles). A developed B2 version was designed for low-level penetration, though only the prototype (WJ954) was built. From early 1964 all V-bombers were allocated a low-level role, but at the end of January 1965 Valiants were officially withdrawn from first-line service due to metal fatigue in all main wing spars. The production total of 107 Valiants includes all prototypes.

Vickers Varsity

Type: multi-role advanced crew trainer.
Crew: two/four.
Power plants: two 1950 hp Bristol Hercules 264.
Dimensions: span 95 ft 7 in; length 67 ft 6 in; height 23 ft 11 in.
Weights: empty 27,040 lb; loaded 37,500 lb (maximum).
Performance: maximum speed 288 mph at 10,000 ft; initial rate of climb 1400 ft per min; service ceiling 28,700 ft; range 2650 miles.

The Varsity, with its patent similarity in configuration to the Valetta, was nevertheless virtually a fresh concept, in that it was designed as an updated crew trainer to replace such existing wartime – converted trainers as the Wellington T10 in the postwar RAF. Slightly larger than the Valetta, the Varsity had a tricycle undercarriage, and was even adaptable by means of a pannier attachment to the role of bombing instructor if required. The prototype Varsity first flew in July 1949, and first deliveries to the RAF were in October 1951. For more than 20 years Varsities provided excellent facilities for navigational and signals instruction to RAF crews; while individual Varsities became relatively common as RAF station hacks and general internal communications aircraft. Total Varsity production amounted to 163 aircraft.

Westland Wyvern S.4

Type: naval strike; torpedo bomber.
Crew: one.
Power plant: 4110 hp Armstrong Siddeley Python ASP3.
Dimensions: span 44 ft; length 42 ft 3 in; height 15 ft 9 in.
Weights: empty 15,608 lb; loaded 24,500 lb (maximum).
Performance: maximum speed 383 mph at sea level; service ceiling 28,000 ft; range 900 miles.
Armament: four 20 mm Hispano cannon in wings; maximum bomb load 3000 lb, or 16 3-inch rockets, or one torpedo.

The initial Wyvern torpedo/fighter first flew in December 1946 with a Rolls-Royce Eagle piston engine, though the design was intended to have turboprop power from its conception. Delays, and a succession of (mainly) unproven power plant installations prevented the Wyvern from entering FAA service until May 1953, from which date the type equipped four operational and several training squadrons. Wyverns of No. 830 Squadron FAA saw brief active use during the Suez Crisis operations, as ground attack aircraft, but the type was withdrawn from squadrons in mid 1958.

Left: **the RAF's three V-bomber designs fly in formation. The Vickers Valiant is in the foreground, with the Avro Vulcan leading the formation and the HP Victor in the background.**
Right: **a Westland Wyvern 4.**

Part Five
HELICO

OPTERS

Below: the Westland Belvedere was the RAF's first twin-engined helicopter to attain squadron service.

XG 452

Above: a Bristol Sycamore HR13 search and rescue helicopter.

Bristol Sycamore

Type: search and rescue; anti-submarine warfare.
Crew: two.
Power plant: 550 hp Alvis Leonides.
Dimensions: rotor diameter 48 ft 7 in; length 42 ft; height 14 ft 7 in.
Weights: empty 3810 lb; loaded 5600 lb.
Performance: maximum cruising speed 132 mph; cruise range 330 miles; endurance 3½ hrs.

The Sycamore prototype (Bristol Type 171 Mark 1) first flew in July 1947, and improved variants were first delivered to the RAF for operational use in April 1953 with No. 275 Squadron. As such the Sycamore was the first British-designed helicopter to see RAF service. Its initial role was as a search and rescue vehicle for Fighter Command, but in later years the type was used to good effect in Malaya; Cyprus, Kenya, Aden and Borneo on active operations. Seven squadrons were Sycamore-equipped eventually.

Westland Dragonfly

Type: casualty evacuation; communications.
Crew: one (plus three passengers).
Power plant: 520 or 550 hp Alvis Leonides 50.
Dimensions: rotor diameter 49 ft; length 40 ft 10 in; height 12 ft 11½ in.
Weights: empty 3800 lb; loaded 5500 lb.
Performance: maximum speed 95 mph at sea level; service ceiling 13,200 ft; maximum range 300 miles.

Though the first helicopter built in Britain to enter RAF use, the Dragonfly was of American design, built under licence by Westland. It was a British version of the Sikorsky S-51 for which Westland obtained manufacturing rights in December 1946. The initial RAF Dragonfly (WF308, an HC2) was delivered in 1950, and in April of that year several were sent to Malaya for jungle rescue and casualty evacuation duties. These Dragonflies and their crews later formed No. 194 Squadron, the RAF's first-ever helicopter squadron from February 1953. Dragonflies were ultimately replaced in first-line use from July 1956.

Westland Belvedere

Type: short-range tactical transport/freighter.
Crew: two (accommodation for 18 troops).
Power plants: two 1465 hp Napier Gazelle.
Dimensions: rotor diameter 48 ft 11 in; height 54 ft 4 in; height 17 ft.
Weights: empty 11,085 lb; loaded 19,000 lb (maximum).
Performance: maximum cruising speed 138 mph; cruise range 460 miles; service ceiling 17,000 ft.

Designed by the Bristol company as its Type 192, the Belvedere prototype first flew on 5 July 1958, and two examples were sent to the RAF Trials Unit at Odiham in October 1960. This latter unit became No. 66 Squadron in August 1961, by which date the Bristol Helicopter Dept had become part of Westland Aircraft Ltd. As the RAF's first twin-engined helicopter in squadron service, the Belvedere equipped only three squadrons (Nos. 26, 66 & 72), and operated in Aden and the Far East. In Aden several accidents led to the temporary dis-

Below: **Major-General RE Urquhart, General Officer Commanding Malaya District, climbs aboard a Westland Dragonfly helicopter at Kuala Lumpur.**

Above: **a Belvedere of No. 66 Sqn, Borneo.**

bandment of No. 26 Squadron, but with necessary modifications the type gave good service later in Borneo with No. 66 Squadron from 1962–66, and was finally retired from RAF use in early 1969.

Westland Whirlwind

Type: search and rescue; communications.
Crew: three (up to eight passengers).
Power plant: 600 hp Pratt & Whitney R-1340-40 (HAR2–8); 1050 shp Bristol Siddeley Gnome turbine (HC10).
Dimensions: rotor diameter 53 ft; length 41 ft 9 in; height 13 ft 3 in (15 ft 7½ in overall).
Performance: maximum speed 105 mph at sea level; service ceiling 10,000 ft (HC10); range 360 miles.
Armament: four Nord AS11 air-ground anti-tank missiles (HC10).

Below: **a Whirlwind HAR10 of No. 22 Sqn.**

The Whirlwind, a Westland-built version of the Sikorsky S-55, was piston-engined in its earliest models (HAR2-8), but the later HAR/HC10 variants were turbine-powered; many earlier marks being retrospectively modified to Mark 10 engine standards. The first Whirlwind HAR1 was delivered to the Royal Navy in 1953, while the first RAF version (HAR2) began deliveries in 1955. Improved HAR4s began service from 1955. Gnome-engined Mark 10s first entered RAF squadron use in late 1961, and later operated successfully in Borneo, Cyprus, Malaysia and the Middle East generally, apart from Britain and Germany.

Westland Wessex

Type: tactical transport; ground assault.
Crew: two/three (accommodation for 16 passengers).
Power plants: two coupled 1350 shp Bristol Siddeley Gnome turbines.
Dimensions: rotor diameter 56 ft; length 38 ft 6 in (folded); height overall 16 ft 2 in.
Weights: empty 8304 lb; loaded 13,500 lb.
Performance: maximum speed 132 mph at sea level; service ceiling 14,100 ft; maximum range 480 miles.
Armament: Nord anti-tank missiles (ground assault version).

Virtually a re-engined Sikorsky S-58 initially, the Wessex HAS1 entered first-line service with the Royal Navy with No. 815 Squadron in July 1961. From January 1967 Wessex HAS3s came into service. RAF HC2s, with coupled Gnome engines, entered service with No. 38

Below: **a Westland Whirlwind HAR2.**

Helicopters

Above: a Westland Wessex HC2 of No. 18 Squadron based at Gutersloh, Germany.
Left: Wessex HC2s of No. 28 Sqn, Hong Kong.
Right: a Sea King HAR3 of No. 202 Sqn.

Group in February 1964 and in the same year HU5s began service with the RN as commando-carrier assault transports. Two Mark 2s were converted to HCC Mark 4 VIP transports for use by the Queen's Flight. Wessex helicopters have served in virtually every part of the globe.

Westland Wasp

Type: multi-role.
Crew: two (accommodation for three passengers).
Power plant: 710 shp Rolls-Royce Nimbus 103/104 shaft-turbine.
Dimensions: rotor diameter 32 ft 3 in; length overall 40 ft 4 in; height 11 ft 8 in.
Weights: empty 3452 lb; loaded 5500 lb (maximum).
Performance: maximum speed 120 mph at sea level; maximum rate of climb 1440 ft per min (not vertical); service ceiling 12,400 ft; range 270 miles.
Armament: two homing torpedoes on external racks; or depth charges; or air-to-surface missiles.

Designed originally by Saunders-Roe, the Wasp became a Westland product after a merger. Intended for small-ship, platform-launch, short-range maritime roles for both defensive and offensive duties, the Wasp entered FAA service in 1963. More than 100 Scouts (the original title for the design) were built for Army use, with roughly the same number for RN use. They were gradually superseded by the Lynx from 1976–77, in RN units.

Left: a Whirlwind HAR9 of the FAA exercises with the Holyhead lifeboat.
Below: a Sea King HAS1 of No. 826 Sqn FAA.

Westland Sea King

Type: anti-submarine; strike; search and rescue.
Crew: four (accommodation for 25 troops).
Power plants: two 1500 shp Rolls-Royce Gnome H.1400 free-turbine; two 1795 shp Rolls-Royce Gnome H.1400-3 (HAS2).
Dimensions: rotor diameter 62 ft; length overall 72 ft 8 in; height 16 ft 10 in.
Weights: empty 15,474 ib; loaded 21,000 lb (maximum).
Performance: maximum speed 143 mph (HAS1); maximum rate of climb 1770 ft per min (not vertical); approved service ceiling 10,000 ft (HAS1); maximum range 937 miles.
Armament: four homing torpedoes on external racks; or nuclear depth charges.

A licence-built version of the Sikorsky S-61, the Sea King was first tested by the FAA in 1969, and entered operational use with the FAA when No. 824 Squadron was formed in February 1970. Initial RN orders were for 56 aircraft, followed by orders for a further 21 aircraft by 1976. Becoming the FAA's primary anti-submarine attack helicopter, the Sea King was further improved with the HAS2 version, with up-rated Gnome turbo-shaft engines and six-blade tail rotor. HAS2s entered FAA service in December 1976, while a rescue version is the HAR3. Its highly sensitive array of submarine detection equipment, including 'dunking' sonar and automatic flight control system means that the Sea King is one of the world's most effective submarine hunter/killers.

Westland-Aerospatiale Lynx

Type: multi-role.
Crew: two (accommodation for up to 10 troops).
Power plants: two 900 shp Rolls-Royce Gem 10001.
Dimensions: rotor diameter 42 ft; length overall 49 ft 9 in; height overall 12 ft.
Weights: empty 5225 lb; loaded 9250 lb (army), 9500 lb (navy).
Performance: maximum speed 207 mph; maximum rate of climb 2370 ft per min (not vertical); maximum range 860 miles.
Armament: two homing torpedoes; or depth charges; or external racks for air-to-surface missiles.

Another of the three helicopter designs agreed by the 1968 Anglo-French contract, the Lynx supersedes the Wasp as the FAA's standard submarine hunter/killer, and general purpose operational aircraft. The Lynx first entered FAA service in September 1976, and in its HAS2 form entered full operational service with No. 702 Squadron FAA in December 1977. Renowned for its agility, the Lynx is adaptable to a bewildering variety of maritime and land-based roles for both army and navy duties. Claimed to be the world's most manoeuvrable combat 'chopper', the Lynx can roll at over 100 degrees per second, and can fly backwards at 80 mph.

Westland-Aerospatiale Puma

Type: tactical assault; troop transport.
Crew: two (accommodation for 20 troops).
Power plants: two 1328 hp Turbomeca Turmo IIIC4.
Dimensions: rotor diameter 49 ft 2½ in; length overall 59 ft 6½ in; height 16 ft 10½ in.
Weights: empty 7795 lb; loaded 15,430 lb (maximum).
Performance: maximum speed 174 mph at sea level; maximum cruising speed 159 mph; maximum range 390 miles.

A development of the French SA300, the Puma resulted from a 1968 Anglo-French manufacturing agreement, and the first British-produced Puma HC1 made its initial flight in November 1970. The first Service example was delivered to the RAF in January 1971, and No. 33 Squadron became the first Puma squadron from September 1971. Capable of many roles, the Puma has served as freighter, trooper, ambulance, and ground-attack gun-ship – both by day and by night.

Below: a Westland-Aerospatiale Puma HC1 in service with No. 33 Squadron based at Odiham.

Part Six
AIRS

Below: **HMA C.10 pictured at RNAS Airship Station Longside, Aberdeen.**

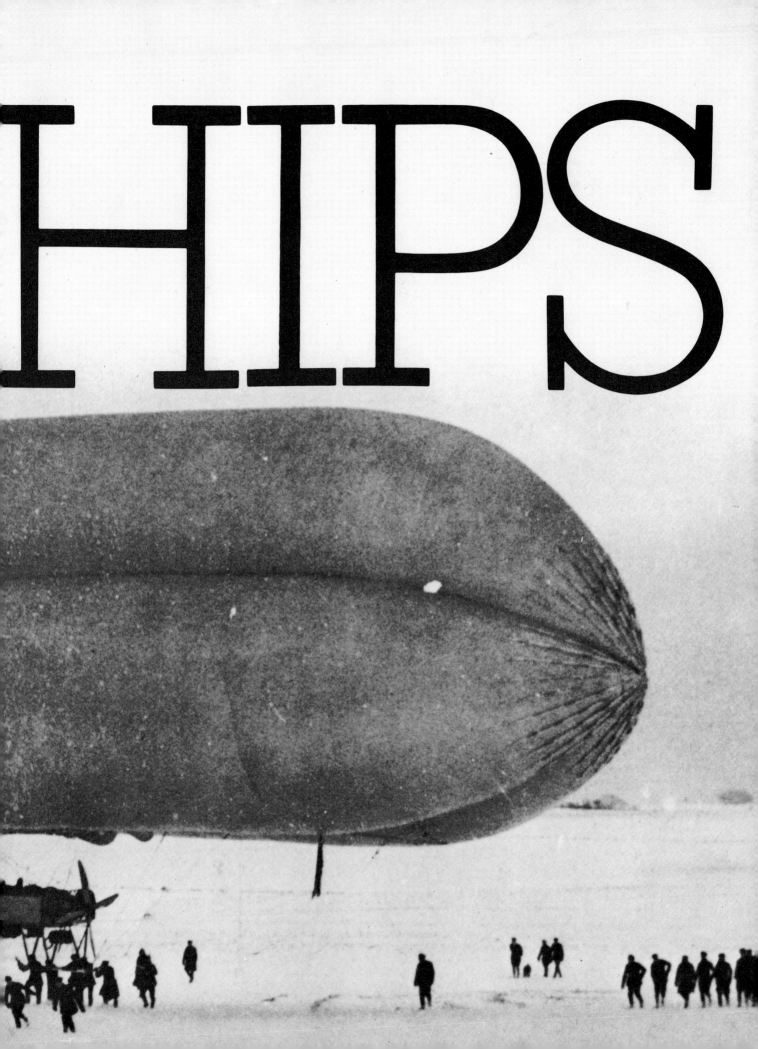

Above: Nulli Secundus II at Farnborough.

Nulli Secundus, Army Dirigible No. I.

Volume fully inflated: 55,000 cu ft.
Length: 122 ft.
Maximum diameter: 26 ft.
Engine: 50 hp Antoinette.
Crew: two or three.
Trial speed: 16 mph.

The first British Army airship, Dirigible No. 1, popularly titled *Nulli Secundus*, first flew on 10 September 1907. It was designed by Colonel J L B Templer, Superintendent of the Balloon Factory at Farnborough until May 1906. Flights in the following months proved successful, but *Nulli Secundus* suffered severe damage on 10 October 1907 due to unusually strong gusts of wind while picketed in the open. The airship was rebuilt and redesigned, emerging as *Nulli Secundus II*, which made its first flight on 24 July 1908, but made its ultimate flight on 15 August that year; again due to undue winds causing damage. Later officialdom attempted to retitle the *Nulli Secundus* as *Alpha* to make it the first in a series of Greek alphabetic names to be given to army dirigibles, but the retrospective name was seldom used in practice.

Baby, Army Dirigible II; later, Beta, Dirigible IIa.

Volume: 24,000 cu ft (*Baby*); 35,000 cu ft (*Beta*).
Length: 81 ft (*Baby*); 104 ft (*Beta*).
Maximum diameter: 24 ft (*Baby*); 35 ft (*Beta*).
Engines: two coupled 8 hp Buchet (*Baby*); one 25 hp REP (*Baby*); one 35 hp Green (*Baby*, Nov–Dec 1909), later *Beta*; one 45 hp Clerget (*Beta*).
Crew: two (*Baby*); three (*Beta* with Clerget).
Maximum speed: 35 mph (*Beta* with Clerget).

The Army's second dirigible, built by Farnborough, was the *Baby*, which first flew on 11 May 1909. It was fatally damaged on 21 December 1909 during a brief ascent. Reconstructed and lengthened, the airship re-emerged as the

Right: Beta in flight.

Beta I in May 1910, and in this form performed a long series of useful flights, including night sorties, and various trials with wireless equipment. In May 1912 *Beta* was on the strength of No. 1 Airship and Kite Squadron, Royal Flying Corps, and in August 1914 was on charge to the Royal Naval Air Service (RNAS), after all airships had been transferred from the Army to the Royal Navy. After an accident in 1911, the *Beta I* was given a fresh envelope, re-engined, and retitled *Beta II*.

HMA Gamma.

Volume: 72,000 cu ft; later, 101,000 cu ft.
Length: 160 ft.
Maximum diameter: 46 ft.
Engines: 80 hp Green (1911); two 45 hp Iris (1912).
Endurance: 8 hrs.
Crew: five.
Maximum speed: 32 mph.

His Majesty's Airship *Gamma* was launched in February 1910. Its envelope was of French Astra cotton and rubber, thereby progressing from the goldbeater's skin used in previous airships and balloons. In 1912 *Gamma* was reconstructed to give increased capacity, and its Green engine replaced by two Iris power plants, while two swivelling, four-bladed propellers were fitted. In the 1912 Army Man-

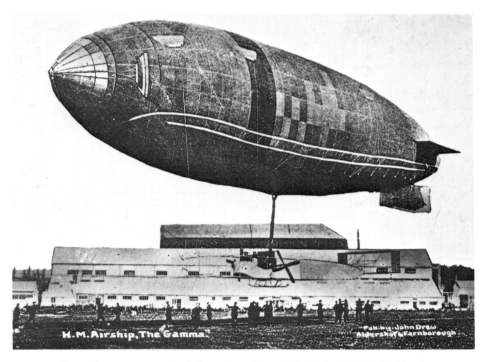

oeuvres *Gamma's* crew transmitted from its radio over a distance of 35 miles above East Anglia. In January 1914 HMA *Gamma* was transferred to the Royal Navy, but was broken up in late July 1914.

No.1 Rigid Naval Airship (Mayfly).

Volume fully inflated: 640,000 cu ft.
Length: 512 ft.
Diameter: 48 ft.
Useful lift: 3 tons.
Engines: two 180 hp Wolseley water-cooled.

On 14 August 1908 the Admiralty asked Vickers, Sons and Maxim Ltd to submit a price for construction of a rigid airship ('Zeppelin type') to the design of the Director of Naval Construction. The firm's tender was accepted on 7 May 1909. Admiralty specifications included the ability to maintain a speed of 40 knots for 24 hours, to reach a height of 1500 feet, to carry wireless telegraphy apparatus, with 'comfortable' accommodation for the crew. Construction commenced, and framework was of a new alloy,

Above: **His Majesty's Airship *Gamma* pictured at Farnborough.**

duralumin. The hull was twelve-sided, and the envelope was doped with aluminium dope on its top side, and yellow pigment on its lower sections. On the morning of 22 May 1911, the *Mayfly* (its unofficial soubriquet) was drawn out of her shed and for next three days was moored to a pontoon in Cavendish Dock, Barrow-in-Furness, successfully riding out gusty winds of more than 40 mph. Returned to her shed for modifications, the *Mayfly* was in the process of being transferred from her shed to a mooring raft on 24 September 1911 when a wind gust drove it against the shed door, breaking its back. The airship was a total loss, and the subsequent court of inquiry established that *Mayfly*'s hull was too weak, and recommended that the Royal Navy should have no more rigid airships built, a view which effectively banned such construction for the next two years.

Below: **His Majesty's Airship No. 1, 'Mayfly', pictured approaching its mooring post on Cavendish Dock, Barrow-in-Furness, on 22 May 1911.**

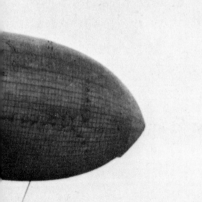

THE "DELTA".

THE "BETA".   THE NEW NAVAL AIRSHIP.

Above: HMA *Delta* pictured at Farnborough with *Beta* and *Baby* in the background.

HMA Delta.

Volume: 175,000 cu ft.
Length: 150 ft.
Maximum diameter: 29 ft.
Engines: two 55 hp White and Poppe.
Crew: up to six.
Maximum speed: 42 mph.

Design of HMA *Delta* commenced at the Balloon Factory in 1910, and it was originally intended to be a semi-rigid airship of 160,000 cubic feet capacity. It eventually emerged as a non-rigid airship of increased capacity in the autumn of 1912. *Delta* participated in the 1913 Army Manoeuvres and the Naval Review at Spithead in July 1914, being by then on charge of the Royal Navy. During 1913 *Delta*'s several flights included the sending of many wireless messages while airborne. In the same year Captain (later Air Commodore) E M Maitland, often referred to as the 'Father of British Airships', made a free-fall parachute descent from the *Delta*.

Sea Scout (SS).

Volume: 65,000 cu ft (SS).
Length: 144 ft (SS); 143 ft (SSZ).
Maximum diameter: 28 ft (SS); 39 ft (SSZ).
Engines: one 70 hp Renault and one 100 hp Green (AW Class).
Useful lift: 1236 lb (SS).
Armament: up to 450 lb of bombs; Lewis machine gun(s) if required.

The need for cheap, quickly-produced, non-rigid airships for coastal anti-submarine patrol work was appreciated early in the war by Admiral Fisher who, in the spring of 1915, ordered production of such aircraft. The Sea Scout (SS) was the first of three main classes of non-rigid airships to be built during the 1914–18 war, the others being Coastal and North Sea Classes. It was the SS type which first acquired

Above: the crew car of an SS-Z Class airship equipped with bombs, ballast bags, mooring ropes and Lewis machine gun.
Below: an SS Class 'blimp'.

The Coastal Class of non-rigid airship was an improved and larger version of the basic blimp configuration, being of tri-lobe envelope format. Coastal C1, the first of the type, was tested in May 1915, and the first C Class airship entered RNAS operational service in June 1916. Only 27 C-type airships were built, but these gave continuous and hardy service until the end of World War 1. The Coastal-Star (C*) was a slightly improved, larger variant which entered first-line service with the RNAS in January 1918. By the Armistice only 10 C* non-rigids had been completed, although about 20 had been ordered originally.

North Sea (NS).

Volume: 360,000 cu ft.
Length: 262 ft.
Maximum diameter: 58 ft 9 in.
Engines: two 250 hp Rolls-Royce Hawks, or two 240 hp Fiats.
Trial speed: 40 mph.
Armament: bomb load up to 800 lb; three 0.303 in Lewis machine guns.

The North Sea Class of non-rigid airship underwent initial trials in February 1917, and was in general the largest of the non-rigid airships made in 1914–18. Problems accrued from the complicated coupling of the engines to the propellers with the Hawk installation; hence the use of Fiat engines in some later craft. A total of 18 NS Class non-rigids were built for the Admiralty; though NS 17 and NS 18 were never actually delivered, and NS11 was sent to the USA. This latter NS established an endurance record for non-rigid airships in 1919 by remaining aloft for 101 hours during a 4000-mile cruise.

HMA R.9.

Volume: 890,000 cu ft.
Length: 526 ft.
Maximum diameter: 53 ft.
Engines: four 180 hp Wolseley Maybach (originally); two 180 hp Wolseley Maybach and one 250 hp Rolls-Royce.
Trial speed: 42.5 mph.

The rigid R.9 was initially ordered from the Vickers firm in June 1913, and the final contract signed in March 1914. Intended to be able to attain a speed of 45 mph, lift a minimum of five tons disposable weight, and have a ceiling of 2000 feet, the R.9 followed much of the basic design of the German Zeppelin Z.IV, plans of

Below: HMA R.9 uncovered to show the gas bags, Pulham, 30 May 1918.

the nickname 'Blimp' – thereafter applied generically to all non-rigids. Crew accommodation for an SS airship was basically an aircraft fuselage, duly modified to accommodate wireless set, armament, handling gear, and crew, suspended below the airship envelope. A wide variety of crew-car designs were used, partly depending on the airship maker involved; as indeed the types of engines fitted varied. The improved SS Zero offered slightly higher performance and improved crew-accommodation car. Total deliveries to the RNAS included at least 36 SS-types and 76 SSZ-types, apart from other variants.

Coastal (C).

Volume: 170,000 cu ft (C); 210,000 cu ft (C-Star).
Length: 195 ft 9 in (C); 210 ft (C-Star).
Maximum diameter: 39 ft 6 in (C); 44 ft (C-Star).
Engines: two 150 hp Sunbeam (early types); one 240 hp Fiat and one 100–110 hp Berliet (some later types).
Maximum speed: 50 mph.
Armament: bomb load up to 400 lb (C), 660 lb (C-Star); two 0.303 in Lewis machine guns.
Cruise endurance: approximately five hours.

which had been made available to Vickers. Changes in design and official policy delayed final construction, and R.9 only made its first flight on 27 November 1916. In April 1917 R.9 was accepted for service and served at Howden and Pulham airship stations, mainly on training duties and some experimental trials of airship handling and mooring equipment. R.9 was eventually broken up at Pulham in June 1918.

HMA R.23.

Volume: 940,000 cu ft.
Length: 535 ft.
Maximum diameter: 53 ft.
Engines: four 250 hp Rolls-Royce.
Trial speed: 54.5 mph.
Useful lift: 13,400 lb.

One of three rigid airships ordered from the Vickers firm in October 1915, all slightly bigger versions of the R.9, the R.23 was delivered for service at Pulham in September 1917. In 1918 the airship was used for experiments in carrying defensive fighters under its keel, two Sopwith 2F.1 Camels, but had proved virtually useless for normal aerial operations of war. It was dismantled at Pulham in September 1919.

Below: **His Majesty's Airship R.23.**

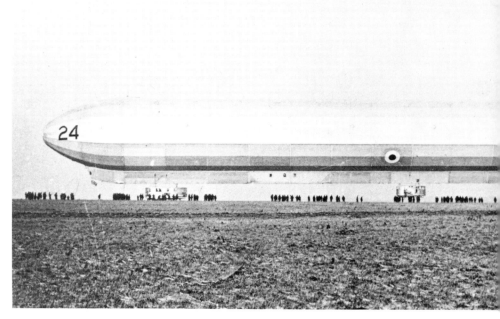

Left: **His Majesty's Airship R.24.**

HMA R.24.

Volume: 940,000 cu ft.
Length: 535 ft.
Maximum diameter: 53 ft.
Engines: four 250 hp Rolls-Royce.
Trial speed: 54.5 mph.
Useful lift: 13,800 lb.

Second of the '23 Class' trio of rigid airships ordered in October 1915, the R.24 was built by the Beardmore firm and eventually proved to be overweight and operationally unworthy. Delivered to East Fortune naval air station in October 1917, the R.24 was used for training purposes only, and was dismantled at Pulham in December 1919.

HMA R.25.

Volume: 940,000 cu ft.
Length: 535 ft.
Maximum diameter: 53 ft.
Engines: four 250 hp Rolls-Royce.
Useful lift: 13,000 lb.
Trial speed: 54.5 mph.

Third of the initial '23 Class' rigid airships ordered in 1915, the R.25 maintained the poor showing of its stablemates, her construction permitting fore and aft surging of the internal gas bags making it statically unstable. It was delivered to Howden in October 1917, relegated to training duties only, and was dismantled at Cranwell in September 1919.

Below: **His Majesty's Airship R.27.**
Bottom: **a rear threequarter view of His Majesty's Airship R.26.**

HMA R.26.

Volume: 940,000 cu ft.
Length: 535 ft.
Maximum diameter: 53 ft.
Engines: four 250 hp Rolls-Royce.
Trial speed: 54.5 mph.
Useful lift: 14,050 lb.

First of a second batch of '23 Class' rigid designs, the R.26 was ordered in January 1916, and emerged for service on 20 March 1918. It inherited the defects of its predecessors and was used mainly for training and experimental trials, though on 20 November 1918 it was airborne over Harwich to witness the surrender of German U-Boats. It was eventually scrapped in March 1919.

HMA R.27.

Volume: 990,600 cu ft.
Length: 539 ft.
Maximum diameter: 53 ft.
Engines: four 250 hp Rolls-Royce.
Trial speed: 56.5 mph.
Useful lift: 16,800 lb.

In June 1916 an improved '23 Class' design was approved, and four rigids of this new '23X Class' were to have been built. R.27, R.28, R.29, and R.30. In the event R.28 and R.30 were cancelled due to a later policy change. The first 23X type built was R.27, by Beardmore in Renfrew, which was commissioned on 29 June 1918 and based at Howden. Its career was relatively brief. After logging nearly 90 flying hours it was destroyed in flames on August 16 that year when burning petrol spilled on a nearby SS Class non-rigid spread to the R.27 and two other SS type blimps.

HMA R.29.

Volume: 990,600 cu ft.
Length: 539 ft.
Maximum diameter: 53 ft.
Engines: four 250 hp Rolls-Royce.
Trial speed: 56.5 mph.
Useful lift: 19,400 lb.

The other 23X Class rigid airship was the R.29, built by Armstrong Whitworth at Selby. It was commissioned on 20 June 1918 and based at East Fortune on the Firth of Forth. During 1918–19 the R.29 logged a total of nearly 438 flying hours; its longest patrol being 32 hours 20 minutes on 3/4 July 1918. R.29 was employed on anti-submarine patrols during the closing months of the war, and was part-credited officially with the ultimate destruction of *UB-115* on 29 September 1918. It remained at East Fortune after the Armistice, and was dismantled there on 24 October 1919.

HMA R.31.

Volume: 1,535,000 cu ft.
Length: 614 ft 8 in.
Maximum diameter: 64 ft 10 in.
Engines: six 250 hp Rolls-Royce.
Trial speed: 70 mph.
Useful lift: 37,000 lb.

R.31 and its stablemate R.32 were both built by Short Brothers at Cardington, and both marked a progressive step in design. They were designed with wooden girder hulls, inspired by the German Schütte-Lanz airships, and both were initially ordered in May 1916. R.31 made its first flight in August 1918, and was formally commissioned on 6 November 1918, on which date it started a flight to East Fortune. En route wooden girders started breaking and the airship made an emergency landing at Howden. After being housed in the same burned hangar in which R.27 had been destroyed, R.31 was later examined and found to be rotting from moisture damage. Accordingly, the airship was dismantled in February 1919; having a total flight time of only 8 hours 55 minutes.

HMA R.32.

Volume: 1,535,000 cu ft.
Length: 614 ft 8 in.
Maximum diameter: 64 ft 10 in.
Engines: five 250 hp Rolls-Royce.
Trial speed: 65 mph.
Useful lift: 37,000 lb.

R.32 was not commissioned until 3 September 1919, and was used mainly for tests at the National Physical Laboratory, before being loaned in 1920–21 for training the crew of the R.38, then under construction for eventual sale to the USA. In April 1921 the airship was then subjected to over-pressurisation of one of its gas cells in a test-to-destruction, and the wreck dismantled. Total flight time amounted to 212 hours 45 minutes, apart from time logged in American hands.

HMA R.33.

Volume: 1,950,000 cu ft.
Length: 643 ft.
Maximum diameter: 78 ft 9 in.
Engines: five 250 hp Sunbeam Maori.
Trial speed: 60 mph.
Useful lift: 58,100 lb.

Built by Armstrong Whitworth, the R.33 was an overt copy of the German Zeppelin L.33 which had force-landed in England in September 1916. Production was authorised in November 1916, and the R.33 first flew on 6 March 1919. Based at Howden, R.33 was sent to Pulham in

Above: **His Majesty's Airship R.33.**

1921 for mooring mast experimental trials, but ceased flying in June that year. Refurbished at Cardington, it was again flown to Pulham in April 1925, but two weeks later, on 16 April, R.33 tore away from its mooring mast in a gale, damaging the nose structure, and was flown in that condition for nearly 30 hours – stern-first to Holland – before eventually regaining its Pulham base next day. Repairs lasted until August, and further flights in 1926 included experiments with carriage and release of two Gloster Grebe fighters from under its hull. Evidence of fatigue in the metal frame resulted in R.33 being grounded, and it was eventually broken up in May 1928.

HMA R.34.

Volume: 1,950,000 cu ft.
Length: 643 ft.
Maximum diameter: 78 ft 9 in.
Engines: five 250 hp Sunbeam Maori.
Trial speed: 60 mph.
Useful lift: 58,100 lb.

Another copy of the German Zeppelin L.33, the R.34's construction commenced in December 1917, and first flight was on 14 March 1919. On 2 July 1919 the R.34 set out to fly the Atlantic to New York; the first-ever east-to-west aerial crossing of the Atlantic. This first leg of the crossing was accomplished in 108 hours 12 minutes. On 10 July R.34 set out again, this time

from New York, for the return flight to England, arriving at Pulham in the early hours of 13 July; thus establishing the first double crossing by air of the Atlantic. R.34 did not fly again until February 1920, and then only briefly, but on 27 January 1921, while on a training flight from Howden, it struck a hill, causing serious damage in the forward section. It was then dismantled.

HMA R.38 (ZR2).

Volume: 2,274,000 cu ft.
Length: 699 ft.
Maximum diameter: 85 ft 6 in.
Engines: six 350 hp Sunbeam Cossack.
Trial speed: 71 mph.
Useful lift: 102,144 lb.

Originally ordered in September 1918, R.38 was intended to be a heavily-armed coastal patrol rigid airship. Projected armament included four 520 pound bombs, eight 230 pound bombs, a one-pounder gun on a forward top platform, and a total of 12 machine guns (presumably Lewis or Vickers 0.303-in) paired in various locations. Performance requirements included ability to patrol the North Sea for six days up to 300 miles from base. Construction started (apparently) in February 1919, but official policy delayed, then nearly cancelled its completion. Then in October 1919 it was agreed to sell R.38 (completed) to the USA for £300,000, in whose service R.38 would be retitled ZR2. R.38 flew for the first time on 23 June 1821, and in the next eight weeks flew several trial flights, during which a number of

Left: **HMA R.34 made the first double crossing of the Atlantic by air.**
Below: **His Majesty's Airship R.80.**

defects became apparent. On 23 August 1921, R.38 left Howden with 50 men on board for a ferry trip to Pulham, where it was to be loaded for the trans-Atlantic delivery flight to the USA. Remaining in the air that night, owing to fog at Pulham, R.38 next day was over Hull at some 2500 feet when it was put through a series of over-violent control moves, at full engine power. The airship broke into two, and both sections fell into the river Humber, exploding on impact. Only five men survived.

HMA R.80.

Volume: 1,200,000 cu ft.
Length: 535 ft.
Maximum diameter: 70 ft.
Engines: four 230 hp Wolseley Maybach.
Trial speed: 60 mph.
Useful lift: 39,900 lb.

In November 1917 the Vickers firm was given permission by the Admiralty to proceed with an airship design of their own. The firm's chief airship designer then was Barnes Wallis who, with a virtual free hand, conceived and designed the perfect streamlined shape of a rigid airship destined to become R.80. Construction began late in 1917, but its first flight was not until 19 July 1920, during which excess gas pressure caused some damage. In January 1921 the R.80 was officially commissioned by the RAF, and in the following month flown to Howden – ostensibly for scrapping. A reprieve came when R.80 was made available as a training vehicle for American airship crews at Howden, but on 20 September 1921 the airship made its last flight, to Pulham where it was laid up after logging a total flying time of 73 hours. In 1925, still at Pulham, R.80 was dismantled.

Index

Page numbers in italics refer to illustrations.

Page numbers in bold type indicate major references.

ABC Dragonfly engine 56
Albacore (Fairey) **115**, *115*, 116
Albemarle (AW) 93, **93–4**
Alcock, J and Brown, AW 84
Aldershot (Avro) 72
Allison engines 107, 131, 189
Alpha (*Nulli Secundus*) 214
Alvis Leonides engines 188, 197, 206
Andover (Avro) *151*, **151–2**
Anson (Avro), 21, **62**, *62*, *63*, 188
Antoinette engines 10, 214
AR1 engine 36
Argosy (AW-HS) **148**, *148*, 189
Armstrong Siddeley engines
    Cheetah 62, 92
    Double Mamba 168
    Jaguar 60, 68, 71
    Lynx 61
    Panther 69
    Python 203
    Sapphire 170, 177
    Serval 81
    Tiger 65, 92
    Viper 156
Atlas (AW) **60**, *60*, 79
Attacker (Supermarine) 23, 180, *199*, **199–200**
Auster (British Taylorcraft)
    I–V *103*, **103**, **105**, 149
    AOP6–9 *148*, **149**
Australian Flying Corps 56
Avenger (Grumman) **119**, *119*

Baby (Sopwith) 40, 48, **49**
Baby (airship) 10, 11, **214–15**
Baffin (Blackburn) 63, **64**, *64*
Ball, Albert 35, 44, 45
Balloon School 10, 11
ballons 10, 13
Baltimore (Martin) 128, *128*, **129**
Barker, Major WG 56
Barnwell, F 35
Barracuda (Fairey) **116**, *116*
Bat Boat (Sopwith) 14
Battle (Fairey) 21, **113**, *113*
BE2 series 13, 16, **34**, *34*, 45
Beardmore engines 32, 40, 43, 44
Beauchamp-Proctor, A 45
Beaufighter (Bristol) 22, 100, *102*, **102–3**, *103*
Beaufort (Bristol) **101–2**, *102*
Beaumont, Capt F 10
Belfast (Short) 26, *198*, **199**
Belvedere (Westland) *205*, **206–7**, *206–7*
Berliet engines 217
Beverley (Blackburn) **157**, *157*
BHP engines 37, 38, 39
Bishop, WA 44
Bisley (Bristol) 101
Bison (Avro) **61**, *61*, 63
Black Arrows team 177
Blackburn engines 103, 149
Blackburn (Blackburn) **63**, *63*
Blenheim (Bristol) 20, 21, 79
    I 21, *100*, **100–101**
    IV **101**, *101*
    V *100*, **101**
Blue Diamonds team 177
Blue Herons team 177
Bolingbroke (Bristol) 101
Boston (Douglas) **111**, *111*
Botha (Blackburn) **99**, *99*
BR engines 56, 80
Brigand (Bristol) **159**, *159*
Bristol engines
    Centaurus 88, 127, 143, 157, 159
    Hercules 88
    Hercules II, IV 133, 134

Hercules III 102, 142
Hercules VI 95, 96, 102, 142
Hercules X 102
Hercules XI 93, 102, 142
Hercules XVI 95, 96, 102, 134, 142
Hercules XVII 102, 142
Hercules 106 170
Hercules 230 201
Hercules 264 203
Jupiter 65, 66, 71, 73, 74, 89
Mercury VIS2 71
Mercury VIII 100, 117
Mercury IX 99, 117
Mercury XII 143
Mercury XV 101
Mercury XX 129, 131, 143
Mercury XXX 131, 143
Mercury 23/30 101
Olympus 152
Pegasus IM3 64, 88
Pegasus IIL3 85
Pegasus IIM3 65, 88, 113
Pegasus II–VI 135
Pegasus III, IX 65
Pegasus X 81, 83
Pegasus XVIII 133, 142
Pegasus XX 73, 88
Pegasus XXII 133
Pegasus XXX 113
Perseus VIII 88
Perseus X 99
Perseus XII 99, 143
Taurus 101, 115
Bristol Siddeley engines
    BS605 rocket engine 157
    Gnome Turbine 207
    Olympus 152
    Orpheus 181
    Pegasus 103, 183
    Proteus 160
    Sapphire 200 173
    Viper 102, 201 156
    Viper 520 turbojet 181
Britannia (Bristol) 26, **160**, *160*
Buccaneer (Blackburn) 29, *157*, *158–9*, **159**, *190*, 194
Buchet engines 214
Bulldog (Bristol) **66**, *66*, 71

Camel (Sopwith) *13*, 16, 18, 50, **51**, *51–3*, **53**, 56, 218
Camm, Sydney 78
Campania (Fairey) *39*, **39–40**
Campbell, F/O K 102
Canberra (EE) 26, **165**, *165–7*, **167**
Catalina (Consolidated) 22, 83, **105**, *105*
Central Flying School 12, 32, 61, 92, *92*, 120, *169*, 188, *188*
Chipmunk (DH) **161**, *161*
Chitral (HP) 73
Churchill, Winston 11
Clark-Hall, R 14
Clerget engines 35, 36, 40, 41, 49, 56, 214
Clive (HP) 73
Cloud (Saro) **81**, *81*
Coastal (airship) **217**
Cody, Samuel Franklin 10
Collishaw, Ray 51
Comet (DH) 26, **161**, *161*, *162*, 187
Corsair (Chance-Vought) *104*, **105**
Cuckoo (Sopwith) **56**, *56*
Culley, Lt SD 53
Curtiss, Glenn 14, 42
Curtiss engines 38, 68

Dakota (Douglas) *9*, **112–13**, *113*
Dallas, R 44
Dart (Blackburn) **63**, *63*
Defence, Ministry of 28
    White Papers on 26
Defiant (BP) 99, **99–100**, *100*
de Havilland, Geoffrey 13, 34, 37, 38
de Havilland engines
    Ghost 162, 164
    Gipsy Major 107, 129, 149, 161
    Gipsy Queen 194
    Goblin 162

Gyron Junior 157
Demon (Hawker) **78**
Dirigible No. I 10, 214
Dirigibles II, IIa 11, *214*, **214–15**
Dolphin (Sopwith) 54, *55*
Dominie (HS) **181**, *181*
Dragonfly (Westland) **206**, *206*
Duke, Sqn Ldr Neville 177
Dunne, Lt JW 10

E.28/39 (Gloster) 22
Elephant (Martinsyde) *43*, **43–4**
Esmonde, Lt Cdr E 114

F-111K (General Dynamics) 28
F2A/F2B (Bristol) 16, *31*, **36**, *36*, 69, 89
Fawn (Fairey) **67–8**, *68*
FB5, FB9 (Vickers) **56–7**
Fe2, Fe2a 40
Fe2b/2d 40, *41*
Fe8 16, **41**, *41*
Felixstowe F2A **41–2**, *42*
Felixstowe F3 70, 83
Felixstowe F5 **70**, *70*, 83
Fiat engines 38, 217
Firebrand (Blackburn) **157**, *157*
Firefly I (Fairey) 23, **116**, *116*, 167
Firefly FR.4-AS.6/7 (Fairey) **167**, *167*, *199*
FK3, FK8 (AW) **32**, *32*
Fleet Air Arm 23, 99, 105, 114, 115, 116, 119, 135, 157, 161–8 *passim*, 176, 180, 183, 190, 199, 200, 203, 209
    408 Flt 77
    423 Flt *61*
    702 Sqn 209
    800 Sqn 23, 99, *183*, 199, *199*
    801 Sqn 157, 161
    803 Sqn 99, 200
    804 Sqn 119
    806 Sqn 116, 180, *180*
    807 Sqn 176
    809 Sqn *158–9*
    810 Sqn 167
    811 Sqn *64*
    813 Sqn 157
    815 Sqn 207
    824 Sqn 209
    825 Sqn 114, 167
    826 Sqn 115, 168, *209*
    827 Sqn *115*
    830 Sqn 203
    832 Sqn 119
    849 Sqn 168
    892 Sqn 165, *190*
Flycatcher (Fairey) **68**, *68*, 69
Fokker *Eindecker* 40
Fortress (Boeing) **99**, *99*
Fox (Fairey) 20, **68–9**, *69*
Fulmar (Fairey) 23, **116**, *116*
Fury (Hawker) 19, **75**, *76–7*, *77*

Galloway Adriatic engines 43
Gamecock (Gloster) **71**, *71*, 74
Gamma, airship 11
Gannet (Fairey) **168**, *168*
Gannet (Grumman) 120
Gauntlet (Gloster) **71**, *71–2*, 117
General Electric engines 194
Gladiator (Gloster) 21, 77, **117**, *117*, *118*
Gnat (HS) **181**, *181*, *182*, 187
Gnome engines 32, 35, 48, 49
Gnome Monosoupape engines 32, 37, 41, 49, 56
Gordon (Fairey) 69, **69–70**
Grebe (Gloster) **71**, *71*, 220
Green engines 214, 215, 216
Grover, Capt GE 10

Halifax (HP) 20, 21, *120*, **121**, *121*, *122*, **123**
Hamble Baby (Fairey) **40**, *40*
Hampden (HP) 20, 21, **120–21**, *121*
Hardy (Hawker) **79**, *79*
Harrier (HS) 29, *179*, **183**, *183–5*
Harrow (HP) **73–4**
Hart (Hawker) *19*, 74, **74–5**, *75*, 78, *78*, 79, 89

Harvard (NA) **130**, *131*
Hastings (HP) **170**, *172*, *172*
Havoc (Douglas) *111*, 111, **111–12**
Hawk (HS) 181, *186*, **187**
Hawker, Capt LG 35
Hawker-Siddeley Group 7, 148, 151
Hector (Hawker) **79–80**
Hellcat (Grumman) **120**, *120*
Hendon (Fairey) **70**, *70*
Hercules (Lockheed) 28, **189**, *189*
Hereford (HP) 121
Heyford (HP) **73**
Hinaidi (HP) **73**
Hind (Hawker) 75
Hispano-Suiza engines 34, 36, 44, 45, 54, 56
HMA No. 1 11, **215**, *215*
HMA C.10 *213*, **217**
HMA *Delta* **216**
HMA *Gamma* **215**
HMA R.9 *217*, **217–18**
HMA R.23 **218**, *218*
HMA R.24 **219**, *219*
HMA R.25 **219**
HMA R.26, R.27 **219**, *219*
HMA R.29 *16*, **220**
HMA R.31, R.32 **220**
HMA R.33 71, **220**, *220*
HMA R.34 **220–21**, *221*
HMA R.38 **221**
HMA R.80 **221**, *221*
Hornet (DH) **160–61**, *161*
Horsley (Hawker) **74**, *74*, 88
HS 681 28
Hudson (Lockheed) 21, **127**, *127*
Hunter (Hawker) 7, 26, *147*, 154, **177**, *177*, *179*, **180**, 187, 194, 201
Hurricane (Hawker) 20, 21, 22, 77, 109, **123**, *123–5*, **125**
Hyderabad (HP) **72**, 73

Immelmann, Max 40
Indian Air Force 89, 144
Insall, Lt GSM 57
Iris (Blackburn) 64, **64–5**
Iris engines 215

Jaguar (SEPECAT) 29, 190, 194, *198*, **199**
Javelin (Gloster) 26, *27*, 165, *166*, **170**, *170*
Jet Provost (BAC) *156*, **156–7**, 181, 187

Kangaroo (Blackburn) **35**, *35*
Kestrel (Miles) 131
Kestrel (HS) **183**, *184*
Kitchener, Lord 11
Kittyhawk (Curtiss) **107**, *107*

Lancaster (Avro) 20, 22, 23, 26, **95–6**, *95–7*, 109, 134, 149, 150, 151
Lee, Capt HP 10
Le Rhône engines 32, 35, 36, 37, 38, 41, 44, 49
Lerwick (Saro) **132**, *133*
Liberator (Consolidated) 22, **106**, *106*
Liberty engines 36, 37, 38, 42, 43, 66, 67, 70
Lightning (BAC) 26, **154**, *154–5*, *175*
Lincoln (Avro) 26, **150**, *150*, 151, 159
London II (Saro) **81–2**, *82*
Lycoming engines 103
Lynx (Avro) 32, **61**, *61*
Lynx (Westland-Aerospatiale) **209**
Lynx engines 61
Lysander (Westland) **143–4**, *144–5*

McCudden, J 45
Mackenzie, Lt RHL 10
Macmillan, Norman 69
Magister (Miles) **129**, *129*
Maitland, Capt EM 216
Manchester (Avro) 20, 21, 94, **94–5**, 96

Mannock, E 44, 45
Marauder (Martin) **129**, *129*
Martinet (Miles) **131**, *131*
Martlet (Grumman) **119**, *119*
Maryland (Martin) **128**, *128*
Master (Miles) *21*, **129**, *129*, **131**
Mayfly, airship 11, **215**, *215*
Meteor I, F.3 (Gloster) *22*, 23, **117**, **119**, *119*, 169
Meteor 8 (Gloster) 148, 169
Meteor F.4-PR.10 (Gloster) *169*, **169–70**, *170–71*
Meteor NF.11–14 (AW) *148*, **148–9**
Mitchell, Reginald J 22, 83, 136
Mitchell (NA) **131–2**, *132*
Mohawk (Curtiss) **106–7**, *107*, 107
Moorhouse, Lt WB Rhodes 34
Mosquito (DH) 22, *108*, **109**, *110*, **111**, 112, 132, 161
Mottershead, Flt Sgt T 40
Mustang (NA) **131**, *131*

Napier engines
Dagger 79, 131·
Gazelle 206
Lion 38, 43, 63, 66, 69
Lion II 61, 63, 67, 72, 84
Lion V 63, 67, 82, 84
Lion XI 85
Rapier 115
Sabre 126, 127, 157
Neptune (Lockheed) **188**, *188*
Nimrod (Hawker) *77*, **77–8**, 78
Nimrod (HS) 26, 29, **187**, *187*
Norn (Hawker) 77
North Sea, airship **217**
NT2B (Norman Thompson) **44**, *44*
Nulli Secundus 10–11, **214**, *214*

1½ Strutter (Sopwith) 16, *46*, **49**, *49*
Osprey (Hawker) **78**, *78*
Overstrand (BP) **65–6**, *66*
Oxford (Airspeed) **92**, *92*

P.1154 28
Packard Merlin engines 95, 96, 131, 136, 150
Panther (Parnall) **80–81**, *81*
Pembroke (Hunting Percival) **188**, *188*
Perth (Blackburn) *17*, **64–5**
Petter, WEW 154
Phantom (McDonnell Douglas) 28, 29, **190**, *190–93*
Pintail (Fairey) 68
Pioneer (Scottish Aviation) **197**, *197*
Porte, Sqn Cdr 42
Pratt & Whitney engines
Double Wasp R-2800 105, 119, 127, 129, 132, 143
Twin Wasp R-1830 112, 119, 133, 142
Twin Wasp S3C4G 101, 105, 111, 119, 127, 128
Wasp R-1340 131, 207
Wasp Junior 62, 92, 129
Prentice (Percival) 188, **194**, *194*
Provost (Hunting Percival) 156, **188**, *188*, 194
Puma (Westland-Aerospatiale) **209**, *211*
Pup (Sopwith) 16, *49*, **49–50**, 50, 53

RAF engines 32, 34, 38, 40, 44, 45
RE1 and series 13
RE5 44
RE7 **44–5**, *45*
RE8 16, **45**, *45*
Red Arrows team 181, *182*, 187
Rees, Major Lionel 37
Renault engines 34, 38, 46, 216
Ripon (Blackburn) **63**, 64
Roc (Blackburn) **99**, *99*
Rolls-Royce engines
250hp 218, 219, 220
Avon 154, 161, 165, 200, 201
Buzzard 64
Condor 64, 74
Conway 156, 173

Dart 148, 151
Derwent 117, 148, 169
Eagle 203
Eagle III 37, 46, 47
Eagle V 39
Eagle VI 37
Eagle VII 37, 70
Eagle VIII 37, 39, 41, 42, 43, 66, 67, 84
Falcon 35, 36, 44, 56
Gem, Gnome 209
Griffon 116, 136, 151, 167
Hawk 217
Kestrel *21*, 79
Kestrel I 74, 78, 79
Kestrel II 75, 77, 78
Kestrel III 73, 83
Kestrel V 77, 78, 79
Kestrel VI 70, 73, 75
Kestrel VIII, IX 82
Kestrel X 79
Kestrel XXX 129
Mark II 42, 57
Mark III 40, 44
Mark IV 39, 42
Merlin I, II 113, 123, 136
Merlin III 99, 113, 123, 136
Merlin IV 92, 113
Merlin VIII 116
Merlin X 92, 142
Merlin XX 95, 99, 102, 103, 123
Merlin 21, 23, 25, 72 109
Merlin 24, 27 123
Merlin 30, 32, 116
Merlin 45, 63 136
Merlin 73, 76 109
Merlin 85/102 95, 150
Merlin 130/131/133/134 160
Merlin 502 149
Merlin T.24 149
Nene 180, 199, 200
Nimbus 209
Peregrine 145
Spey 157, 187, 190
Tyne 199
Vulture 94, 95
Welland 117, 119
Royal Air Force
Air Support Command *189*
Bomber Command 21, 23, 26, 96, 99, 111, 112, 121, 132, 142, 152
Coastal Command 21, 22, 23, 26, 29, 62, 82, 88, 92, 96, 99, 101, 103, 106, 111, 121, 127, 128, 133, 142, 143, 151, 159, 188
Fighter Command 21, 22, 23, 117, 137, 206
Strike Command 152
1 Sqn *19*, 77, *77*, 183
2 Sqn 131, *131*, 201
3 Sqn 61, *66*, 71, 74, 194
4 Sqn 79
5 Sqn 89, *89*, *106*, 144
6 Sqn *69*, 79, 144, 190
7 Sqn 85, 134
8 Sqn 88, 151, 159
10 Sqn 72, 92, *122*, 156, *156*, 173
11 Sqn 74, 75, 164
12 Sqn *68*, 69, *69*, 75, *75*, 113, 157, *165*
13 Sqn *167*
14 Sqn *88*, 129, *129*
15 Sqn 74, *95*, *134*, *159*, *173*
16 Sqn 144
17 Sqn 71, 74, *190*
18 Sqn 66, *209*
19 Sqn 71, 137
20 Sqn 144, *184*
21 Sqn 79, *110*, 127, *127*
22 Sqn 88, 101, 102, *207*
23 Sqn *27*, 71, 78, *78*, 111, *164*
24 Sqn 16, *74*
25 Sqn 71, 77, *77*
26 Sqn 60, *60*, 206, 207
27 Sqn *9*, 16, 89, 103, 111, 152, *165*
28 Sqn 144, *145*, *208*
29 Sqn 16, 149, *154*, *175*
30 Sqn 79, *79*, *132*, 157

31 Sqn *32*, *87*, 112
32 Sqn 16, 71, 72
33 Sqn 74, 75, 161, 209, *211*
34 Sqn 157
35 Sqn 32, 121
36 Sqn 74, 88, 159, 188, 189
37 Sqn 74
38 Sqn 70, 207
39 Sqn 75
40 Sqn *101*
41 Sqn *66*, 170
42 Sqn 88, *88*, 101, *101*, 159
43 Sqn 56, *60*, 71, *71*, 77, 177, 190
44 Sqn 96
45 Sqn *88*, 143, 159, 161, *161*
46 Sqn *71*, *148*, 151, *151*, 170
47 Sqn 157, 172
48 Sqn 62
49 Sqn 120, 201
50 Sqn *80*
51 Sqn 161
53 Sqn 157, *198*, 199
54 Sqn 162, *163*, 199
55 Sqn 16, 129, *175*
56 Sqn *155*, 201
57 Sqn 150, 173
58 Sqn 84
60 Sqn 67, 89, 132, 188
62 Sqn 101
64 Sqn 161
66 Sqn *170*, 206, 207, *207*
67 Sqn 194
71 Sqn 194
72 Sqn *37*, 117, *118*, 206
74 Sqn 154
75 Sqn 74
76 Sqn 88
78 Sqn 197
79 Sqn 201
80 Sqn *117*, *136*, 161
81 Sqn 132, 188
82 Sqn 143
83 Sqn *94*, *121*, 152
84 Sqn 89, 143, *143*, 157, 159, *159*
85 Sqn *125*
86 Sqn *102*
87 Sqn *117*
90 Sqn 99, 101
92 Sqn 177
93 Sqn 74
94 Sqn *123*
96 Sqn 67
98 Sqn 132
99 Sqn 66, *67*, 72, *72*, 73, 142, 160
100 Sqn 74, 88
101 Sqn 65, 66, 165
102 Sqn 73, *93*
105 Sqn *110*, 111
106 Sqn *97*
107 Sqn *111*
108 Sqn *106*
110 Sqn *14*, 66, 143
111 Sqn 60, 71, 125, 177
112 Sqn 107, *194*
114 Sqn 100, 148, *148*
115 Sqn 74
120 Sqn *25*, 67, 151
135 Sqn 132
137 Sqn 145
138 Sqn 201
139 Sqn *31*, 101
144 Sqn 66
149 Sqn 159
150 Sqn *113*
151, 152 Sqns 53
157 Sqn 111
179 Sqn *143*
180 Sqn 132
185 Sqn 56
192 Sqn 161
194 Sqn 206
196 Sqn *134*
201 Sqn *83*, *133*
202 Sqn *59*, 82, *209*
203 Sqn *52*, *187*, 188
205 Sqn 66, 82, 134
207 Sqn *42*, 95
208 Sqn 36, *36*, 56, 144, *147*
209 Sqn *53*, 64, *64*, 65, *132*, 133, *197*

210 Sqn 53, *84*, *133*, 188
211 Sqn *100*
214 Sqn *42*, 74, *142*
215 Sqn 74
216 Sqn *85*, 161, *162*
217 Sqn 37, 188, *188*
220 Sqn 62
223 Sqn 129
224 Sqn 127
226 Sqn *113*
230 Sqn *82*, 134
237 Sqn 79
240 Sqn 133
245 Sqn *171*
247 Sqn 162
249 Sqn *126*
260 Sqn *107*
261 Sqn 132
263 Sqn 145
264 Sqn 99, *99*, 100
267 Sqn 197
269 Sqn 127, *127*
274 Sqn *124*
275 Sqn 206
276 Sqn *144*
295 Sqn 94
307 Sqn *103*
511 Sqn 160
551 Sqn 149
617 Sqn 152, *152*
640 Sqn 120
651 Sqn 105
Royal Aircraft Establishment 18
Royal Aircraft Factory, Farnborough 12, 14, 44
Royal Australian Air Force 103, 107, 129, 134, 170
1 Sqn 150
10 Sqn *133*
462 Sqn *122*
Royal Auxiliary Air Force 144 162, 169
504 Sqn *74*, 117
604 Sqn *102*
608 Sqn 99
609 Sqn *126*
613 Sqn 80
616 Sqn 117
Royal Canadian Air Force 60, 65 83, 96, 134
1 Sqn 54, *55*, 78
403 Sqn *107*
407 Sqn *142*
422 Sqn 133
425 Sqn *142*
426 Sqn *95*
Royal Engineers 11, 12
Royal Flying Corps 11–16
1 Sqn 12, 214
2 Sqn 12, 34
3, 4, 5 Sqns 12
6 Sqn 12, 40
7 Sqn 12
8 Sqn 34
11 Sqn 56, 57
12 Sqn 40
19 Sqn 34, 54, 56
20 Sqn 40
21 Sqn 34, 44
23 Sqn 54, 56
24 Sqn 37
25 Sqn 40
27 Sqn 43, 44
30 Sqn 56
32 Sqn 37, *37*
40, 41 Sqns 41
46 Sqn 50
48 Sqn 36
52 Sqn 45
54 Sqn 50
55 Sqn 37
56 Sqn 45
60, 63 Sqns 56
66 Sqn 50
70 Sqn 49, 51
72 Sqn 56
79, 87 Sqns 54
Royal Naval Air Service 12–13, 14, 16, 32, 215, 217
4 Sqn 51
5 Sqn *49*

7 Sqn 48
10 Sqn 51
3, 5 Wings 48
Royal New Zealand Air Force 71 82, 107

Sabre (NA) 26, **194**, *194*
Samson, Charles R 14
Scapa (Supermarine) **83**, *83*
Scarf, Sqn Ldr 101
Schneider (Sopwith) 40, *48*, **49**
Schwann, Cdr Oliver 14
Scimitar (Supermarine) **200**, *200*
Scout (Bristol) *35*, **35–6**
Scout (Nieuport) 13, 16, **44**, *44*
Scout (Westland) 209
SE5/SE5a 16, **45**, *46*
Sea Fury (Hawker) *176*, 176, 180
Sea Gladiator (Gloster) 78, 117
Sea Harrier (HS) **183**, *183–5*
Sea Hawk (Hawker) 27, **180**, *180*, 199, 200
Sea Hornet (DH) 161
Sea Hurricane (Hawker) *124*
Sea King (Westland) **209**, *209*
Sea Scout, airship **216–17**, *217*
Sea Vampire (DH) 162
Sea Venom (DH) 164, 165, 199
Sea Vixen (DH) *165*, *165*
Seafire (Supermarine) 137, *137*, 138
Seafox (Fairey) **115**, *115*
Seal (Fairey) *69*, **69–70**
Shackleton (Avro) 25, 26, 29, **151**, *151*, 187, 188
Shark (Blackburn) **65**, *65*

Siddeley engines 36, 37, 38
Sidestrand (BP) **65**, *65*, 66
Singapore (Short) 65, **82**, *82*
Siskin III, IIIA (AW) **60**, *60*, 71
Skua (Blackburn) 23, 78, **99**, *99*
Skyraider (Douglas) *199*
Smith, R and K 84
Snipe (Sopwith) **56**, *56*
South African Air Force 107, 129
60 Sqn *128*
Southampton (Supermarine) 70, **82–3**, *83*
Spad 7, **56**, *56*
Spitfire (Supermarine) 7, 20, 21, 22, 83, 109, **136–8**, *136–41*
SS, airship **216–17**, *217*
SS18 (Gloster) 71
Stirling (Short) 20, 21, 121, **134**, *134–5*
Stranraer (Supermarine) **83**, *84*
Sunbeam engines
  150hp 217
  225/260hp 44, 46, 47
  Arab 36, 44, 56
  Cossack 42, 46, 221
  Maori 39, 42, 46, 57, 220
Sunderland (Short) 21, *133*, **133–4**
Superfortress (Boeing) 159
Swift (Blackburn) 63
Swift (Supermarine) 26, **201**, *201*
Swordfish (Fairey) 23, **113–14**, *113–15*
Sycamore (Bristol) **206**, *206*

Tabloid (Sopwith) 40, **48**, *48*, 49
Tarpon (Grumman) **119**, *119*

Tempest (Hawker) *126*, **127**, 176
Templer, Capt JLB 10, 214
Thunderbolt (Republic) **132**, *132*
Tiger Moth (DH) 91, 92, **107–8**, *108*, 129, 131, 161, 194
Tomahawk (Curtiss) **107**, *107*
Tornado (Panavia) 29, **194**, *194–6*, 199
Trenchard, Sir Hugh 18, 39
Trent, Sqn Ldr LH 128
Triplane (Sopwith) **50–51**, *50–51*
TSR2 (BAC) 28
Turbo-Union engines 194
Tutor (Avro) 34, **61–2**, *62*
Twin Pioneer (Scottish Aviation) **197**, *197*
Typhoon (Hawker) 22, **126**, *126*, 126, 145

V/1500 (HP) *14*
Valentia (Vickers) 85, *87*, 201
Valetta (Vickers) **201**, *201*, 203
Valiant (Vickers) 26, **201**, *202*, **203**
Vampire (DH) 23, **162**, *162–3*, 164, 165, 181, 188
Varsity (Vickers) **203**, *203*
VC10 (BAC) **156**, *156*
Vengeance (Vultee) **143**, *143*
Venom (DH) **164**, *164*, 165
Ventura (Lockheed) *127*, **127–8**
Vernon (Vickers) **84**, *84*, 85, 201
Victor (HP) 26, **173**, *173–5*, 201, *202*
Victoria (Vickers) 84, **85**, *85*, 201
Vildebeest (Vickers) **88**, *88*
Vimy (Vickers) 72, **84**, *84*, 85
Vincent (Vickers) **88**, *88*

Virginia (Vickers) 72, **84–5**, *85*
Vulcan (Avro) 26, 29, **152**, *152–3*, 194, 201, *202*

Wallis, Sir Barnes 143, 221
Walrus (Supermarine) *135*, **135–6**
Wapiti (Westland) 78, 88, **89**, *89*
Warwick (Vickers) **143**, *143*
Washington (Boeing) 26, **159**, *159*
Wasp (Westland) **209**
WBIII (Beardmore) 50
Wellesley (Vickers) **88**, *88*
Wellington (Vickers) 20, 21, 70, *142*, **142–3**, 143, 203
Wessex (Westland) **207**, *209*
Whirlwind (Westland) fighter **145**, *145*
Whirlwind (Westland) h/c **207**, *207*
White and Poppe engine 216
Whitley (AW) 20, 21, **92**, *93*
Wight Seaplane **57**, *57*
Wildcat (Grumman) **119**, *119*, 120
Wolseley engines 11, 36, 45, 56, 215, 217, 221
Woodcock (Hawker) **74**, *74*
Wright, O and W 13
Wright Cyclone engines
  G-205 119
  GR-1820 127
  GR-2600 111, 119, 129, 131, 143
  R-1820 99, 106
  R-3350 159, 188
Wyvern (Westland) 157, **203**, *203*

York (Avro) **149**, *149*, 172

Picture Credits

Wg Cdr Annand pp 78 (top), 78–79
RCB Ashworth pp 188–89
R Athey pp 1, 50
Author's Collection pp 8–9, 10–11, 12–13, 14, 14–15, 16–17, 17, 19, 20–21, 22–23, 24–25, 27, 28–29, 32, 32–33, 33 (top), 34, 34–35 (top), 34–35 (bottom), 35, 36–37, 38–39, 40, 41 (top and centre), 42–45, 46 (bottom), 46–47, 48, 49 (top), 50–51, 53, 55–60, 60–61 (top), 61–65, 66 (top), 66–67, 68, 68–69, 69 (centre and bottom), 70, 71 (centre), 72–73, 74 (top), 74–76, 78 (bottom), 79, 80 (top), 84 (centre and bottom), 85–87, 88 (top), 88–92, 93–94, 94–95, 95 (top), 98, 99 (top and bottom), 100 (centre and bottom), 100–101, 102–103, 103 (top), 105 (top), 106 (top), 107 (centre), 108 (top), 110 (bottom two), 111, 112, 114, 115, 116 (bottom), 116–117, 118–120, 121–3, 124 (bottom), 126 (top and centre), 127, 129 (top two), 130, 131, 132 (top two), 133 (top two), 134, 134–135 (bottom), 136, 137 (top), 142 (top two), 143 (top), 145–147, 148 (top), 148–150, 150–151, 151 (top and bottom left), 152 (top), 153, 156–157, 157, 159 (bottom), 161 (top and centre), 162 (bottom), 162–163, 165, 166–167, 167 (top two), 168–169, 170 (bottom), 170–173, 176, 180 (bottom), 181 (bottom), 183 (bottom), 184 (bottom), 187, 188 (top), 190–191, 199, 200, 200–201, 201 (top), 202, 203 (bottom), 204–205, 206, 206–207, 207 (centre), 209 (top

left and bottom), 212–213, 214–215, 215 (top), 216, 216–217, 217 (top), 218–219, 220–221
Sqn Ldr CPO Bartlett DSC p 49 (lower)
Boeing Aircraft Corporation p 105 (lower)
CE Brown pp 120–121 (bottom)
RA Brown p 194 (top)
V Cashmore p 128 (top)
S Challen p 106 (centre)
L Clarke p 113 (centre)
Courtesy OC XV Sqn RAF p 95 (bottom)
L Crocker pp 60–61 (bottom)
JB Cynk p 103 (bottom)
Sqn Ldr L Davies pp 18–19
OG Davies p 128 (bottom)
S Edwards p 107 (bottom)
Wg Cdr GM Elvin p 69 (top)
A Fairbairn p 197
Flight International pp 71 (top and bottom), 82–83, 106 (bottom), 110 (top)
M Gidman p 116 (top)
Via W Gunston pp 194–195, 196–197
Via EA Harlin pp 30–31
Hawker-Siddeley pp 74 (bottom), 77 (bottom), 80 (bottom), 176–177
Imperial War Museum pp 100 (top), 101 (centre), 104, 129 (bottom), 132, 143 (bottom)
Sqn Ldr CG Jefford p 88 (bottom)
EG Jones p 194 (bottom)
P Kilduff pp 33 (bottom), 41 (bottom)
GS Leslie pp 81 (top), 217 (bottom)

Wg Cdr G Lewis DFC pp 37, 46 (top)
Mann, Egerton Co. p 47
MOD (Air) pp 26–27, 36, 66 (centre), 81 (bottom), 82 (bottom), 151 (bottom right), 159 (centre), 160–161, 164, 170 (top), 181 (top), 201 (bottom)
Via EB Morgan pp 83, 84 (top), 135, 221
RAF Museum, Hendon pp 51, 117 (top)
K Munson p 188 (bottom), 214
B Robertson pp 82 (top), 103 (centre), 144–145, 148 (centre)
Vickers pp 203 (top), 215 (bottom)
R J Wilson pp 2–3, 4–5, 6–7, 108 (lower), 112–113, 137 (bottom), 138, 140–141, 152 (bottom), 154–155, 156, 156–157 (bottom), 158, 159 (top), 160, 161 (bottom), 162 (top), 164–165, 166, 167 (bottom), 174–175, 177, 178–179, 180 (top), 182, 183 (top), 185, 186, 189, 190, 192–193, 195, 198, 207 (top and bottom), 208, 209 (top right), 210–211

Artwork

Mike Badrocke pp 52–53, 54, 96–97, 108–109, 124 (top), 124–125, 138–139, 184 (top), 184–185
Mike Bailey pp 66 (bottom), 77 (top), 92–93, 97, 99 (centre), 101 (top), 102, 113 (top and bottom), 117 (bottom), 120–121 (top two), 125, 126 (bottom), 133 (bottom), 134–135 (top), 139, 142 (bottom), 144